JOURNAL FOR THE STUDY OF THE NEW TESTAMENT
SUPPLEMENT SERIES
230

COPENHAGEN INTERNATIONAL SEMINAR
11

Sheffield Academic Press
A Continuum imprint

The New Testament as Reception

edited by
Mogens Müller & Henrik Tronier

Journal for the Study of the New Testament
Supplement Series 230

Copenhagen International Seminar 11

Copyright © 2002 Sheffield Academic Press
A Continuum imprint

Published by Sheffield Academic Press Ltd
The Tower Building, 11 York Road, London SE1 7NX
370 Lexington Avenue, New York NY 10017-6550

www.SheffieldAcademicPress.com
www.continuumbooks.com

British Library Cataloguing-in-Publication Data

A catalogue record for this book is available from the British Library

Typeset by Sheffield Academic Press
Printed on acid-free paper in Great Britain by MPG Books Ltd, Bodmin, Cornwall

ISBN 1-84127-314-7

CONTENTS

PREFACE

On 12–16 June, 1999, nearly 60 New Testament scholars from Scandinavian universities and other educational institutions met for the Sixth Nordic New Testament Conference at Grundtvigs Højskole Frederiksborg in Hillerød, north of Copenhagen.

The history of these Nordic Conferences, of which the first took place at the University of Aarhus back in 1978, has been definitively written by Sigfred Pedersen;[1] he founded the conference and was its leader through the first years.

The topic for the 1999 Conference, 'New Testament as Reception', was chosen based on the conviction that it represents a fruitful angle of approach to New Testament studies. It means that New Testament writings can be viewed as reception in relation to the Old Testament, ancient Judaism, contemporary Hellenistic-Roman culture and philosophy, the 'historical Jesus', and—concerning the Acts of the Apostles—Paul. But recognition of the New Testament writings as the result of ancient reception invites the further question of what it means for the continuing reception of the New Testament in the Christian Church. For just as the New Testament writings are to be seen as more or less the result of a creative transformation process, so their continuing reception in the history of the Church is an ongoing transformation interplaying with cultural development.

The following ten articles represent main papers and papers delivered in seminar groups at the conference.

It is a pleasure here—on behalf of the commitee that organizes the Conference—to thank Gads Fond, Clara Lachmanns Fond, Københavns Universitets Almene Fond, and Statens Humanistiske Forskningsråd for substantial financial support in holding the Conference. Generous support and help with all the practical arrangements was also given by the Department of Biblical Exegesis at the Theological Faculty at the University of

---

1. See Sigfred Pedersen, 'Scandinavian New Testament Conferences, 1978–1994', in Gunnlaugur A. Jónsson et al. (eds.), *The New Testament in its Hellenistic Context* (Studia theologica islandica, 10; Reykjaviks: Hásteóli Íslands, 1996), pp. 15-36.

Copenhagen. Thanks also have to be given to Dr Greg Doudna for correcting the English translations of the manuscripts, to PhD student Nicolai Techow for standardizing the Greek and Hebrew quotations and proofreading, and last but not least to the secretary at the Department for Biblical Studies at our faculty, Anne-Lise Pemmer, for the extensive and detailed work of preparing the manuscript for press.

Mogens Müller
Henrik Tronier

ABBREVIATIONS

AB	Anchor Bible
AGJU	Arbeiten zur Geschichte des antiken Judentums und des Urchristentums
AthD	Acta theologica Danica
AV	Authorized Version
BA	*Biblical Archaeologist*
BARev	*Biblical Archaeology Review*
BETL	Bibliotheca ephemeridum theologicarum lovaniensium
BEvT	Beiträge zur evangelischen Theologie
BFCT	Beiträge zur Förderung christlicher Theologie
BGBE	Beiträge zur Geschichte der biblischen Exegese
BHT	Beiträge zur historischen Theologie
Bib	*Biblica*
BibInt	*Biblical Interpretation: A Journal of Contemporary Approaches*
BJS	Brown Judaic Studies
BT	*The Bible Translator*
BZ	*Biblische Zeitschrift*
BZAW	Beihefte zur *ZAW*
BZNW	Beihefte zur *ZNW*
CBQMS	*Catholic Biblical Quarterly*, Monograph Series
CIS	Copenhagen International Seminar
ConBNT	Coniectanea biblica, New Testament
CRINT	Compendia rerum iudaicarum ad Novum Testamentum
DJD	Discoveries in the Judaean Desert
DSD	Dead Sea Discoveries
DTT	*Dansk Teologisk Tidsskrift*
EKKNT	Evangelisch-Katholischer Kommentar zum Neuen Testament
FBE	Forum for Bibelsk Eksegese
FzB	Forschung zur Bibel
FRLANT	Forschungen zur Religion und Literatur des Alten und Neuen Testaments
HBT	*Horizons in Biblical Theology*
HNT	Handbuch zum Neuen Testament
JAOS	*Journal of the American Oriental Society*
JBT	Jahrbuch für biblische Theologie

JQR	*Jewish Quarterly Review*
JSNT	*Journal for the Study of the New Testament*
JSOTSup	*Journal for the Study of the Old Testament*, Supplement Series
JSPSup	*Journal for the Study of the Pseudepigrapha*, Supplement Series
KD	*Kerygma und Dogma*
KEK	Kritisch-exegetischer Kommentar zum Neuen Testament
LEC	Library of Early Christianity
NEB	*New English Bible*
NIGTC	The New International Greek Testament Commentary
NIV	New International Version
NRSV	New Revised Standard Version
NTAbh	Neutestamentliche Abhandlungen
NTS	*New Testament Studies*
OTP	James Charlesworth (ed.), *Old Testament Pseudepigrapha*
PVTG	Pseudepigrapha Veteris Testamenti graece
RB	*Revue biblique*
RevQ	*Revue de Qumran*
RHPR	*Revue d'histoire et de philosophie religieuses*
RSV	Revised Standard Version
RV	Revised Version
SBL	Society of Biblical Literature
SBLSP	SBL Seminar Papers
SC	Sources chrétiennes
SEÅ	*Svensk exegetisk årsbok*
SJOT	*Scandinavian Journal of the Old Testament*
SNTSMS	Society for New Testament Studies Monograph Series
ST	*Studia theologica*
THKNT	Theologischer Handkommentar zum Neuen Testament
TS	*Theological Studies*
TU	Texte und Untersuchungen
WBC	Word Biblical Commentary
WUNT	Wissenschaftliche Untersuchungen zum Neuen Testament
ZAW	*Zeitschrift für die alttestamentliche Wissenschaft*
ZNW	*Zeitschrift für die neutestamentliche Wissenschaft*
ZTK	*Zeitschrift für Theologie und Kirche*

Mikael Winninge, TD, Associate Professor, Umeå University, Institutionen för religionsvetenskap, S-901 87 Umeå, Sweden

Troels Engberg-Pedersen, Associate Professor of New Testament Exegesis, University of Copenhagen, Institut for Bibelsk Exegese, Købmagergade 44-46, DK-1150 København K., Denmark

Renate Banschbach Eggen, Doctoral candidate, Tutor, Department of Religious Studies, Norwegian University of Science and Technology, Trondheim, Department of Religous Studies, Norwegian University of Science and Technology, Trondheim, N-7034 Trondheim, Norway

Samuel Byrskog, Professor of New Testament and Hermeneutics, Department of Religion, University of Göteborg, Institutionen för religionsvetenskap, Box 200, S-405 30 Göteborg, Sweden

Niels Hyldahl, Professor Emeritus of New Testament Exegesis, University of Copenhagen, Nivåvænge 20-6, 2990 Nivå, Denmark

Håkan Ulfgard, TD, Associate Professor, Department of Theology and Religious Studies, Linköping University, SE-581 83 Linköping, Sweden

Jorunn Økland, Lecturer, Department of Biblical Studies, University of Sheffield, Department of Biblical Studies, University of Sheffield, Arts Tower, Sheffield S10 2TN, UK

Tord Fornberg, Director of the Swedish Theological Institute in Jerusalem, Israel, Associate Professor in New Testament Exegesis at Uppsala University, Sweden, The Swedish Theological Institute, P. O. Box 37, IL - 91000, Jerusalem, Israel

Thor Strandenæs, Associate Professor of Missiology, School of Mission and Theology, Stavanger, Norway, Misjonshøgskolen, Misjonsveien 34, N-4024 Stavanger, Norway

THE NEW TESTAMENT RECEPTION OF THE OLD TESTAMENT

Mogens Müller

Introduction

For the authors of the New Testament the holy writings of Judaism were a basic generator of meaning in their conceptual universe. In their eyes Jesus Christ was not just someone who appeared in his own right; his life story was believed to be deeply integrated in the revelation embodied in the collection of books later called the Old Testament.

Consequently the New Testament cannot be read as independent or self-sufficient literature. On the contrary, according to their internal self-understanding the New Testament writings confirm that they are to be understood as both the continuation and the fulfilment of the history that began in the Old Testament books (Heb. 1.1; 1 Pet. 1.10-12). The holy books of Judaism quite simply were the first Bible of the Church. Seen in its proper perspective New Testament literature can be characterized as an attempt to maintain a specific interpretation of the Old Testament.

Early Christianity did not depart from contemporary groups within ancient Judaism in being dependent on other writings, but persisted in maintaining a common basis. What distinguished Christians was solely the starting point of interpretation, that is, the belief that Jesus Christ was the revelation of the true meaning of Holy Writ. Or, to put it another way, salvation history—which the Christian Church believed it embodied and continued—gave 'pre-history' a new significance. The new schematic category developed by Christian interpretation made this very clear. Where ancient Judaism interpreted its books basically as 'the Law', Christians tended to read the same books as 'promise'. The centre of gravity thus shifted from the Mosaic Law to the Prophets. Seen from the outside, church and synagogue appeared as two brotherhoods whose dissimilarity was founded in their different ways of interpreting the same writings.

Reception of the Scripture as Expressive of a Process of Historical Consciousness

Over the last few decades the recognition of these points of departure has resulted in an ever-increasing interest in the reception history that suc-ceeded the final redaction of the Old Testament books and the formation of the Jewish canon in the Hellenistic-Roman period. The first evidence of such redaction or canon-formation is found in the prologue to the book of Sirach, Josephus in *Apion* 1.37-41, and *4 Ezra* 14. For biblical exegesis the focus on reception has generated an intense preoccupation with extra-canonical Jewish literature as expressing a consciousness-historical devel-opment of the religion or ideology embedded in the writings that were later canonized.

Where Old Testament exegetes used to concentrate their efforts on a traditio-historical reconstruction of the origin and original meaning of the various traditions, many are now focused instead on the people responsible for the final redaction. The centre of gravity has been transferred from a study of the narratives to a study of a posterity which strove to legitimize itself by these narratives. At the same time the narratives are not treated as isolated phenomena but as transitional phases in a process that continued in post-canonical literature. In a biblical-exegetical context this has led to the realization that the texts' reception is the foundation for our under-standing of Scripture and its subsequent utilization in the New Testament writings.

One example of this changing centre of gravity is the attention given to the genre called 'rewritten Bible'. Where biblical-historical paraphrases such as, for example *Jubilees*, the first 11 books of Josephus's *Antiquities of the Jews* and Pseudo-Philo's *Liber Antiquitatum Biblicarum* were for-merly considered to be secondary and, in a traditio-historical respect, of minor interest compared to the 'original' text, they are now being treated as important first-hand evidence of how ancient Judaism read and under-stood its holy books. In the research carried out by the Swedish exegete Håkan Ulfgard on the Feast of Tabernacles, it is symptomatic of this new paradigm that what interests him is not the 'history' of this feast but its 'story', which expresses an altered attitude to its significance.[1]

The focus on how deeply New Testament writings are rooted in con-temporary Jewish Scripture reception has occasioned a renewed interest in

---

1.   See H. Ulfgard, *The Story of Sukkot: The Setting, Shaping, and Sequel of the Biblical Feast of Tabernacles* (BGBE, 34; Tübingen: J.C.B. Mohr [P. Siebeck], 1998).

the Dead Sea Scrolls. In the first decades after the sensational find of these texts the scrolls were studied primarily as evidence of a specific sectarian aspect of ancient Judaism, which of course they are. But this was based on a research paradigm which axiomatically presupposed Christianity to be different. According to this paradigm Jesus' and his first followers' 'religion' was not Jewish at all. In connection with an analysis of the theological contents of the Dead Sea Scrolls an exegete such as Herbert Braun succeeded in formulating it almost as a concession that the greater part of the Jewish elements in the Gospel traditions expressed a re-Judaization, 'Although also with regard to Jesus himself we of course have to reckon with a takeover of a certain quantity of Judaism'.[2] Today this attitude seems almost absurd; it has been replaced by a willingness to understand the group of people behind the Dead Sea Scrolls as a devout society whose self-understanding and use of Scripture to a great extent had formal parallels to the Christian society.

A similar tendency is evident in Philo research. From a position as a marginal figure in ancient Judaism,[3] the Jewish-Alexandrian philosopher and exegete is today considered the exponent of a paradigm of interpretation which greatly helps to explain the structure of reality and significance which, for example, Paul advocates. The apparent parallels are so far from being accidental as to clearly indicate that both are rooted in Hellenistic Judaism.[4]

---

2.   'wenngleich natürlich auch für Jesus selber mit der Übernahme eines gewissen Quantums Judentum gerechnet werden muss'. See H. Braun, *Spätjüdisch-häretischer und frühchristlicher Radikalismus. Jesus von Nazareth und die essenische Qumransekte*, II (BHT, 24; Tübingen: J.C.B. Mohr [P. Siebeck] 1957; 2nd edn, 1969), p. 1. See also J. Jeremias, *Jesu Verheissung für die Völker, Franz Delitzsch-Vorlesungen 1953* (Stuttgart: W. Kohlhammer, 1956), p. 33, where the author, in connection with his demonstration of the fact that Jesus was not minded to go beyond the borders of Israel, asks almost in astonishment: 'Blieb Jesus im Judentum stecken?'

3.   See, e.g., B. Otzen, *Judaism in Antiquity: Political Developments and Religious Currents from Alexander to Hadrian* (The Biblical Seminar, 7; Sheffield: Sheffield Academic Press, 1990), p. 62, where he says of Philo: 'He was an isolated phenomenon, and his significance was greater for the early fathers of the church than it was for Judaism.' However, the fact that Philo's impact on Judaism was inconsiderable says nothing about his importance for his contemporaries. See also the critique in G. Græsholt, 'Er Filon bare et sidespor?', *DTT* 56 (1993), pp. 19-34.

4.   This has ben exemplarily proved by H. Tronier in a number of essays and in his *Transcendens og transformation i Første Korintherbrev* (Tekst & Tolkning, 10; Copenhagen: Akademisk Forlag, 1994).

The transfer of focus from traditionalist and text-archaeological questions to reception history has suddenly brought the old Greek translation of the holy books of Judaism, the Septuagint, into favour again; from a theologically Cinderella-like existence this edition of the Old Testament has again become what it was in the beginning: the first Bible of the Church.[5] Where formerly it was considered a rather unreliable translation, which might at best be used as textual evidence in cases where the Hebrew Bible text was deadlocked, the Septuagint is now treated as a creative version of the Bible in transmission made for Hellenistic Diaspora Jews in the last centuries before the beginning of our era. The early Christians adopted it as their authentic Bible text.

It is worth noting that even though the Septuagint text was adopted as *the* biblical text this did not mean that the Apocrypha was acknowledged as Holy Writ in line with the books that made up Biblia Hebraica. The New Testament has not one apocryphal quotation cited as Holy Writ.[6] This argument should be taken into account before putting a date on a final delimitation of the holy books of Judaism. Apparently Josephus was not the only one to realize that only books written before Artaxerxes were truly prophetic. The oldest Christian enumeration of Old Testament books is the one ascribed to Melito from the end of the second century (see Eusebius, *Hist. eccl.* 4.26.13-14). This list does not include the Apocrypha; its canonical status was generally disputed in the first centuries of the Church.[7]

All translation is interpretation and the Septuagint is thus, like the ancient Jewish Bible interpretation, proof of how Holy Writ was understood in the period predating the creation of the New Testament books.[8] But a static perception of the text has put difficulties in the way of this insight, even though the New Testament has examples of Old Testament quotations that are meaningful only if considered on the basis of the Septuagint. The classic example of this is the quotation from Isa. 7.14 in Mt. 1.23. The word used by the Greek text, 'virgin', is an essential precondition for the evangelists'

---

5. See M. Müller, *The First Bible of the Church: A Plea for the Septuagint* (JSOTSup, 206; CIS, 1; Sheffield: Sheffield Academic Press, 1996); *idem*, 'Die Septuaginta als die Bibel der neutestamentliche Kirche', KuD 42 (1996), pp. 65-78.

6. The exception that proves the rule is Jude 14-15, quoting from *1 En.* 1.9.

7. See, e.g., B. Otzen, 'Das Problem der Apokryphen', *SJOT* 10 (1996), pp. 258-70.

8. A fine example of the value of understanding the Septuagint as an attempt at cultural translation is M. Rösel, *Übersetzung als Vollendung der Auslegung: Studien zur Genesis-Septuaginta* (BZAW, 223; Berlin: Walter de Gruyter, 1994).

use of the word and for the tradition created about Jesus' mother, Mary, as a virgin. Some translators of the Bible would deal with this problem and others of the same kind by translating from the Septuagint instead of Biblia Hebraica as an exception. Only the latest generation of translators of the Old Testament have given up this practice, even with respect to 'Church Bibles'.[9]

The reception of the Old Testament into the New Testament books did not start from scratch. As the Christian congregation grew out of Judaism, the collection of holy books, which from the very beginning enjoyed—and retained—a status as divine, was already an 'interpreted Bible'.[10] The New Testament authors not only related to the text, but they were also tied to an exegetical tradition which meant constantly having to adapt the biblical text to new situations and preconditions. To both Jewish and Christian interpreters it was unquestionably God who spoke through the Holy Writ (cf. 2 Tim. 3.16; 2 Pet. 1.21). This meant that there were never any conflicts or dissociations; it was only a question of reinterpretation.

It has also become increasingly apparent that the final redaction of extant Old Testament writings aimed at more than just a description of past history and reiterations of divine speeches in past situations. Already the transmission process, which was provisionally concluded in the various Old Testament books as we know them from Biblia Hebraica and the Septuagint, is influenced by theological and ideological ideas; these do not reflect a tendency that should first be recognized and then preferably eliminated in order to reshape the texts into sources of the history they refer to; theology and ideology instead are the raison d'être of these texts. When the author of *Aristeas* by means of a relatively primitive allegorical reading succeeds in making the food prescriptions relate to ethics, and Philo—thanks to a refined allegorical interpretation—tries to uncover the spirituality behind or underneath the literal significance, this has been done

9. Thus the *Zürcher Bibel* (1955); The *New English Bible* with the Apocrypha (1970); *La Bible: Traduction oecumenique* (1988); New Revised Standard Version (1989); and the authorized Danish Bible from 1992. In the *Jerusalem-Bibel* (1966), the Norwegian Bible translation from 1978, *Einheitsübersetzung* (1980), and the latest edition of the *Luther-Bible* (1984), the Virgin still appears.

10. In a number of more recent investigations an analysis of this 'interpretation' has been attempted. Two anthologies are worth mentioning: M.J. Mulder (ed.), *Mikra: Text, Translation, Reading and Interpretation of the Hebrew Bible in Ancient Judaism and Early Christianity* (CRINT, 2.1; Assen: Van Gorcum, 1988), and M. Sæbø (ed.), *Hebrew Bible/Old Testament. The History of its Interpretation*, Part I vol. 1 (Göttingen: Vandenhoeck & Ruprecht, 1996).

in accordance with the tendency of the transmission process. The religious content of the texts has determined their status.

Vetus Testamentum in Novo Receptum

Early Christianity's reception of Judaism's holy books takes place in this universe of preconception and interpretation; but even if the reception according to the Christian congregation's self-understanding reveals the true meaning of the Scripture, it is on condition that this true meaning only becomes apparent with Jesus' life and fate. The moment it was recognized that the foundation of interpretation was the belief that God had finally revealed himself in his Son, a factor outside Scripture turned the pointer of the compass in another direction, as it were to a magnetic pole. Without a magnetic pole Old Testament traditions point in several directions. Besides the Law a number of prophecies predict that in the last days God will interfere and alter his people's conditions; this expectation is described as the new covenant.

It is this susceptibility to a new future that the New Testament reception of the holy books of Judaism exploits. Because the New Testament writings take it for granted that its own events are the fulfilment of the prophecies, the biblical history illuminates the true meaning of Scripture, and the meaning of it changes in Christian reception. It is to Hans Hübner's merit that these problems have been put on the Bible theological agenda; he has formulated the thesis that *Vetus Testamentum* is *Vetus Testamentum in Novo receptum*,[11] thus emphasizing that Christian reception, of which the New Testament books are evidence, has given the Bible of Judaism another significance than it had before. Hans Hübner distinguishes between *Vetus Testamentum* per se and *Vetus Testamentum in Novo receptum*, but this provokes the question whether *Vetus Testamentum* per se is the *Old* Testament at all. In a manner of speaking this collection of books only became the Old Testament when it became a Christian book.

The term 'Old Testament' to describe a certain collection of books is not in evidence until the second century, but at least one of its preconditions is Paul's words in 2 Cor. 3.14. It should be emphasized that because of the

---

11. See H. Hübner, 'Vetus Testamentum und Vetus Testamentum in Novo receptum: Die Frage nach dem Kanon des Alten Testaments aus neutestamentlicher Sicht', *JBT* 3 (1988), pp. 147-62; repr in *idem, Biblische Theologie als Hermeneutik* (ed. A. and M. Labahn; Göttingen: Vandenhoeck & Ruprecht, 1995), pp. 175-90; *idem, Biblische Theologie des Neuen Testaments* (3 vols.; Göttingen: Vandenhoeck & Ruprecht, 1990, 1993, 1995), I. pp. 62-70.

obvious authority of Scripture the first generations of Christians realized on the one hand the necessity of legitimizing themselves in relation to it, whereas on the other hand they interpreted the significance of the life of Christ within the world of ideas pertaining to the Scripture. Inasmuch as the utilization of Scripture in the New Testament is punctual and highly selective, it became necessary in the course of the second century to take possession of the entire Scripture by means of an *interpretatio Christiana* in order to preclude an *interpretatio Judaica*; an early example is the *Letter of Barnabas*. Later on a number of commentaries on entire Old Testament books sprang up, intent on maintaining their 'Christian' significance.

The New Testament writings have not been created to supercede the Old Testament ones. The New Testament authors took it as a matter of course that the same God spoke through the Old Testament as through Jesus Christ (cf. Heb. 1.1). Marcion was the first to make the new collection of writings independent of the Judaic Bible on the basis that there was no continuity between the Old Testament creator of the world, the demiurge, and the Father of Jesus Christ. In opposition to this the New Testament authors were determined in their interpretation to abide by the Judaic Bible as Holy Writ. When the Old Testament is quoted in the New Testament there seems no distance. The apparent discontinuity is ascribed to the historical level as expressions of salvation *history*.

The Reception of the Old Testament as Biblical Theology

In this sense the New Testament authors engage in biblical theology, and this brings us face to face with the all-important question concerning the New Testament reception of the Old Testament which is theologically so important for a modern perception of this collection of books as part of the Christian Bible. Is it the New Testament that decides the significance of the Old Testament, or has the Old Testament an independent significance —as being also part of the canon of the Christian Church? For today's research the alternatives seem to be either a perception of biblical theology as an 'all-embracing' theology or an understanding of biblical theology as a process that commences in the New Testament writings, that is a New Testament theology whose 'text' is the Old Testament.

The first alternative is represented by Peter Stuhlmacher's *Biblische Theologie des Neuen Testaments*.[12] Stuhlmacher defines New Testament

---

12. *Biblische Theologie des Neuen Testaments* (2 vols.; Göttingen: Vandenhoeck & Ruprecht, 1992, 1999). See also by P. Stuhlmacher, *Schriftauslegung auf dem Wege*

theology in the sense that it is rooted in and open to the Old Testament, as a part of a biblical theology that comprises both the Old and the New Testaments.[13] Stuhlmacher follows Hartmut Gese's perception of the relationship between the Old and the New Testaments as the expression of a tradition process which for the Old Testament was concluded with the events described in the New Testament. Gese advocated the thesis that the Old Testament owes its existence to the birth of the New Testament; the New Testament becomes the cornerstone of a tradition process that consists of one unit: a continuum.[14]

Opposed to this is Hans Hübner's work in three volumes of the same title, which appeared between 1990 and 1995; here the two Testaments are seen as a unity only in so far as the New Testament authors' argumentation with the Old Testament is part of the theological reflection according to which biblical theology is primarily an analysis of their theological dealings with the Old Testament.[15]

Even though, from a history-of-religion viewpoint, there is a marked continuity in the way the Jesus movement and the Early Church manifest themselves within ancient Judaism, their self-understanding was reflected in an interpretation of Scripture that points to a new beginning, that is discontinuity. This discontinuity does not express itself in a fundamentally new hermeneutics, but rather in an awareness of representing a new chapter in salvation history. As the eschatological fulfilment of the prophecies this means that previous events can be characterized as past history and 'obsolete' (Heb. 8.13; Mk 2.21-22 par.).

---

zur biblischen Theologie (Göttingen: Vandenhoeck & Ruprecht, 1975); *idem,* *Versöhnung, Gesetz und Gerechtigkeit: Aufsätze zur biblischen Theologie* (Göttingen: Vandenhoeck & Ruprecht, 1981); and *idem, Wie treibt man Biblische Theologie* (Biblisch-Theologische Studien, 24; Neukirchen–Vluyn: Neukirchener Verlag, 1995).

13. See Stuhlmacher, *Biblische Theologie*, I, pp. 5.9.38.

14. See H. Gese, 'Erwägungen zur Einheit der Biblischen Theologie', *ZTK* 67 (1970), pp. 417-36; repr. in, *Vom Sinai zum Zion: Alttestamentliche Beiträge zur biblischen Theologie* (BevT, 64; Munich: Chr. Kaiser Verlag, 1974), pp. 11-30, here p. 14: 'Das Alte Testament entsteht durch das Neue Testament; das Neue Testament bildet den Abschluss eines Traditionsprozesses, der wesentlich als eine Einheit, ein Kontinuum ist'. Cf also p. 30: 'Das Neue Testament an sich ist unverständlich, das Alte Testament an sich ist missverständlich.' In this respect Gese continues the argumentation by Gerhard von Rad, *Theologie des Alten Testaments* (2 vols.; Munich: Chr. Kaiser Verlag, 1957, 1960).

15. See Hübner, *Biblische Theologie*, I, p. 28.

Examples of the Reception of the Old
Testament into the New Testament

The oldest concrete witnesses of the reception of the Bible of Judaism are the letters of Paul. It is certainly remarkable that Paul only quotes the Old Testament in his so-called main letters; there are no Old Testament quotations in Thessalonians, Colossians, Philippians and the Letter to Philemon.[16] All existing Pauline letters can be traced back to the older Paul and have presumably been written within a few years.[17] Galatians, Corinthians and Romans all betray how Paul struggles to do justice to the revelation which he presumes the Scripture represents.

These letters represent a development that confirms that Paul was a biblical theologian in the sense of interactive interpretation of Scripture. The apostle did not quote examples from a fully developed 'theology'. On the contrary it is apparent that at this late time of Paul's life his theology was still developing. For Paul, Scripture is still very much a creative thing. It is not only that faith in Christ sheds light on Scripture; Scripture also sheds light on the content of the faith.

In a salvation-historical connection this is apparent in the way Paul places the Mosaic Law in Galatians and 1 Corinthians in one way and in 2 Corinthians and Romans in another way.[18] In Galatians the point of departure is a static two-room-thinking which forces Paul to a negative judgment of the Mosaic Law (Gal. 3.19-20), whereas an intensive exegetical study of the Scripture in 2 Corinthians gives a positive judgment of the role of the Mosaic Law in salvation history. 2 Corinthians 3.7-11 says that there was a splendour in the dispensation of death and condemnation,

16. In the Deutero-Pauline letters the Old Testament is quoted in Ephesians and the Letters to Timothy, but not in Titus.

17. Cf N. Hyldahl, *Die paulinische Chronologie* (AthD, 19; Leiden: E.J. Brill, 1986), in which Hyldahl argues that Thessalonians are from 51, and the other genuine letters from 54–55.

18. Cf. the following three essays by H. Tronier: 'Virkeligheden som fortolkningsresultat—om hermeneutikken hos Filon og Paulus', in M. Müller and J. Strange (eds.), *Det gamle Testamente i jødedom og kristendom* (FBE, 4; Copenhagen: Museum Tusculanum, 1993), pp. 151-82; 'Loven og dæmonmagterne ifølge Galaterbrevet—en hermeneutisk forklaring', in L. Fatum and M. Müller (eds.), *Tro og historie* (Festschrift Niels Hyldahl; FBE, 7; Copenhagen: Museum Tusculanum, 1996), pp. 264-84; 'Allegorese og universalisme—erkendelse som gruppemarkør hos Filon og Paulus', in N.P. Lemche and H. Tronier (eds.), *Etnicitet i Bibelen* (FBE, 9; Copenhagen: Museum Tusculanum, 1998), pp. 67-107.

although this splendour was fading, having been limited by the coming of the new covenant.

Behind this realization is an exegetical combination of the mentioning of a new covenant in Jeremiah 31, and the statements of Ezekiel 11 and 36 that in due time God will remove the stone heart from the body of his people and insert a heart of flesh and blood and put in a new spirit that they may keep his statutes and keep his ordinances. Thanks to the hermeneutical rule *gezerah shavah* (Hillel's second rule), Paul thus succeeds in connecting the new covenant with the concept of the new spirit. The same rule also allows him to use the mentioning of the stone tables in Exodus 34 so that the commandments of these stone tables could also be seen to be imprinted on the stone hearts of Ezekiel 11 and 36. This very combination precludes Paul from quoting one single scriptural passage.

The exploitation of the idea of a new covenant gave Paul the opportunity to speak about the old covenant as commandments that were justified at the time. On the whole it was the idea of a new covenant that became the basis of the reception of the—by now—Old Testament in the New Testament writings. Although seldom mentioned directly, it may still be seen as a kind of a basic structure.[19] It cannot be taken for granted that the reception of the Old Testament is consistent, but it may be present in various shapes.[20] In Paul's writings, Scripture is essentially used in argumentation, whether this be in the shape of direct quotations or through allusions, but in later New Testament writings it is also sometimes incorporated in hidden typologies and as 'rewritten Bible'.

The basic idea is that Jesus' deeds and fate, and also the Christian Church, unfold the intention of the Scripture. In this connection the find of the *pesher* commentaries among the Dead Sea Scrolls have pushed research forwards. The *pesher* commentaries confront us with a topical

19. See M. Müller, 'The Hidden Context: Some Observations to the Concept of the New Covenant in the New Testament', in T. Fornberg and D. Hellholm (eds.), *Texts and Contexts* (Festschrift Lars Hartman; Oslo: Oslo University Press, 1995), pp. 649-58.

20. See among the comprehensive literature the survey by D. Moody Smith, 'The Use of the Old Testament in the New', in J.M. Efird (ed.), *The Old Testament in the New and Other Essays* (Festschrift William Franklin Stinespring; Durham, NC: Duke University Press, 1972), pp. 3-65; the anthology by D.A. Carson and H.G.M. Williamson (eds.), *It is Written: Scripture Citing Scripture* (Festschrift Barnabas Lindars; Cambridge: Cambridge University Press, 1988); and H. Hübner, 'New Testament Interpretation of the Old Testament', in M. Sæbø (ed.), *Hebrew Bible/Old Testament: The History of its Interpretation,* (Göttingen: Vandenhoek and Ruprecht, 1996), pp. 332-72.

interpretation of particular prophetic literature, written with the thought in mind that the last days referred to by the prophecies were near, which made their importance acute. It was generally thought that the Scripture was inexplicable in itself, and that a new revelation was needed to explain it.[21] Thus a new perspective was added to the old construction prophecy-fulfilment, for while it had hitherto been perceived as proof of Holy Writ, it was now seen as *expansion*.

This is a fertile approach to understanding Paul's Scripture reception as it appears in 1 Cor. 10.11; Rom. 4.23-24; 15.4; cf. also 2 Cor 1.19b-20; and Rom. 1.2. To what degree the expansion was able to decide the reading can be seen in Rom. 10.5-9, where righteousness by faith is the subject of a midrashic exegesis on Deut. 30.12-13. The same reasoning is behind the so-called fulfilment quotations so characteristic of the Gospel of Matthew. As proof of Holy Writ they fail, for they prove nothing. But as explanation of the real purpose of the text they demonstrate the text's realization and thus also the coming of the eschatological era.

However, it is not only in the form of quotations that we find the Scripture in the Gospels. It is also present in the form of narratives typologically related to 'models' in the Old Testament. The recurrent precondition is what is expressed in the 'more than' sayings (Mt. 12.41, 42 = Lk. 11.32, 31; cf. Mt 12.6). In Matthew Jesus is portrayed as the new Moses.[22] Other illustrations of this idea can be seen in the miracles of the fish and loaves and the raising of the dead.[23] The creative influence of Psalm 22 also shows through the Passion. The introductory genealogy of the Gospel of Matthew, like the one in 1 Chronicles 1-9, serves the purpose of maintaining Old Testament history as the necessary *pre*history of what follows.

---

21. See B. Ejrnæs, 'Pesher-litteraturen fra Qumran', in N. Hyldahl and T.L. Thompson (eds.), *Dødehavsteksterne og Bibelen* (FBE, 8; Copenhagen: Museum Tusculanum, 1996), pp. 27-39.

22. Cf. D.C. Allison, *The New Moses: A Matthean Typology* (Philadelphia: Fortress Press, 1993).

23. Already D.F. Strauss saw this clearly; see *Das Leben Jesu: kritisch bearbeitet*, I (Tübingen, 1835; repr. Darmstadt: Wissenschaftliche Buchgesellschaft, 1969), pp. 72-73: 'Den reichsten Stoff zu dieser mythischen Verzierung lieferte das alte Testament, in welchen die erste, vornehmlich aus dem Judenthum gesammelte Christengemeinde lebte und webte. Jesus als der grösste Prophet musste in seinem Leben und seinen Thaten Alles vereinigt und überboten haben, was die alten Propheten, von welchen das A.T. erzählt, gethan und erlebt hatten, er als der Erneurer der hebräischen Religion durfte hinter dem ersten Gesetzgeber in keinem Stücke zurückblieben sein...'

The genre of historical reflection also intrudes. As proved by Marius Reiser, the New Testament writings, in particular the Gospels, are part of the literary conventions built up by ancient Judaism in the Hellenistic-Roman period.[24] Thus the question about the position of the Gospels in ancient literary history is best answered in terms of the flow of traditions which sprang from the Old Testament, particularly the Septuagint.[25]

The book of Revelation occupies a place of its own. In regard to genre it belongs to apocalyptic Judaism to such a degree that the book was formerly taken to be a mediocre Christianized Jewish apocalypse. The peculiarity of Revelation is that in spite of being the New Testament book that contains the most quotations from the Old Testament—in particular from Daniel, Ezekiel and Psalms[26]—the book never once uses a *formula quotationis*. In other words Revelation presupposes familiarity with Scripture, which it then writes into its own text. The author of this book took inspiration in the world in which he lived.[27]

The Letter to the Hebrews is a typical example of the New Testament reception of the Old Testament in the shape of biblical theology. On the one hand it is true that although part of Hebrews is made up of quotations

24. Cf. M. Reiser, '*Die Stellung der Evangelien* in der antiken Literaturgeschichte', *ZNW* 90 (1999), pp. 1-27, in which he says: 'Die literarischen Formen des Neuen Testaments sind fast ausnahmlos bereits in dieser Literatur geläufig und belegt. In ihr findet sich auch die nächsten Analogien zur literarischen Form der Evangelien (p. 7).'

25. See Reiser's conclusion, 'Die Stellung der Evangelien', p. 20: 'Der Blick auf die pagan-griechische und die jüdisch-griechische Erzählliteratur macht deutlich, dass die Evangelien, ganz abgesehen von Inhalt und Funktion, in sprachlich-stilistischer wie formaler Hinsicht am meisten Gemeinsamkeiten mit den biographischen Erzählungen des Alten Testaments bzw der Septuaginta aufweisen... Was ihre Form betrifft, sind sie vor allem der jüdischen Historiographie und ihren biographischen Topoi verpflichtet; der Zusammenhang mit Formen der griechischen Biographie "ist dagegen weniger deutlich und teilweise wohl erst durch die Rezipenten hergestellt"' (quote from H. Cancik).

26. See, e.g., C.K. Beale, 'Revelation', in D.A. Carson and H.G.M. Williamson, *Its is Written: Scripture Citing Scripture* (Festschrift Barnabas Lindars; Cambridge: Cambridge University Press, 1988), pp. 318-36. According to various criteria the number of scriptural quotations in Revelation fluctuates between c. 200 to c. 1000; see n. 1.

27. Cf. Hübner, *Biblische Theologie*, III, p. 207: 'Vielleicht darf man sogar so weit gehen, dass man sagt, das Alte Testament sei für ihn vor allem ein *Buch der Bilder* gewesen; doch muss soloit hinzugelügr wer den, dass es für ihn *die eine göttliche Realität repräsentierenden Bilder* waren—nicht nur Bilder, *die diese Realität zum Ausdruck bringen, sondern Bilder*, die als Bilder am Realitätsgehalt des von ihnen Dargestellten partizipieren.'

from the Scripture, of which nearly all have been consistently taken from the Septuagint, they are nowhere cited as something already written, but rather as something spoken, for according to this letter it is God himself who speaks. On the other hand this does not mean that the Old Testament sayings have been allowed to retain their original meaning. On the contrary they are incorporated in a new context which considerably alters their meaning. In this case Holy Writ does indeed become the *Old* Testament.[28]

Conclusion

In conclusion it may be said that as to contents the Old Testament becomes another book in the New Testament reception due to its name: the Bible of Judaism becomes *Vetus Testamentum in Novo receptum*. Jesus Christ is perceived as the revelation of the true content of Scripture, which earlier used to be hidden. This does not mean, though, that what might be termed the intrinsic value of the Old Testament text disappears. By contrast, the Scripture that has given the New Testament literature its range of ideas retains its influence on its contents, thus making it possible to speak of an interactive relationship between Scripture and the interpretation of the Christ revelation.[29]

As to the Mosaic Law it may be seen that its intrinsic value was still so strong that the apologetic attitude towards this Law, which was recognized in the second century, was germinating already in the New Testament; it was realized that it was levelled at the Jews because of their particular callousness and obstinacy (cf. Mk 10.5 = Mt. 19.8). The interpretation of the *Letter to Barnabas*, which was probably apologetically decided, is an

---

28. Cf. H.-F. Weiss, *Der Brief an die Hebräer* (KEK, 13; Göttingen: Vandenhoeck & Ruprecht, 1991), p. 181: 'Hier, im Hebr, wird die Schrift [...] in der Tat als "Altes" Testament gelesen und verstanden, in seiner Zuordnung zum "Neuen" Testament und in seiner Ausrichtung auf die neue Heilsordnung...Schriftauslegung, das ist im Hebr. nach Massgabe des hermeneutischen Kanons von Hebr 1.1f nichts anders als Christusverkündigung. Das Alte ist hier ganz in das Neue hineingekommen.'

29. It is thus a disparagement of the constituent significance of the Old Testament for the New Testament to say with B. Lindars, 'The Place of the Old Testament in the Formation of the New Testament Theology' *NTS* 23 (1977), pp. 59-66 (66): 'The place of the Old Testament in the formation of New Testament theology is that of a servant, ready to run to the aid of the gospel whenever it is required, bolstering up arguments, and filling out meaning through evocative allusions, but never acting as the master or leading the way, nor even guiding the process of thought behind the scenes.'

indirect testimony of the same intrinsic value; the letter consistently denies the literal importance of the commandments (see esp. *Barn.* 9).[30]

Finally it should be said that in the long term the reception of the Old Testament into the New Testament meant an end to the ancient Judaeo-Greek flow of traditions, which—based primarily on the Septuagint—resulted in the literature later categorized as the Old Testament Pseudepigrapha. It is suggestive that not only the Gospels and other New Testament literature, but also all the ancient Judaeo-Greek literature was segregated in the course of the second century from rabbinic Judaism to survive only in the Christian tradition; thus it becomes possible, as Martin Reiser has done, to define the writings of the New Testament as the apex of this flow of traditions.[31]

---

30. Cf. M. Müller, 'Jøder og jødedom som teologisk problem i oldkirken', in N.P. Lemche and M. Müller (eds.), *Fra Dybet* (Festschrift John Strange; FBE 5; Copenhagen: Museum Tusculanum, 1994), pp. 180-92.

31. See Reiser, 'Die Stellung der Evangelien', p. 6, where it is said: 'Man kann das Neue Testament geradezu als den literarischen Höhepunkt dieses Traditionsstroms betrachten.' Cf. p. 20.

The New Testament Reception of Judaism in the Second Temple Period

Mikael Winninge

The Literature Considered

If New Testament reception of Judaism is to be discussed, it is necessary to define what Jewish literature shall be considered. Moreover, it is a case of labelling this literature. To begin with the latter, the term 'intertestamental literature' is often used, but it is problematic since it implies a Christian pre-understanding. That would involve speaking of Jewish literature in Christian terms.[1] It is more useful to speak about 'Jewish literature between the Hebrew Bible and the Mishnah'.[2] The only minor difficulty with such a label is the fact that parts of the literature referred to are older than the youngest books in the Hebrew Bible, for example, Sirach and some passages in *1 Enoch*. An alternative label wold be 'Jewish writings of the Second Temple period'.[3] An objection against this label could be that the temple was destroyed in 70 CE, whereas some of the books normally included are from a later period, for example *4 Ezra* and *2 Baruch*. However, such an inconvenience can be accepted since this period designation is widely accepted. With the label decided, it is of greater importance to delimit the literature intended. The translation, reading, and interpretation of the Hebrew Bible is of great interest when New Testament reception of Judaism is studied. The use of the Hebrew Bible can be viewed in several literary corpora, for example in the Targumim and the Midrashim, but rabbinic literature in general poses special problems. Even if the Mishnah, for instance, certainly contains older material,

---

1. G.W.E. Nickelsburg, *Jewish Literature between the Bible and the Mishnah: A Historical and Literary Introduction* (Philadelphia: Fortress Press, 1981), pp. 2-3.
2. Cf. the title of Nickelsburg's book in the preceding footnote.
3. Cf. the title of M.E. Stone (ed.), *Jewish Writings of the Second Temple Period: Apocrypha, Pseudepigrapha, Qumran Sectarian Writings, Philo, Josephus* (CRINT, 2.2; Assen: Van Gorcum; Philadelphia: Fortress Press, 1984).

it is difficult to tell what is true pre-70 Judaism.[4] This leaves us with the following corpora: Apocrypha; Old Testament Pseudepigrapha; Qumran sectarian writings; Philo; and Josephus.[5]

Theoretical Considerations; Three Kinds of Reception

After the decision of what Jewish texts to consider as a basis for New Testament reception, it is important to reflect on what is meant by *reception*. Without making the claim of comprehensiveness, for practical reasons I prefer thinking of three main kinds of reception, each with their own subcategories:

Literary Dependence

Literary dependence can be more or less difficult to prove. The dependence might result in brief accounts, abstracts, excerpts, quotations, allusions or redactional arrangement. Whatever sort of literary dependence there might be, the relation to or the attitude towards the literature used can be of various kinds:

  a.   Proof, confirmation, ideological solidarity.
  b.   Modification, application, revision, adaptation.
  c.   Repudiation, contesting, reinterpretation.

Common Ideological Basic View

In many cases it is impossible to speak about literary dependence, but still the term *reception* can be felt appropriate. One text can be interpreted as providing an adequate background for another. Different texts can be viewed as emerging from the same socio-political and religious stream. Such an ideological stream can contain major and minor groups and subgroups, the structure of which can vary from time to time.

That the author of one text has been acquainted with an older text is often plausible and sometimes even probable, although absolute certainty might be beyond reach. At any rate, the question of reception can be modified and made meaningful nonetheless. When focusing on a common ideological basic view, which can be extracted and reasonably reconstructed from one or more older texts, it is possible to study and evaluate the reception of this tradition in a subsequent text. The basic view can

---

4.   See, e.g., E.P. Sanders, *Judaism: Practice and Belief 63 BCE—66 CE* (London: SCM Press; Philadelphia: Trinity Press International, 1992), p. 10.

5.   Stone, *Jewish Writings*, pp. xvii-xxiii.

either be of a broad cultural mainstream character or of a narrower group-specific kind. In the latter case the results are prone to be more fruitful and interesting. The received common ideological basic view can be treated in various ways:

    a.   Ideological congeniality.
    b.   Situational modification of the basic view.
    c.   Partial contesting of the basic view.

Ideological Deprecation
When a common ideological basic view is shared, reception is not at all surprising. The point in reading texts belonging to other groups in society, let alone opponents, is less obvious. Nevertheless, the question of *reception* can be relevant even if there is no clear literary dependence. Ideological deprecation can be of at least two kinds:

Deprecative 'Contribution to the Debate'. It is important to avoid anachronistic conclusions when speaking in terms of a *debate* in society, but such an analogy cannot be regarded as completely irrelevant, if the Hellenistic spirit of 'openness' is considered. Several competing philosophies were possible. Josephus's description of the Jewish religious parties is a significant example.[6] Reception in a case like this can be described as a common knowledge of an alternative view or lifestyle, which is repudiated in a general manner.

Immediate Criticism of Specific Ideological View. Here reception involves a direct attack and a clear target. The ideology of the opponents is the focal point. In order to understand fully the text in which the reception takes place it is necessary to reconstruct the socio-political and religious provenance of the opponents.

    In this article I will connect to the three kinds of reception described above by giving New Testament examples of each and discussing what subcategory can be used best as a means of interpretation in each case. The following main section of the article therefore consists of three separate parts. First, a rather short and uncomplicated example of New Testament literary dependence on Jewish literature from the Second Temple period. Second, a somewhat longer but quite manageable example of reception of a common ideological basic view. Third, a more extensive

---

6.   Josephus, *Ant.* 18.11-25; *Life* 10–12.

and very complicated example of ideological deprecation of contemporary Judaism in the New Testament.

Example of Literary Dependence

Jude and the Testament of Moses

Jude 9. The fallen angels and Sodom (Jude 6-7) are accompanied by dreamers (v. 8). They slander the good angels, maybe by denying their significance, maybe by using them in magical formulae. In Jude 9 a lost passage from the *Testament of Moses* is adduced. This passage obviously reported how the archangel Michael, while contending with the devil, renounced condemnation of him by leaving judgment to God. The raison d'être of the story is probably found in the fact that the tomb of Moses was unknown according to Deut. 34.5-6. Presumably, the matter in dispute was whether Moses could be taken up to heaven or have his body handed over to the devil because of his killing of the Egyptian (Exod. 2.11-12). According to Philo, angels buried Moses.[7] The missing section of the Testament of Moses might well have reported how the archangel buried Moses in a secret place appointed by God. The literary dependence in Jude 9 is of the confirmative kind, portraying a righteous and exemplary behaviour. Thus we can speak of ideological solidarity here. A detail of special interest is the fact that the text quoted or alluded to is lost.

Jude and 1 Enoch

Jude 14-15. In these verses *1 En.* 1.9 is quoted. The exact wording of the original Hebrew or Aramaic text cannot be reconstructed with certainty. The Ethiopic version of *1 En.* 1.9 can be translated as follows: 'Behold, he will arrive with ten million of the holy ones in order to execute judgment upon all. He will destroy the wicked ones and censure all flesh on account of everything that they have done, that which the sinners and the wicked ones committed against him.'[8] It is also meaningful to compare this version with an Aramaic fragment from Qumran (4Q204) and a Greek fragment.[9] As a matter of fact, the quotation in Jude 14-15 more resembles

---

7. Philo, *Vit. Mos.* 2.291.

8. This is the translation by E. Isaac in *OTP*, I, p. 13-14.

9. For the Aramaic text (4Q204) see J.T. Milik and M. Black, *The Books of Enoch: Aramaic Fragments of Qumrâm Cave 4* (Oxford: Clarendon Press, 1976). For the Greek fragment see M. Black (ed.), *Apocalypsis Henochi Graeci* (PVTG, 3; Leiden: E.J. Brill, 1970), p. 19.

these fragments, the most obvious similarity being the conviction for 'the harsh things that ungodly sinners have spoken against him' (Jude 15). The point of interest here, however, is the way in which 'Jude' obviously has changed the meaning of the original text. Whereas all the mentioned texts report that he (God) will come with his holy ones, 'Jude' exchanges the actor by inserting 'the Lord': 'See, *the Lord* is coming with ten thousands of his holy ones' (Jude 14). For 'Jude' the Lord is Christ. Such a revision is probably polemically meant, since the opponents seem to have questioned the traditional expectations concerning the return of Christ. Therefore it is reasonable to understand the reception of *1 En.* 1.9 in Jude 14-15 as an instance of 'modification, application, revision, or adaptation', inasmuch as 'Jude' modifies the quoted text, adapting it for the specific situation of the original recipients of his letter. It is worth noting that 'Jude' says that Enoch *prophesied*, thereby indicating that *1 En.* was understood to comprise prophecies, the implication of which is that the book was regarded as holy scripture in one sense or another. The concept of canonicity within Judaism was not fixed once and for all at this time. Ironically, because of this, the value of Jude was anachronistically questioned in the subsequent canonical process within Christianity.

As an example of New Testament reception of Old Testament Pseudepigrapha the letter of Jude is illustrative. The patristic reception of the Letter of Jude, however, sometimes became problematic, inasmuch as *1 Enoch* was viewed as holy scripture by 'Jude', but not in early Christianity.[10]

Example of Common Ideological Basic View

Galatians and the Psalms of Solomon

A good reason for comparing Galatians with the *Psalms of Solomon* is that both texts were written by persons of Pharisaic background.[11] In the following I will develop an aspect of my previous research on the *Psalms of Solomon*.

Pss. Sol. 10.4; 14.2-3. According to the *Psalms of Solomon*, piety of everyday life was very important. Through sincere pious living unintentional sins could be forgiven and the devout could even atone for unknown sins

---

10. E.g. Jerome, *De Vir. Illust.* 4.

11. M. Winninge, *Sinners and the Righteous: A Comparative Study of the Psalms of Solomon and Paul's Letters* (ConBNT, 26; Stockholm: Almqvist & Wiksell, 1995), p. 180.

('sins of ignorance') by humble fasting (*Pss. Sol.* 3.6-8). For such a pious life the Torah was significant. In *Pss. Sol.* 14.2 the devout are 'those who live in the righteousness of his commandments, in the Law [i.e. the Torah], which he has commanded for our life [i.e. that we may live]'. Indeed, 'the Lord's devout shall live by it [the Torah] forever' (*Pss. Sol.* 14.3) Thus, a 'positive' role is ascribed to the Torah, a guiding and life-giving function.[12] The Torah provides the means for remaining within the covenantal sphere and it testifies that the devout are remembered in mercy (*Pss. Sol.* 10.4).[13]

How does Paul view this 'positive' role of the Torah? In one sense Paul recognizes it. This is obvious in Rom. 7.12: 'So the law is holy, and the commandment is holy and just and good'.[14] So far we may speak of ideo-logical congeniality. In Galatians Paul is more reserved. The validity of the Torah is clearly restricted and its positive potential less evident: 'for if justification comes through the law, then Christ died for nothing' (Gal. 2.21; cf. 3.17-18). It is more adequate to label this attitude situational modification. In a certain perspective Paul completely denies the positive force of the Torah. Without hesitation he rejects the view that the Torah can make alive (Gal. 3.21; cf. 3.11-12). Paul's words in Rom. 7.10 are revealing: 'and I died, and the very commandment that promised life proved to be death to me'. These expressions show that Paul at this point dissociates himself from the Pharisees and the views he once shared. Instead he speaks of 'the law of the Spirit of the life in Christ Jesus' (Rom. 8.2). This is partial contesting of the basic view. What can be made of this at least seemingly inconsistent picture? Since Paul emphatically maintains that the Torah is not opposed to the promises of God (Gal. 3.21), we probably should conclude that Paul *modifies* his former Pharisaic view of the 'positive' role of the Torah, at least if we choose to regard him as a coherent thinker. In sum, this is a situational modification of the basic view then.

Pss. Sol. 7.9; 10.1-4; 14.1-2. Several times the *Psalms of Solomon* demon-strate how an individual or a whole community can be cleansed from sin and guilt by means of discipline (*paideia*). To be forgiven the devout have to confess their sins, acknowledge the Lord as their disciplinarian (*Pss. Sol.* 8.29), and endure his chastisement. This view was characteristic of the

---

12. Winninge, *Sinners*, pp. 119-20
13. Winninge, *Sinners*, pp. 79-80, 202, 323-24.
14. Cf. Rom. 7.14, 16, 21-23.

Pharisees. Also in this context the importance of the Torah was significant. In *Pss. Sol.* 10.1-4 a unique combination of the words 'whip' (*mastix*) and 'discipline' (*paideia*) can be found in explicit connection with the Torah (*nomos*), which through its testimony functioned as a critical examinator of men's lives in continuous supervision (*en episkopēi*). In a similar manner the law is portrayed as a yoke according to *Pss. Sol.* 7.9: 'we are under your everlasting yoke and the whip of your discipline'. The description of the yoke as everlasting is notable, not least because it gives hints for a correct interpretation. As a matter of fact, the Torah is often described as a yoke in rabbinic literature.[15] The yoke of the law is basically understood as a privilege. The remarkable thing about the *Psalms of Solomon* is that whips and discipline are mentioned at the same time. Indeed, 'those who endure the Lord's discipline' (*Pss. Sol.* 14.1) are the same as 'those who live in the righteousness of his commandments' (*Pss. Sol.* 14.2). Consequently, the Torah does not only have a 'positive' life-giving function according to the *Psalms of Solomon*, but also a 'negative' chastising one. Here it must be emphasized that 'negative' by no means is a valuation. It is only a way of defining the restrictive role of the Torah and keeping it logically distinct from the 'positive' guiding role. Ultimately, however, the 'negative' function serves a 'positive' purpose.[16]

Gal. 3.21-25. I do not consider it likely that Paul, the Pharisee, felt uncomfortable and dissatisfied with his Jewish religion before he became a Christian.[17] Nevertheless, I think it is time to realize that Paul, even as a Pharisee, could assign the Torah a 'negative' role.[18] As a matter of fact, I think this is exactly what he does in Gal. 3.24 when he speaks about the law as a *paidagōgos*. The combination of *nomos* and *paideia* becomes understandable against the background of the *Psalms of Solomon*. The *paidagōgos* was the slave who brought the boy to school and back again. In school the boy would get training and education (*paideia*) from his teacher (*paideutēs*). The two words *paideia* and *paideutēs* normally have to do with rearing of children, learning and teaching, but sometimes they can have the more specific denotation of 'discipline' and 'disciplinarian'

---

15. *M. Ab.* 3.5; *b. Sanh.* 94b. Cf. *2 En.* 48.6-9 and *2 Bar.* 41.3. See also Mt. 11.28-30; Acts 15.10; and *Did.* 6.2. See further Winninge, *Sinners*, pp. 116-17.

16. Winninge, *Sinners*, pp. 139, 205-206, 324-25.

17. So correctly, e.g., K. Stendahl, *Paul among Jews and Gentiles and Other Essays* (Philapelphia: Fortress Press, 1976).

18. Winninge, *Sinners*, p. 325. See also pp. 296-97 in connection with Rom. 3.19-20.

respectively, as in the *Psalms of Solomon*. If Paul was thinking of the Torah in those terms, he might have chosen the less ambiguous and somewhat rougher *paidagōgos* on purpose. To find a suitable translation of the word and a reasonable interpretation of the metaphor are classic exegetical issues. At any rate the meaning is not teacher or tutor, as the choice of *paideutēs* could have implied. Custodian (RSV) is one possibility, disciplinarian (NRSV) another. The idea of supervision is clearly at hand (cf. the *episkopē* of the law in *Pss. Sol.* 10.4).[19] Although the purpose of the Torah is basically 'positive' according to Paul, just as the role of the *paidagōgos* ultimately was, we should recognize the 'negative' function of it. A significant difference is that, whereas the chastising yoke in the *Psalms of Solomon* was everlasting, the disciplinary role of the Torah was temporary according to Paul. Thus the expression *eis Christon* can be translated 'until Christ came' (NRSV).[20] For at least two reasons it is notable that Paul in Galatians also speaks about the law as 'a yoke of slavery' (Gal. 5.1). First, the description of the Torah as a yoke occurs here, just as in the *Psalms of Solomon*. Second, the slavery image corresponds to the use of the term *paidagōgos* (a slave) and strengthens its 'negative' connotation, that is, the idea of discipline and supervision. To sum up, as far as the 'negative' restrictive function of the Torah is concerned, surprisingly enough we find clear ideological congeniality.

Excursus on the 'Negative' Role of the Torah

It is worthwhile to reflect on what 'whips' and 'discipline' meant to Paul. Before the experience on his way to Damascus Paul was involved in the persecution of Christians and in taking strong disciplinary measures because of negligence of the law in Diaspora synagogues. Were disciplinary measures and preaching circumcision (cf. Gal. 5.11) a typical Pharisaic business? It is notable that Paul in one breath can say 'as to the law, a Pharisee; as to zeal, a persecutor of the church' (Phil. 3.5-6). (By the way, persecution seems to be the single obvious sin in his life.)[21] As a Christian, Paul himself experienced persecution and severe disciplinary measures taken against him in Diaspora synagogues. Five times he received 'the forty lashes minus one' (2 Cor. 11.23-25). When Paul says, 'through the law I died to the law... I have been crucified with Christ' (Gal. 2.19-20),

19. Cf. the translation 'under the supervision of' (NIV).
20. E.g. Stendahl, *Paul*.
21. Cf. Gal. 1.13-14 and 1 Cor. 4.4.

he is perhaps reflecting on a paradox—Christ as the end of the 'negative' role of the Torah on the one hand, and his own suffering on the other. His words in Gal. 6.17 are characteristic: 'I carry the marks of Jesus branded on my body'. Maybe this is what the author of Colossians wants to express on Paul's account: 'I am now rejoicing in my sufferings for your sake, and in my flesh I am completing what is lacking in Christ's afflictions for the sake of his body, that is, the church' (Col. 1.24).

Example of Ideological Deprecation

Galatians and 4QMMT
Until recently the Pauline *erga nomou* in Gal. 2.16 was considered to be a philological innovation. Paul uses the expression as many as three times in Gal. 2.16 and thereafter in Gal. 3.2, 5 and 10. Elsewhere the expression only occurs in Rom. 3.20 and 28. There have been different opinions concerning the reference of the expression and its conceptual contents. It has even been claimed that Paul either misunderstood his own Jewish heritage or for polemical reasons deliberately misconstrued the piety of his Jewish contemporaries. At any rate, at the focal point of the debate was the interpretation of the Torah and its practical implications. Already at the philological level there is uncertainty with regard to the expression *erga nomou*. A literal translation of the Greek genitive construction would be 'works of the law'.[22] If the genitive is understood as a genitive of quality, *nomos* must be some kind of attributive, 'legal works'.[23] Another option is the objective genitive, which might give the translation 'observing the law'.[24] An additional possibility is the subjective genitive, denoting origin or cause, as in the following translations: 'works required by the law' or 'works originating from the law'.[25] Irrespective of translation an important question has to be answered: what is meant by the law (*nomos*)? Is it the Torah, materialized by the five books of Moses? Is it the whole Hebrew bible? Is it doctrine, like an abstract sum of the contents of the holy

---

22. E.g. NRSV. See also H.D. Betz, *Galatians* (Hermeneia; Philadelphia: Fortress Press, 1979), p. 113; and J.D.G. Dunn, *A Commentary on the Epistle to the Galatians* (London: A. & C. Black, 1993), p. 131. Cf. the German translation 'Werke des Gesetzes' in *Einheitsübersetzung*.

23. E.g. F.F. Bruce, *The Epistle to the Galatians: A Commentary on the Greek Text* (NIGTC; Exeter: Paternoster Press, 1982), p. 136.

24. E.g. NIV.

25. Cf. the French translation 'il accomplit ce qu'ordonne la loi [de Moïse]' in *La bible en français courant*.

scriptures; only the ten commandments; the Jewish ceremonial law; the specific *halakhic* laws functioning as Jewish identity markers; or a Platonic idea?[26] At any rate, there can be no doubt that the concept of *erga nomou* is central in Paul's thought. This can easily be detected in the antithesis of the idea. According to Gal. 2.16, it is a matter of being justified or put right 'by the works of the law' or 'through faith in Jesus Christ'.[27]

After too much secretiveness among the initiated the Polish scholar Z.J. Kapera boldly decided to make the important Qumran document 4QMMT public in the first issue of *The Qumran Chronicle* (1990). Two years later R.H. Eisenman and M.O. Wise presented a Hebrew text with translation and interpretation in their not so reliable bestseller *The Dead Sea Scrolls Uncovered* (1992).[28] Another two years, and eventually the text-critical edition by E. Qimron and J. Strugnell, *Miqsat Ma'ase Ha-Torah*, was published (1994).[29] The whole document 4QMMT has been named by the key expression *miqsat ma'ase ha-torah*, which according to Qimron's and Strugnell's translation is 'some of the precepts of the Torah' (4QMMT C27).[30] However, this translation is far from self-evident. M.G. Abegg has claimed that 'this translation unfortunately obscures MMT's relationship to Paul's letters'.[31] He has suggested the translation 'pertinent works of the law'.[32] A similar and perhaps even better rendering of the word *miqsat* is 'selection',[33] which might lead us to the translation 'a selection of works of the Torah'. Of course, this presumably implies that these works also are

26. E.g. Winninge, *Sinners*, pp. 214-18.

27. In Gal. 3.2 and 5 the antithesis is 'hearing of faith', which can be translated in several ways, but most probably 'hearing with faith' (genitive of quality), and means believing what you hear.

28. R.H. Eisenman and M.O. Wise, *The Dead Sea Scrolls Uncovered* (Shaftesbury: Element Books, 1992). For severe criticism of their book see, e.g., *K. Berger, Qumran und Jesus: Wahrheit unter Verschluss?* (Stuttgart: Quell, 1993), pp. 20-40.

29. DJD, 10; Oxford: Clarendon Press.

30. See 4QMMT C27 in Qimron and Strugnell, *Miqsat*, p. 63. The same translation occurs in 4QMMT 113 according to F. García Martínez, *The Dead Sea Scrolls Translated* (Leiden: E.J. Brill, 1994), p. 79.

31. M.G. Abegg, 'Paul, "Works of the Law" and MMT', *BARev* 20 (1994), pp. 52-55. See also *idem*, '4QMMT C27, 31 and Works Righteousness', DSD 6 (1999), pp. 139-47.

32. Cf. P. Grelot, 'Les oevres de la Loi', *RevQ* 16 (1994), pp. 441-48.

33. This was suggested during a seminar discussion at the Society for New Testament Scholars (SNTS) meeting in Birmingham, 1997.

the most pertinent. The translation by G. Vermes is 'some of the observances of the Law'.[34] The choice of 'observances' better captures the meaning than 'precepts', because the focus is more on practice than on rules as such. At any rate, 4QMMT with its key expression *ma'ase hatorah* provides us with the exact Hebrew equivalent of Paul's *erga nomou*. Consequently, the concept 'works of the law' now can be considered as firmly rooted in Jewish pre-Christian soil. Even if the full significance of the concept can only be determined by a deeper study of 4QMMT, it is obvious that a comparison is meaningful, not least because the concept is so central in both 4QMMT and Galatians. Moreover, it should be noted that in 4QMMT C31 (in the same context as the expression *ma'ase hatorah*, 4QMMT C27) a reference to Abraham is made: 'he believed the Lord; and the Lord reckoned it to him as righteousness' (Gen. 15.6). The same biblical verse appears in Gal. 3.6, a single verse after one of the instances of 'works of the law' (Gal. 3.5).[35] Thus, it is not merely a matter of similar expressions in use, but of both conceptual and contextual likeness. Both texts concern covenant and eschatology.[36] It might even be the case that both texts are letters.[37]

If a comparative study of 4QMMT and Galatians is to be meaningful it is necessary to reflect on some questions of background. First of all, the historical background of 4QMMT has to be discussed. Since Eisenman and Wise wrote their controversial *The Dead Sea Scrolls Uncovered* several hypotheses have appeared. Eisenman made the unlikely claim that Qumran was an early Christian community of former Zealots with James, the brother of Jesus, as the teacher of righteousness.[38] According to Qimron

34. G. Vermes, *The Complete Dead Sea Scrolls in English* (Harmondsworth: Penguin Books, 1997).

35. Yet, in 4QMMT C31 righteousness depends on action, 'when you perform what is right and good', whereas Gal. 3.6 focuses on belief.

36. N.T. Wright, '4QMMT and Paul: The Contexts of Justification' (seminar paper from the SNTS meeting in Copenhagen, 1998).

37. So according to Qimron and Strugnell, *Miqsat*. However, Strugnell later changed his mind on this issue. R.H. Eisenman, on the other hand, has maintained the idea of a letter. See also M. Bachmann, '4QMMT und Galaterbrief, *ma'ase ha-torah* und *erga nomou*', *ZNW* 89 (1998), pp. 91-113. For opposition to this view see, e.g., F. García Martínez, '4QMMT in a Qumran Context', in J. Kampen and M.J. Bernstein (eds.), *Reading 4QMMT: New Perspectives on Qumran Law and History* (Atlanta: Scholars Press, 1996), pp. 15-27.

38. R.H. Eisenman, *James the Just and the Habbakuk Pesher* (Leiden: E.J. Brill, 1986). Cf. N.A. Silberman, *The Hidden Scrolls* (New York: Grosset/Putnam, 1994).

and Strugnell 4QMMT consisted of a letter from Qumran, maybe by the teacher of righteousness, to their opponents in Jerusalem, the high priest included ('the wicked priest'). The purpose of the letter was to make clear differences in Torah interpretation and urge change. The tone of the letter is relatively polite. The opinions in the letter collide with Pharisaic views and accord with those of the Essenes, and sometimes with those of the Sadducees.[39] H. Stegemann has another hypothesis, according to which the teacher of righteousness was high priest during the period 159–152 BCE, but was removed by Jonathan Maccabaeus, who usurped power and the position of high priest. In exile the teacher of righteousness sought to organize an encompassing national Essene movement with aims such as true Torah interpretation and legitimately practised cult. Not least because of the fact that Jonathan was not a Zadokite, he could not be accepted by the teacher of righteousness. According to 4QpPs[a] Jonathan received a letter, which Stegemann identifies with 4QMMT. This resulted in an attempted assassination of the founder of Essenism.[40] A fourth hypothesis has been presented by F. García Martínez, who places the formative period of Essenism at the end of the third century BCE To his mind there was a schism among the Essenes in the second century. In this situation the teacher of righteousness wrote 4QMMT, addressed not to the political establishment in Jerusalem but to the larger Essene group, from which the Qumran group split. The leader of the other group was designated 'the liar' (e.g. 4QpPs[a]). The dispute behind 4QMMT was about biblical interpretation. The main topics of controversy were the calendar, rules of ritual purity pertaining to the temple and Jerusalem, *halakhoth* about impurity, tithes, and marriage.[41] A fifth hypothesis worth mentioning is the one suggested by L.H. Schiffman, who with reference to the interpretation of Torah claims a Sadducean background for 4QMMT. The document can

39. Qimron and Strugnell, *Miqsat*. This quite common view is shared also by, e.g., J.C. VanderKam, *The Dead Sea Scrolls Today* (Grand Rapids: Eerdmans, 1994), pp. 59-60. According to J.M. Baumgarten, at least some of the halakhic rules are clearly Sadducean. ('The "Halakha" in MMT', *JAOS* 116 [1996], pp. 512-16. For criticism of Qimron's and Strugnell's historical interpretation see, e.g., S. Medala, 'Some Remarks on the Official Publication of MMT', *The Qumran Chronicle* 4 (1994), pp. 193-202, and B.W.W. Dombrowski, '4QMMT after DJD X: Qumran Cave 4. Part V', *The Qumran Chronicle* 5 (1995), pp. 151-71.

40. H. Stegemann, *Die Essener, Qumran, Johannes der Täufer und Jesus: Ein Sachbuch* (Freiburg: Herder, 4th edn, 1994), pp. 148-51, 198-226.

41. F. García Martínez, *The People of the Dead Sea Scrolls* (Leiden: E.J. Brill, 1995), pp. 91-96.

explain the origin of the Qumran group in terms of priestly disputes concerning the impact of Hellenism on society, different positions during the Maccabean revolt and conflicting attitudes towards the Hasmoneans and their high priestly ambitions.[42] One of the difficulties with Schiffman's hypothesis is how the reconstruction of Sadducean views is made.[43] More problematic is another kind of hypothesis, maintained by N. Golb, according to whom the site of Qumran is not related to the production of the scrolls. Qumran was only a Jewish fortress, and the scrolls discovered in the vicinity were documents brought from Jerusalem and saved from destruction in the Jewish war.[44] After all this, in the light of all of the conflicting hypotheses the critical question by P.R. Davies is understandable: 'Was there really a Qumran Community?'[45] I do not intend to answer the question about the historical background of 4QMMT in this article but one thing is sure: the question is relevant to a comparative study of the 'works of the law' in 4QMMT and Galatians. As a matter of principle it cannot be excluded that Paul was fighting against opponents who one way or other were related to the movement behind 4QMMT. For instance, Paul blames the Galatians for 'observing special days, and months, and seasons, and years' (Gal. 4.10). I am not arguing that this is likely, but all similarities must be considered. If Paul's opponents can be identified, and if it can

---

42. L.H. Schiffman, *Reclaiming the Dead Sea Scrolls* (AB; Garden City, NY: Doubleday, 1994). See also *idem*, 'Origin and Early History of the Qumran Sect', *BA* 58 (1995), pp. 37-48.

43. See, e.g., O. Betz, 'The Qumran Halakhah Text Miqsat Ma'ase Ha-Torah (4QMMT) and Sadducean, Essene, and Early Pharisaic Tradition', in D.R.G. Beattie and M.J. McNamara (eds.), *The Aramaic Bible: Targums in their Historical Context* (JSOTSup, 166; Sheffield: JSOT Press, 1994), pp. 176-202. Baumgarten, 'The "Halakha"', gives him some support. So does I. Gruenwald, '4QMMT: Its Significance for the Study and Understanding of Ancient Judaism and Early Christianity' (seminar paper from the SNTS meeting in Copenhagen, 1998). It is interesting that 4QMMT C10 mentions both the book of Moses and the books of the Prophets and David (Psalms), since the latter did not have the same status according to what are generally considered as Sadducean views, at least if we believe Josephus.

44. N. Golb, *Who Wrote the Dead Sea Scrolls? The Search for the Secret of Qumran* (New York: Charles Scribner's Sons, 1995). Cf. L. Cansdale, *Qumran and the Essenes: A Re-Evaluation of the Evidence* (Texte und Studien zum Antiken Judentum, 60; Tübingen: J.C.B Mohr, 1997). For serious criticim of Golb's theory see, e.g., Stegemann, *Die Essener*, pp. 94-95. For a modification of Golb's views see Silberman, *Hidden Scrolls*.

45. P.R. Davies, 'Was There Really a Qumran Community?', *Currents in Research: Biblical Studies* 3 (1995), pp. 9-35.

be claimed that they spoke about the 'works of the law' in a way similar to that in 4QMMT, we are bound to conclude that Galatians involves immediate criticism of a specific ideological view.

A second question of great significance for a comparative study is the view of the Torah and its interpretation in 4QMMT and in Paul's letters. Much has been written on 'Paul and the law' in the last two decades, since the topic has been regarded as crucial for an understanding of Pauline theology.[46] Scholars have tried to explain Paul's Torah-critical statements in various ways, but some main directions in their efforts of solving the problem can nevertheless be detected. According to the 'qualitative' solution the law simply does not suffice. With the 'quantitative' solution the law is without meaning, since nobody anyhow can fulfil it. The 'backwards-dogmatic' model of explanation maintains that Paul was satisfied with the Torah and the observance of it, but after his experience of a risen Christ he realized that he had to reassess his former perception of the Torah. The plight of humankind was more serious than he previously had believed and the function of the law appeared to be temporary. A fourth explanatory direction is the 'sociological' one, according to which the law was not questioned until the practical problems of dealings between Jewish and non-Jewish Christians in mixed societies were fully realized. Torah observance tended to create a barrier between Christians of different origin. The fifth solution can be described as the idea of 'twofold fulfilment', meaning that the Torah has remaining validity for Jews but has been 'replaced' by Jesus for Gentiles.[47] A radical claim in this connection is that Paul lacks a logically consistent view of the law altogether.[48] To understand Paul is one part of the necessary background discussion. The other is to consider how the Torah is viewed in 4QMMT. It is promising that the question of Torah and *halakhah* at Qumran now more and more is being studied.[49]

46. See, e.g., Winninge, *Sinners*, pp. 214-18.

47. For a good summary see G.M. Smiga, 'Preaching at Risk: Interpreting Paul's Statements on the Law', *New Theology Review* 9 (1996), pp. 74-95. See also K. Snodgrass, 'Spheres of Influence as a Possible Solution to the Problem of Paul and the Law', in S.E. Porter and C.A. Evans (eds.), *The Pauline Writings: A Sheffield Reader* (The Biblical Seminar, 34; Sheffield Readers, 2; Atlanta; Sheffield: Sheffield Academic Press, 1995).

48. H. Räisänen, *Paul and the Law* (WUNT, 29; Tübingen: J.C.B. Mohr, 2nd edn, 1987 [1983]).

49. E.g. P.R. Davies, 'Halakah at Qumran', in *Sects and Scrolls: Essays on Qumran and Related Topics* (Atlanta: Scholars Press, 1996), pp. 113-26.

I consider it quite unlikely that Paul ever read 4QMMT or even knew about it. If we were to assume that he was acquainted with it, it would be more or less impossible to prove.[50] Neither would I dare to make the claim that Paul in Galatians is taking sides against people who adhere to precisely those precepts that can be found in 4QMMT. However, I do believe that the usage of the expression 'works of the law' in 4QMMT and Galatians is closely related. I assume that the concept was important for several contemporary Jewish groups. I deem it plausible that the Pharisees normally used the expression *halakhah*, whereas the Essenes (and maybe the Sadducees) chose to speak about *ma'ase ha-torah*. It may be significant that the Pharisees are often designated in the Qumran texts as 'the seekers of smooth things' (*chalakhoth*), which probably is a pun for 'the seekers of correct behaviour' (*halakhoth*). The Qumran group accused the Pharisees of being too lenient in matters of *halakhah*. They regarded Pharisaic Torah interpretation and observance as 'slippery' and opportunistic. Thus, it would have been surprising if the Essenes (or Sadducees) had chosen the word *halakhah* to denote their own application of the commandments. My hypothesis is that the expression 'works of the law' is a synonym of *halakhah*.[51] That is not to say that the contents are the same—not at all—but that the terms are each other's equivalents in their respective societies. I think it is noteworthy how Paul uses the expression *pneumati peripatein* ('walk by the Spirit') in Gal. 5.16, because this might very well be a deliberate play on words. Is he aiming at outdoing the *halakhah* ('walk', 'practice') of his opponents? This would imply that Paul in Galatians is polemizing against a specific ritual and ethical application of the Torah. Indeed, when the 'works of the law' expression in Gal. 2.16 is interpreted, the *halakhic* context of Gal. 2.11–14 has to be considered.[52] Maybe the attitude of those separating from the mass of the people in 4QMMT C7 corresponds to the fear of Cephas and Barnabas when they separated themselves from the Gentile Christians in Antioch (Gal. 2.12-

50. Cf. J. Kampen, '4QMMT and New Testament Studies', in J. Kampen and M.J. Bernstein (eds.), *Reading 4QMMT: New Perspectives on Qumran Law and History* (SBL Symposium Series, 2; Atlanta: Scholas Press, 1996), pp. 129-44. See also Grelot, 'Les oevres'.

51. So according to A. Finkel during a seminar discussion at the SBL meeting in San Francisco, 1997. According to E. Qimron and J. Strugnell, the term *miqsat* is avoided because of the author's opponents, who were Pharisees. See also Gruenwald, '4QMMT', and Bachmann, '4QMMT'.

52. E.g. 4QMMT B3–9 is about purity and defilement by Gentiles. See J.D.G. Dunn, '4QMMT and Galatians', *NTS* 43 (1997), pp. 147-53. See also Wright, '4QMMT'.

13). The implication of all this is not that Paul sets Jesus against the Torah as such, which commonly is presumed. Rather, the mutually exclusive alternatives are faith (in Jesus) and certain interpretations and applications of the Torah. Thus, it is a matter of *halakhah* versus faith in Gal. 2.16. Consequently, it is not so much a matter of 'getting in' through faith as of 'staying in', since the alternative (*halakhah*) concerns everyday life. To conclude: what then can be said about reception of Judaism in this instance? Since it seems obvious that Paul did not share a common ideological basic view pertaining to Torah observance with the group behind 4QMMT, and since it is quite unlikely that Paul's opponents were closely related to that movement, the most reasonable conclusion is that Paul comes with a deprecative 'contribution to the debate'. In that case, Paul shares a common knowledge of an alternative lifestyle, which he repudiates. However, considering how harsh his attack is, we cannot exclude the possibility that Paul has a very well-defined target of opponents in mind. If so, he is criticizing the specific ideological view of his opponents. Our only problem then is to establish the legacy and precise identity of that group. To sum up, we have to leave the question open whether we ought to speak of a deprecatic contribution to the debate, or an immediate criticism of a specific ideological view here.

Suggestions for Further Study

There is much to be done in the comparative field and a good reason for that is 'the apparent absence of the phrase [works of the law] in other extant Jewish literature'.[53] Some scholars soon emphasized the need of further investigation concerning the relevance of 4QMMT in Pauline studies.[54] Articles began to appear.[55] As can be expected, more has been done with focus directly on 4QMMT.[56] An important perspective, to my mind, is a

53. Kampen, '4QMMT'.

54. See esp. M. Abegg, 'Paul', and Grelot, 'Les oevres'. See also Kampen, '4QMMT'; Dunn, *Galatians*, pp. 78-80, and P.J. Tomson, *Paul and the Jewish Law* (CRINT; Assen: Van Gorcum; Philadelphia: Fortress Press, 1990), p. 66.

55. E.g. D. Flusser, 'Die Gesetzwerke in Qumran und bei Paulus', in P. Schäfer (ed.), *Geschichte—Tradition—Reflexion*. I. *Iudentum* (Festschrift für M. Hengel zum 70. Geburtstag; Tübingen: J.C.B Mohr, 1996) pp. 395-403; Dunn, '4QMMT'; and Bachmann, '4QMMT'.

56. Except those already mentioned e.g. H. Eshel, '4QMMT and the History of the Hasmonean Period', D.R. Schwartz, 'MMT, Josephus and the Pharisees', both in Kampen and Bernstein (eds.), *Reading 4QMMT: New Perspectives on Qumran Law*

text-internal study of 4QMMT with regard to the expression 'works of the law'.[57] This involves focusing on the contextual aspects of the document. Another significant perspective is an investigation of the communicative potential of the text.[58] Experience from the New Testament field demonstrates how appropriate such an approach can be. Reflection on what the implied readers of the text are like will probably also be helpful.

Concluding Reflections

Three main kinds of New Testament reception of Judaism in the Second Temple period have been discussed. Literary dependence is of course the first we think of, but in this article it has been argued that reception can also be understood in terms of ideological backgrounds, either as a common ideological basic view, or as ideological deprecation. 'Paul and the law' is a topic that can exemplify both kinds of background. Paul cannot simply be regarded as a theological innovator, but rather as one who receives and transforms. And the kind of reception varies from case to case.

and History (SBL Symposium Series, 2; Atlanta: Scholas Press, 1996), pp. 67-80; P.R. Callaway, '4QMMT and Recent Hypotheses about the Origin of the Qumran Community', in *Mogilany 1993: Papers on the Dead Sea Scrolls* (Krakow: Enigma Press, 1996) pp. 15-29; A.I. Baumgarten, 'Crisis in the Scrollery: A Dying Consensus', *Judaism* 44 (1995), pp. 399-413; S. Medala, 'The Character and Historical Setting of 4QMMT', *The Qumran Chronicle* 4 (1994), pp. 1-27; J.M. Baumgarten, 'Sadducean Elements in Qumran Law', in E. Ulrich and J.C. VanderKam (eds.), *The Community of the Renewed Covenant* (Notre Dame, IN: University of Notre Dame Press, 1994) pp. 27-36; S. Talmon, 'The Community of the Renewed Covenant: Between Judaism and Christianity', in E. Ulrich and J.C. VanderKam (eds.), *The Community*; I. Knohl, 'Reconsidering the Dating and Recipient of MMT', *Hebrew Studies* 37 (1996), pp. 119-25; and A. Caquot, 'Un exposé polémique de pratique sectaires (4QMMT)', *RHPR* 76 (1996), pp. 257-76.

57. Bachmann, '4QMMT', is working in that direction.
58. This also involves reflecting on the 'we', 'you' and 'they' of the document.

THE RECEPTION OF GRAECO-ROMAN CULTURE
IN THE NEW TESTAMENT: THE CASE OF ROMANS 7.7-25

Troels Engberg-Pedersen

Six General Points

There are two ways of addressing the reception of Graeco-Roman culture in the New Testament: one general and methodological and the other more specific and tied to individual texts. The latter is the important one. This is where relating the New Testament to Graeco-Roman culture proves its value by throwing new light on the New Testament itself. And this is where the comparison allows for the wide range of dissimilarities and similarities vis-à-vis the Graeco-Roman context that go with the particularity of any individual New Testament phenomenon being studied. Nevertheless there are also some general truths in this area, and I shall begin from those. They are by now fairly banal, but perhaps merit a summarizing restatement. Next I shall examine in some detail a single example of the reception of Graeco-Roman culture in the New Testament, namely Paul's account in Rom. 7.7-25 of the relationship between the Mosaic Law and sin. I shall not attempt to give any general, substantive overview of the reception of Graeco-Roman culture in the New Testament as a whole—for example 'How has Graeco-Roman culture been received in the Synoptic Gospels?' (and so forth). To some extent, that has already been done.[1] And in any case it would not highlight the importance of the issue, which is to throw genuinely new light on the New Testament itself and to help us understand *that* better. For that purpose a specific example will serve better.

There are six points at the level of general, methodological reflection.

---

1. See, e.g., the following excellent volumes in the Library of Early Christianity edited by Wayne A. Meeks: J.E. Stambaugh and D.L. Balch, *The New Testament in its Social Environment* (LEC, 2; Philadelphia: Westminster Press, 1986), and D.E. Aune, *The New Testament in its Literary Environment* (LEC, 8; Philadelphia: Westminster Press, 1987).

From Reception to Context

Talk about the 'reception' of Graeco-Roman culture in the New Testament must not be understood to imply that there is something (the New Testament) that may be identified on its own—and may then be said to have 'received' or incorporated aspects of Graeco-Roman culture in such a manner that these might in principle again be shed off while leaving the New Testament 'itself' intact. Instead, the idea should be that the New Testament *belongs within* a context which consists, among other things, of Graeco-Roman culture—but also of (Hellenistic) Judaism, including the Old Testament. The New Testament is the outcome, one might say, of a confluence of impulses. It is clearly not some independently identifiable entity lying alongside this confluence. Nor should we feel comfortable if somebody should choose to speak of the New Testament as constituting a 'creative transformation' of its contextual input in the sense of being something 'new', spectacularly valuable, even 'unique' and thus to be *contrasted* with its Jewish and Graeco-Roman context. We may personally feel that that is just what the New Testament is. But it is an idea that we should attempt to put aside when carrying out dispassionate historical analysis.

The New Testament within Hellenistic Judaism within the Graeco-Roman world

If the basic idea is that of context, one could be tempted to ask how the New Testament relates to what might initially be taken to be its 'two contexts': that of Hellenistic Judaism and that of the Graeco-Roman world more broadly conceived. Such a question would be wrongheaded, however. There is no distinction to be drawn once and for all of a basic, categorical or clearly formulable kind between Hellenistic Judaism and Graeco-Roman culture, a distinction one might then employ to claim that the New Testament belongs primarily within a Hellenistic Jewish context and only secondarily within a Graeco-Roman context. Rather, the New Testament belongs *within* Hellenistic Judaism—which again belongs *within* the Graeco-Roman world.

This point may be made in a different way. It is quite possible to distinguish, in the confluence of impulses issuing in the New Testament, between elements that are specifically 'Jewish-Hellenistic' and others that are specifically 'Graeco- or Roman-Hellenistic'. Thus specifically 'Jewish-Hellenistic' elements are ideas or practices with distinct roots in *pre-*Hellenistic Judaism.[2] Correspondingly, specifically 'Graeco- or Roman-

2. For clarification: let the 'Hellenistic period' proper begin with Alexander.

Hellenistic' elements are ideas or practices with distinct roots in the pre-Hellenistic Greek or Roman world. But once we have drawn this distinction we must hasten to add the following two points. (1) Specifically 'Jewish-Hellenistic' elements do not, of course, turn up in the New Testament in their original, pre-Hellenistic form. Nor do specifically 'Graeco- or Roman-Hellenistic' elements turn up in the New Testament in *their* original, pre-Hellenistic form. The *confluence* of impulses remains a fact. (2) We should not *a priori* expect there to be any contrast between the two types of elements. They need not enter into any kind of friction. It remains to be seen, by careful analysis from case to case, whether there is friction or fusion in the way they are part of the confluence. *A priori* one would expect the probability of fusion or amalgam to be far greater than that of friction, just because they are part of the confluence. But the issue must be determined through an open-minded analysis of the details.

The Purpose of Contextualization

Contextualization of the New Testament may serve many different purposes. As part of New Testament scholarship, however, one purpose should be in focus: that of bringing out the shape and meaning of the New Testament world itself and the New Testament texts. There are two sides to this focus. (1) The aim is not just to take stock of phenomena in the New Testament and compare them wholly from the outside, as one thing with another, with other similar phenomena in antiquity or later. That aim would be perfectly all right, for example, in a history of religion. But as part of New Testament scholarship, contextualization aims to illuminate, elucidate and clarify the shape and meaning of the New Testament itself. (2) However, the aim is certainly not just to adopt the viewpoint of the New Testament texts themselves. Depending on the phenomenon being studied, that might again lead directly to seeing the New Testament phenomenon as unique and to be contrasted with either Judaism or Graeco-Roman culture or both. Contextualization, by contrast, constitutes a perspective 'from the outside in' that is not at all satisfied with merely adopting the viewpoint of the New Testament actors themselves. Still, as part of New Testament scholarship it should be focused on elucidating the New Testament itself.

The Historical-Critical Root of This Approach

The contextualizing approach 'from the outside in' belongs squarely with historical criticism in its basic and broader sense of a method that situates the New Testament historically in its own time and place and critically excludes later dogmatic tenets from influencing its interpretation. But it perhaps takes historical criticism further by consciously declining to seek any 'direct' reading of the New Testament. In the contextualizing approach nobody asks, for example, what Paul says about God and Christ of such a kind that *we* might then also go on to say the same, that is, as something to be *taken over* from Paul. Instead one asks from the outside: *How* does Paul speak of God (etc.)? What does he *mean* by it? And what broader sense does it make within his own context? There is no question here of taking anything over, nor even whether there is anything that *could* be taken over. One is only concerned about understanding and the conditions of intelligibility. The reason for this lies in the genuinely historical realization that a 'direct' reading of major parts of the New Testament is excluded once and for all by the manifest difference in overall worldviews between then and now. Thus the question of 'taking over' and of the conditions governing that (how? by what logical operations?) may only come in—if at all—at a far later stage.

The Profile Shared with Other Modern Approaches
The contextualizing approach shares this profile with other 'modern' approaches whether they be of a social scientific, social anthropological or social historical type or rather of a literary or linguistic one. In all these cases the scholar works 'from the outside in', bringing with him or her a comprehensive perspective that is applied to the New Testament material in order to heighten its intelligibility. There is no wish here—at least not when this kind of scholarship is undertaken with a sufficient degree of sophistication—for taking anything over as a guideline for one's own life. Instead, the scholar adopts a kind of meta-attitude in relation to the object of analysis, being exclusively focused on understanding and intelligibility.

A Special Advantage of the Graeco-Roman Contextualizing Approach
With respect to understanding and intelligibility, however, the Graeco-Roman perspective has a certain advantage that distinguishes it from the other approaches. That is due to a special characteristic of Graeco-Roman culture, which is its immense orientation towards conceptualization. The Greeks were conceptualizers. That, among other things, is what their 'invention' of philosophy is all about. But this approach to the world gradually came to cover more and more sections of it, in rhetoric, linguistics, literary theory, political theory, history and more. The Greeks were 'theorizers'. And it is probably this particular element that had the greatest attraction for the peoples who lived in the periphery—the Romans to the west and the Jews to the east.

This gradual, but highly diversified, dissemination of Greek 'theory' may be observed in Hellenistic Judaism (e.g. Philo) and among the earliest Christians (e.g. Paul). And this is where the Graeco-Roman contextualization of the New Testament proves particularly helpful for making modern scholars understand the New Testament texts. For here the modern wish for intelligibility meets with material in the New Testament itself whose 'Greek', quasi-'theoretical' or philosophical character may provide decisive help in furthering the scholar's basic aim: that of acquiring a deepened understanding of the New Testament texts and world.

In what follows the task is to show by a specific example how knowledge of certain parts of Graeco-Roman culture, in particular the kind of theory that went into Graeco-Roman moral philosophy, may help to elucidate a central New Testament text. If the attempt is successful, it will have shown that one cannot study the New Testament adequately without having acquired a thorough knowledge of those parts of Graeco-Roman culture that have been 'received' in it.

An Example: Romans 7.7-25

The thesis is that the best understanding of the argument of Rom. 7.7-25 comes from situating this text (and Paul as its author) within the context of the Graeco-Roman ethical tradition. In spite of this I have chosen not to bring in the comparative material until the end, and then only rather briefly. The main reason is strategic. It is certainly the case that the reading of the Pauline passage that I shall argue for reflects my own knowledge of what was basically at stake in the intense philosophical discussion of the phenomenon of *akrasia* (weakness of will) that one finds particularly in Aristotle and Stoicism. Indeed, that is the whole point of presenting the reading in this particular essay. However, for strategic reasons I prefer to develop the reading from the text itself and in discussion with major modern interpreters who have in some cases attached relatively little importance to the 'Greek connection'. Only in this way, I suspect, will the reading have any real chance of being found convincing.

Nevertheless, it is appropriate to introduce already here two basic ideas in the ancient discussion of *akrasia* that underlie the following discussion. The first is that *akrasia* was seen by the ancients as a cognitive phenomenon that pertained to a person's self-understanding: why is it that I wish to do one thing but actually do another? How can I make sense of my own behaviour? The second is that *akrasia* was felt to be a major challenge to any attempt at providing a comprehensive and logically coherent explanation of human behaviour: why is it that at the very moment when 'all things considered' (i.e. after having considered all relevant aspects of the situation) I may wish *most* to do one thing—but I then actually do another? How may *any* kind of explanation of human behaviour that we can devise be adequate if it allows for this kind of schizophrenic split?

Traditional Issues

The intensive scholarly discussion of Rom. 7.7-25 has resulted in a number of positions on issues raised by the passage that can now be taken as established. But it has also left over a range of issues that have not been solved in a manner that commands general agreement. Of course, whether one places a given issue in one or the other box very much reflects the individual scholar's own understanding. Also, the notion of 'general scholarly agreement' is a dangerous tool. Still, further work on the passage may reasonably begin from breaking down the traditional issues in the following way.

1. Paul's perspective. It may be taken as established that Paul is describing an experience of living under the Mosaic Law as seen from the Christ-believing perspective that he introduces in 8.1. It is one of the very real advances of twentieth-century scholarship to have established this point beyond reasonable doubt, and scholarship should never go back on it. It is another question exactly how one should understand the 'I' who is speaking throughout the passage. There are differences of emphasis in scholarship on the extent to which Paul may include his own personal self. But there is a fair amount of agreement on a kind of minimalist interpretation to the effect that the 'I' stands for any individual living under the Jewish Law. What the passage describes is the (non-Christ-believing) Jewish experience with the Law—as seen from Paul's new (Jewish) Christ-believing perspective.

2. The function of the passage within the letter. There is general agreement that Paul's aim in the passage is to spell out at long last the exact relationship between the Law and sin, following on a number of hints earlier in the letter (3.20; 4.15; 5.13, 20; 6.1, 15) that there is an especially close relationship between the two. That, of course, is also how he begins the passage (7.7): Is the Law (itself) sin?

2a. An 'apology for the Law'? It is not quite clear in scholarship whether the passage should in fact be seen as an 'apology for the Law'. There is no doubt, of course, that Paul aims to 'save' the Law, God's own law, from being straightforwardly identified with sin. In itself, the Law is certainly not 'sinful'. But scholars also rightly see that this theme recedes somewhat into the background from around 7.15 onwards. In fact, as we shall see, a better account of what Paul aims to say about the Law is this: that *while* the Law is itself certainly holy, just and good (cf. 7.12—the element of 'apology'), its *effect* on (sinful) human beings is quite different. It inescapably 'generates' sin.

2b. 7.7-25 as a negative foil to 8.1-13. Why does Paul wish to spell out the relationship between the Law and sin by going in that particular direction (and describing it with such intensity)? There is fairly general agreement that 7.7-25 and 8.1-13 take up, respectively, 7.5 and 7.6. That means, as many scholars have seen, that 7.7-25 serves as a negative foil to the positive description given in 8.1-13 of the new life in Christ. But again, why spend so much time and energy on drawing a picture of life under the Law in the darkest possible terms—as a mere foil to something else? Elsewhere I have argued that a relatively small group of scholars are right in seeing 7.7-8.13 (and indeed, I would say, the whole of 6.1–8.13) as being basically paraenetic.[3] Thus what Paul does in 7.7-8.11 is to describe, in his usual paraenetic way, the change that 'we' (cf. 7.5) *have* undergone (the 'indicative') as a reminder that leads up to his explicit exhortation in 8.12-13 that his addressees now show that very thing in practice (the 'imperative'). Be that as it may. The present discussion is focused on the argument of 7.7-25 itself. For that purpose it is sufficient to see the passage as a negative foil to 8.1-13.

(3) Adam in Romans 7.7-25? This is an issue that cannot be regarded as settled. W.G. Kümmel, whose classic discussion of the passage (1929) has been the starting point for almost all later treatments, argued against finding Adam anywhere in the passage.[4] But later scholarship has produced an impressive range of counterarguments.[5] The problem is, however,

---

3. See T. Engberg-Pedersen, 'Galatians in Romans 5-8 and Paul's Construction of the Identity of Christ Believers', in T. Fornberg and D. Hellholm (eds.), *Texts and Contexts: Biblical Texcts in their Textual and Situational Contexts* (Festschrift Lars Hartman; Oslo: Scandinavian University Press, 1995), pp. 477-505. also See *idem*, *Paul and the Stoics* (Edinburgh: T. & T. Clark; Louisville, KY: Westminster/John Knox Press, 2000), pp. 187 and 354-55 with references (to Schnackenburg and Byrne).

4. W.G. Kümmel, *Römer 7 und das Bild des Menschen im Neuen Testament* (Munich: Chr. Kaiser Verlag, 1974), pp. 85-87. (This book contains an unaltered reprint—with additions in an appendix—of two treatises by Kümmel: the classic on 'Römer 7 und die Bekehrung des Paulus' from 1929 and an essay on 'Das Bild des Menschen im Neuen Testament' from 1948.)

5. Cf. e.g., G. Theissen, *Psychologische Aspekte paulinischer Theologie* (FRLANT, 131; Göttingen: Vandenhoeck & Ruprecht, 1983), pp. 204-210, with references to the classic advocate of this view, S. Lyonnet. Also U. Wilckens, *Der Brief an die Römer*, II

that these arguments at most show that Paul *could* have had Adam in mind, not that he did. This, then, remains an issue that calls for further discussion.

(4) The structure of the passage. Two issues have not been settled: (a) the position of 7.13 within Paul's line of thought, and (b) the structure of 7.14-20.

(4a) It is usual to take 7.13 as closely attached to 7.7-12. Thus the line of thought runs something like this: The Law is not identical with sin (7.7); for although the Law and sin cooperate in the distressing manner described in 7.7-11, that only means that the Law itself is holy, just and good (7.12) and that it is sin which is responsible for the baleful consequences of that cooperation (7.13). However, a small group of scholars take it that 7.13 introduces the account that follows in 7.14-25.[6]

The issue is a relatively small one and we may already here suggest a solution which should remove it from further discussion: 7.13 may rightly be said to belong both to what precedes and to what follows. In other words, 7.13 is (another) 'Pauline bridge'.[7]

Consider it this way. On the one hand, there is no doubt that the verse belongs closely with what precedes. From the description in 7.7-11 of what actually *happened* with the coming of the Law, Paul aims in 7.12-13 to draw the conclusion (cf. *hōste* at the beginning of 7.12) that whereas the Law is itself good (etc.), it is sin which is responsible for the 'death' that resulted. He first mentions the Law, with a Greek *men* that should have been followed by a corresponding *de* concerned with sin. Paul does bring in sin as the responsible entity, but in a different form. Having stated that the Law is (among other things) good, he breaks off the *men-de* sequence in order to raise in an especially lively form the question that has become pressing: is the good Law then responsible for my 'death'? Answer: No, sin is! In that way Paul has also answered the initial question of whether the Law and sin are the same thing. They do work together. But they can and must be sharply distinguished in themselves. And it is sin, not the

---

(EKKNT, 6; Neukirchen–Vluyn: Neukirchener Verlag, 1980), pp. 78-83, and J.D.G. Dunn, *Romans 1-8*, I (WBC, 38A; Dallas: Word Books, 1988), pp. 379-80.

6.   See, e.g., P. van der. Osten-Sacken, *Römer 8 als Beispiel paulinischer Soteriologie* (FRLANT, 112; Göttingen: Vandenhoeck & Ruprecht, 1975), pp. 196-97, 201.

7.   Van der Osten-Sacken argues that 7.13 belongs *only* with what follows since the phrase with which it begins (*To oun*) introduces something altogether new in the same manner as *Ti oun* in 7.7. That is a mistake, however. The *men* of 7.12 (*hōste ho men nomos* ...) connects directly with v. 13 in the manner I proceed to explain.

Law, that is responsible for their combined effect on the human being: his or her 'death'.

On the other hand, 7.13 also adds an element that points distinctly forward. That is the idea that the cooperation of sin and the Law had a purpose, which is spelt out in the two *hina* clauses of the verse. It is sin that was responsible for the person's 'death'—and it happened in order that sin might itself become *apparent as* sin or, through the Law's commandment, *stand out as exceedingly sinful*. As we shall see, it is the person's own recognition of his or her sinfulness that Paul spells out in 7.14-25. Thus 7.13 also serves as an introduction to what follows. And hence it is a Pauline bridge.

4b. Another unresolved structural issue is more important. Many scholars take it that 7.14-17 go together and are then repeated in 7.18-20.[8] A smaller group of scholars think that 7.14 (or 13) introduces a line of thought that ends with 7.16 and that 7.17-20 then introduces a new thought.[9] The issue is important since it concerns the whole line of Paul's argument from 7.14 (or 13) onwards in a manner that even leads into the next issue, which concerns 7.21-23.

5. Does *nomos* stand for the Mosaic Law all through 7.21-23? This is another famous unresolved issue and one that would initially seem to have some importance. If Paul starts out (7.7) from the question of the relationship between the Law and sin, does he also end his attempt to spell out the effect of their cooperation by talking about the Mosaic Law itself—or about other types of law or lawlikeness?

6. Finally there is the following basic issue. Is Paul in fact speaking in 7.15-25, as one would initially suppose, of the 'problem of *akrasia*' or weakness of will (that of wishing to do A but actually finding oneself to be doing B) in the form in which this was well known, and even central, in the ancient Greek ethical tradition? Or is he only playing on that and instead making a point that is neither 'ethical' nor 'moral psychological', but genuinely 'theological'? There is at least one sub-issue under this more fundamental issue: whether when Paul speaks of 'bringing about' (*katergazesthai*) the bad (7.15, 17, 20) or the good (7.18), he just means 'doing'

8. Thus, e.g., Theissen, *Psychologische Aspektes* pp. 190-91. Also Paul W. Meyer, 'The Worm at the Core of the Apple: Exegetical Reflections on Romans 7', in R.T. Fortna and B.R. Gaventa (eds.), *The Conversation Continues: Studies in Paul and John* (Festschrift J. Louis Martyn; Nashville: Abingdon Press 1990), pp. 62-84, esp. pp. 76-78.

9. Thus, e.g., van der Osten-Sacken, *Römer 8 als Beispiel*, p. 202, and Wilckens, *Der Brief*, p. 74.

it, or whether he sees what is brought about as being some more distant and 'objective' end, namely death (cf. 7.13) or life (for 7.18), respectively.[10] In the first case, he will be quite straightforwardly talking about Greek *akrasia*, but not in the second, or at least not nearly so clearly.

While the second answer to the sub-issue has had many advocates (in Germany) since the time when it was first proposed by Rudolf Bultmann, it has been losing ground with the demise of Dialectical Theology. But it remains on the agenda together with the fundamental issue of whether Paul is basically speaking of ancient Greek-style *akrasia* or not.[11]

That is also the fundamental question that is at issue in this essay. The strategy will be to present a reading of 7.7-25 as the passage will appear to one who knows the ancient Greek discussion of *akrasia* and to show how such a reading may help to resolve the other remaining issues of interpretation. Success in the latter respect will constitute a fairly strong argument in favour of the reading itself and also of adopting the more general perspective that lies behind it.

7.7-13: The Effect of the Law is Full Recognition of Sinful Behaviour as Sin

Heikki Räisänen has helpfully distinguished between three interpretations of the relationship between the Law and sin as stated in 7.7-13.[12] There is first (A) a '*revelatory* or *cognitive* interpretation' to the effect that 'man learns what is sin' in the light of the Law. Next (B), there is a "*definition*" interpretation': the Law 'defines sin as "transgression"'. Finally (C), there

10. There is a long tradition in German theology—going back to Bultmann—for making the claim for a 'transsubjective' interpretation of *katergazesthai*. See R. Bultmann, 'Römer 7 und die Anthropologie des Paulus' (1932), in *idem*, *Exegetica: Aufsätze zur Erforschung des Neuen Testaments* (ed. E. Dinkler; Tübingen: J.C.B. Mohr [Paul Siebeck], 1967), pp. 198-209. Fine arguments against it are listed by Theissen in *Psychologische Aspekte*, pp. 233-34 n. 81. (Though Theissen can hardly claim Wilckens for his own view; see Wilckens, *Der Brief*, pp. 87-88.) The transsubjective interpretation remains alive e.g. in Paul Meyer's accounts (see 'The Worm', p. 76). But the tides are turning. Thus without further discussion Brendan Byrne (rightly) paraphrases the first half of 7.15 as follows: '...the "I" confesses (v 15a) to being totally perplexed (*ou ginōskō*) by its own behavior—that is, what in fact it does, as distinct from what it simply intends'. See B. Byrne, SJ, *Romans* (Sacra Pagina, 6; Collegeville, MN: Liturgical Press, 1996), p. 227.

11. Here too Paul Meyer sides with the German tradition, see 'The Worm', pp. 75-76.

12. H. Räisänen, *Paul and the Law* (WUNT, 29; Tübingen: J.C.B. Mohr, 2nd edn, 1987 [1983]), p. 141.

is a '*causative* interpretation' to the effect that the Law brings about sinning. While not excluding completely elements from the other interpretations, Räisänen himself in principle settles for the causative interpretation.[13] One can understand why. For Paul of course says that sin used the commandment to '*bring about* in me every [form of] desire' (7.8). Furthermore, 'without the law', meaning the Mosaic Law, 'sin was *dead*' (7.8) and it was only with the arrival of the commandment that 'sin sprang to life' (7.9). So, before the Law apparently there was no sinning at all, this being only the result of the 'commandment', meaning the Mosaic Law. Historically and phenomenologically that may seem very strange. Was there no sinning at all before the Mosaic Law was given on Mount Sinai?! And what about Paul's own remark a couple of chapters earlier in Romans that 'until the Law [clearly meaning the Mosaic Law] sin *was* in the world, only sin is not *reckoned* when there is no law' (5.13). If there *was* sin in the world, presumably there also was some actual sinning!

This problem might be solved by taking Paul to be talking in 7.7-25 not of somebody living before the *Mosaic* Laws but of Adam and the commandment given to *him*. For of him it could well be said that as a result of the 'commandment', meaning now God's commandment in Paradise, he was brought to have 'every [form of] desire'. However, there are problems here too. First, in spite of the efforts of scholars it remains very curious that an account of how sinning came into *Adam's* world should answer the question of whether the *Mosaic* Law and sin is the same thing.[14] Second, if that was Paul's idea he should certainly have made it quite explicit, not least in light of his careful distinction earlier in the letter between (1) what happened to Adam (sin and death came into the world and 'everybody sinned', 5.12-13); (2) what the period looked like *between* Adam and 'Moses' (5.13-14); and (3) what then happened with the arrival of the Mosaic Law (5.20).

There is a third argument against finding Adam in 7.7-11. Paul twice says that sin—very actively—'took' or employed the commandment as a

13. Räisänen, *Paul and the Law*, p. 142.

14. The best attempt to give meaning to this apparent tension is Theissen's in *Psychologische Aspekte*, pp. 210-13, who works out how Adam may have served as a 'role model' for Paul. That may or may not be the case. But for the reasons I give, it seems impossible that Paul should have been thinking *directly* of Adam—a fact that makes the authoritarian tone of Käsemann's oft-quoted dictum rather depressing ('Es gibt nichts in unseren Versen, was nicht auf Adam passt, und alles passt nur auf Adam'; E. Käsemann, *An die Römer* [HNT, 8a; Tübingen: J.C.B. Mohr (Paul Siebeck), 1973], p. 186).

sort of military base (*aphormē*) for generating every form of desire in the I-person and for deceiving him or her (7.8, 11). But if sin was active, then no matter how 'dead' it is said to have been, it will also have *been* there *before* 'generating every form of desire'. Now as we know from 5.12, sin *came* into the world *with* Adam. It should follow, if one dare ascribe a coherent position to Paul, that 7.7-13 cannot be intended as describing the very origin of sin with Adam (how it *came into* the world). Instead, Paul must be talking about something new and additional brought about by the Mosaic Law. Furthermore, if from Adam onwards sin was already in the world, that new something cannot be generating sinning from scratch. Thus the causative interpretation fails.

If there was nothing more to be said, one could hardly build much upon this argument. For it would always be open to the interpreter to take Räisänen's line and conclude that Paul just did not have a genuinely coherent position at all. Fortunately, there is more to go on: the verses earlier in Romans that lie behind Räisänen's three fold categorization of possible interpretations. There is, first, 3.20, which in itself points very distinctly in the direction of a *cognitive* interpretation of 7.7-13: 'for *through* [*dia*] the Law there is a *recognition* [*epignōsis*] of sin'. This is of course supported by 7.7-13 itself, which does use distinctly cognitive language both before (7.7) and after (7.13) the statement that every form of desire was 'generated' by the commandment.

Second, there is 4.15, which shows that Paul could claim that where there is no law (and he has just been speaking of the Mosaic Law) neither is there any 'transgression'—at the same time as he goes on to claim (5.13) that while sin is not *reckoned* when there is no law, there *was* sin in the world before the arrival of the (Mosaic) Law. That fits well with a reading of 7.8-11 to the effect that before the arrival of the Mosaic Law sin was 'dead', namely *as* sin (cf. 'there was no [*explicit*] transgression' and 'sin was not *reckoned*'), but there *was* sin in the sense of actual sinning, namely what would later be *seen as* sin. What was missing was precisely the *naming* that would turn an already existing sinning into full, conscious sinning on the part of the sinner. That was only brought in by the Mosaic Law.

Third, there is 5.20. For if 'trespassing' (*paraptōma*), which as the verse itself shows is not different from 'sinning' (*hamartia*), was *multiplied* with the arrival of the Law, then it was obviously there already. And then it cannot have been generated from scratch by the Law. It is true that the Law might well be said to '*generate*' *more* trespassing. But that of course only refers us back to the prior question of what exactly is meant by saying that the Law 'multiplied' trespassing.

What all this points to is the following interpretative task. As we have noted, Paul's scattered remarks about the effect of the Law earlier in the letter cover all three categories identified by Räisänen: the revelatory or cognitive interpretation (A—in particular 3.20); the 'definition' interpretation (B—4.15 and 5.13); and at least partly the causative interpretation (C—5.20). And 7.7-13 itself initially yields a corresponding, somewhat fluctuating picture. If instead of giving up in despair (as Räisänen in effect does) one wishes to give Paul an interpretative benefit of the doubt, the task will obviously be to find some specific *type* of sinning that is of such a kind that one can both understand how it makes sense to say that that particular type of sinning only came into existence with the arrival of the Mosaic Law—and also that it contains cognitive, definitory and causative *elements*. Can such a task be fulfilled?

Here is the suggestion. What came into existence with the arrival of the Law was *sin fully recognized as sin*. Sinning there may well have been before the Law. Indeed, as Paul explicitly says, there *was* sin (5.13-14). But it was not fully recognized *as* sin. Thus there was no explicit 'transgression' (4.15), and consequently the sinning that there was was not 'reckoned' (5.13): people were not held accountable for it (at least not to the same extent as after the introduction of the Law). By contrast, what came with the Law was precisely the *recognition* of sin (3.20, *epignōsis hamartias*) on people's own part. With this dimension added to the pre-existing sinning, it also makes sense to say that with the arrival of the Law sinning was 'multiplied' (5.20). Not only was there sinful behaviour; there also was—and now for the first time—sin fully recognized (by the sinners themselves) as sin. That does imply some multiplication, though not necessarily more *actual* 'sinning'.

Will this also work for 7.7-13? Indeed, yes. 'I did not know sin' before the Law (7.7); this claim makes sense both as straightforward cognitive interpretation (A)—and also as the causative interpretation (C) that some scholars are toying with, that of understanding 'know' to mean 'experience' or even 'have'.[15] For '*full* sinning', sinning fully recognized as sin, only came into existence once the Law had *defined* (cf. B) the sinful behaviour *as* sin. That too will be the correct way to understand Paul's directly causative claim in 7.8 (*kateirgasato*), as well as his point in 7.8-9 about sin's being 'dead' before the arrival of the Law and its coming to life through the Law. What he is talking about is the coming into being of sin *fully recognized as* sin. That *was* brought into being by the Law's

---

15. Cf. e.g., Wilckens, *Der Brief*, p. 78, and Dunn, *Romans*, p. 378.

commandment. And that does constitute a coming to life of sin. Finally, 7.13 of course makes the point explicit: 'in order that sin might become apparent as sin' and even 'in order that sin might become sinful beyond measure'. For the whole point is that the *recognition* of sin *as* sin *makes* sin *sinful*. Sin now stands out in full stature and with flying colours for what it is. Knowledge that an act is one that goes against the Law *makes* it a full case of *sinning*.

What has all this to do with *akrasia*? A great deal indeed. For on the suggested reading of 7.7-13, the experience that Paul is here describing is not just that of a person who is being told, as it were from the outside, that a type of acting to which he has been prone as a matter of fact counts as one of sinning. Rather, a basic point behind Paul's use of the first person singular throughout the passage is to bring out that the person *realizes* that a type of acting to which he or she has been prone is one of real sinning *as is made clear by* that Law to which the person *also* subscribes. That experience alone will constitute the 'death' that Paul states is the result of the coming of the Law. It is the (basically) cognitive *understanding* of the effect of the Law that explains how the Law became 'my death'. And so that death is a cognitive one: the 'death' of *akrasia*.

Scholars will balk at this somewhat sharpened reading of the 'death' Paul is talking of. Is this death not rather an eschatological—and to that extent future—one? One should not deny that this dimension may be present too in what Paul says.[16] But the phrasing of 7.10 strongly suggests that it is the other interpretation that is the primary one. First, Paul speaks of 'death' (*thanatos* at the end of the verse) as being present (cf. the past tense at its beginning *apethanon*: 'I died'). That points distinctly forward to the culmination of Paul's account of *akrasia* (beginning with 7.15): 'Who will rescue me from the body *of this death*?' (again *thanatos*)— which definitely refers to the present. Second, Paul says in 7.10 that the Law's commandment, which was intended for life, was *found by me* (*heurethō moi*) to (lead) to death. That too points distinctly forward to another culminating moment in the full account of *akrasia* that he proceeds to give, namely when he summarizes that experience in the following

---

16. However, it is at least worth pointing out that if that is (also) what Paul means, then the implication will be that even the Jew who fully subscribes to God's holy, just and good law and who (as one may expect) generally keeps it, but from time to time also has the experience of *akrasia* in relation to it—that even this Jew will meet with eschatological damnation and 'death'. That may or may not be what Paul means to imply. But it is, even by his own lights, a very strong claim.

way: 'Thus I *find* that …' (7.21, again *heuriskō*). In both cases it seems to be the present recognition itself of one's inherent sinfulness that constitutes a 'death'.

We should conclude that the connection between the two halves of 7.7-25 (7.7-12/13 and 7.13/14-25) is far closer than it is normally taken. In the first half Paul describes what 'happened' to the representative 'I' when the Mosaic Law was given. In the second half he spells out in more detail the exact content of the very same experience. Why, then, in such detail if the eventual goal ('my death') has already been made clear in 7.10? Let us look more closely at the detailed description in 7.14-25 to see what Paul is up to.

7.14-20: The Two First Steps towards the Recognition of One's Sinfulness
We saw that there is no agreement on the structure of this section. A majority of scholars divide in the way that is also suggested in the Nestle-Aland edition: 7.14-17, 7.18-20. As particularly detailed examples of this we may take Gerd Theissen and Paul Meyer.[17] But ultimately it goes back to Kümmel.[18] A minority of scholars, however, divide as follows: 7.13/14-16, 7.17-20.[19] The issue is important. With the majority division Paul is essentially repeating himself. With the minority division, by contrast, he is making two quite distinct points. Which division is right?

On the majority side there are impressive arguments for finding a repetitive parallelism: a thesis (14, 18a) in both cases followed by a *gar* clause (15a, 18b) that is followed by another *gar* clause with more or less identical content (15b, 19) that is followed by a conclusion introduced in both cases by *ei de* (16, 20). However, a closer look will show that things are not quite so simple. In particular, while the *ei de* of 7.16 looks as if it introduces only the same verse, advocates of the majority view regularly take it as introducing both vv. 16 and 17. That has two unhappy consequences. First, it results in playing down 7.16b, which one might otherwise take to be *the* conclusion introduced by *ei de* at the beginning of the verse. Second, it means that scholars give an altogether inadequate interpretation to *nyni de* at the beginning of 7.17. For that does not have the only mildly adversative, basically 'consecutive' sense that one gets if one takes 7.16b to be only an intermediate concession that is then followed in 7.17 by a statement of the basic point. Rather, *nyni de* is strongly

17. Cf. n. 8.
18. This comes out in Kümmel, *Römer 7 und das Bild*, pp. 59-60.
19. Cf. n. 9.

contrastive. It introduces an altogether new point. And the conclusion introduced by *ei de* at the beginning of v. 16 *is* the one that is stated in that verse itself (16b).[20]

7.15-16 (the first step). The solution lies in realizing that 7.14 recapitulates the preceding two verses (7.12 for 7.14a and 7.13 for 7.14b) and articulates the two sides of what Paul aims to show in the more detailed account of the acratic experience that follows. The first side is that 'we know' that the Law (itself) is spiritual. Or rather, the first side is this external, shared and objective knowledge *as it becomes part of the acratic experience itself*, that is, as it goes into the recognition of the I-person described in 7.14b that he or she is a fleshly being and 'sold under sin'. The first side of this recognition is the one described in 7.15-16. Here Paul describes the I-person's situation as one of perplexity with regard to the person's own acts. 'I' do not 'understand' (*ou ginōskō*) how 'I' act. For 'I' do not do what 'I' wish, but what 'I' hate. But the I-person then draws the following conclusion from this: if 'I' do what 'I' do *not wish*, then it follows that 'I' 'wish for' the Law, that is, agree that it is fine. In other words, it is one element in the I-person's acratic situation that she or he *endorses* the Law—or agrees with 7.14a. Note then that this conclusion is drawn from a description of *akrasia* (in 7.15) that must be intended (cf. *gar* at the beginning of that verse) as an explanation of what was said in 7.14*b*. (Obviously v. 15 cannot be intended as an explanation for 7.14a.) That is the point. For as Paul here wishes to describe the I-person's state of being 'fleshly' and 'sold under sin', it is part of that situation that 'I' *agree* with the *Law* and *wish* to follow *it*. This is one thing that shows he is precisely talking about *akrasia* in relation to the Law.

Apart from making this point—that the understanding of the Law that is described in 7.14a forms part of the situation described in 7.14b (since this is in fact one of *akrasia* in relation to the Law)—7.15-16 only provides one further element in the full description of the experience of *akrasia* that Paul is gradually moving towards giving. That is the point about 'not understanding' one's own behaviour. At this first stage Paul only aims to isolate a *perplexity* (compare *ou gignōskō*) caused by the acratic act to a person who is described as being basically on the side of the Law. The perplexity derives from the fact that while the 'I' is on the side of the Law, he or she still acts *against* it.

---

20. It is revealing that both Kümmel (*Römer 7 und das Bild*, p. 60) and Theissen (*Psychologische Aspekte*, pp. 191 and 213) speak of *nyni de* as a 'concluding particle'. It certainly isn't—as Wilckens saw (*Der Brief*, p. 87).

7.17-20 (the second step). With 7.17 Paul takes a new step in his gradual development of the experience of *akrasia* in relation to the Law. In the two preceding verses the acratic person had been described as being merely *perplexed* by his or her own acratic behaviour. Now, however, Paul has his I-person take a huge step in the direction of recognizing the fact of his or her own acratic behaviour as evidence of a *major split*. For now the I-person of the preceding verses, who was unproblematically described as being on the 'good' side, is identified as an I (*egō*) who is *distinguished* from something else, namely the sin that 'lives in me'. For analytical purposes we may speak of an I-part (the *egō* who belongs on the 'good' side and with whom the speaker basically identifies) and an I-whole, who is precisely the person who speaks, the one who has sin 'in me'. The basic point is that the experience of *akrasia* (as described in 7.18b-19) leads to the realization of a genuine split within the I-whole, between the I-*part* with whom the I-whole identifies and something altogether different: 'sin that lives in me'. This sense of a split is expressed very strongly through Paul's repeated use of the emphatic *egō* (7.17 and twice in 7.20): 'it is in fact no longer I who does it' and so forth.[21] Here the I-whole associates him- or herself very strongly with the I-part and *dis*sociates him- or herself from sin—while at the same time also recognizing and admitting that this sin lives '*in* me' and so constitutes *another* part of the I-whole.

In sum, at the second stage there are three distinct but concomitant movements: (1) that of separating out two opposed parts in the I-whole; (2) that of having the I-whole identify very strongly with one of those parts, the I-part; and finally (3) that of allowing that the *other* part *is* a part of the I-whole too. In comparison with 7.15-16 this does constitute a major step forward in the direction of having a full recognition of a genuine, internal split (1 and 3). But it is noteworthy that the speaker still sees him- or herself as basically belonging on the 'good' side (cf. 2), and the acratic behaviour is still very much described *from* that other perspective. This is clear in itself, but also from the description of the acratic experience in 7.18b: what is 'present to me' (*parakeitai moi*) is the 'good' side, namely willing the good. That is where the 'I' belongs. As we shall see, however, this picture will change.

7.21-23: The Third Step in Recognizing One's Sinfulness

Paul now summarizes (cf. *ara* at the beginning of 7.21). But he does far more than that. First, he reintroduces the Law (left out of account since

---

21. Note the very emphatic, and evidently *logical*, sense of *nyni de* and *ouketi*.

7.16). And second, he concludes the movement towards giving his final account of the inner split of the I-person. While this person remains on the side of the Law, he or she is also forced to recognize the *full* existence of the other side, not only as being 'present to me' (*emoi … parakeitai*, 7.21—now startlingly used of the *bad* side), but also as something present in me (in the limbs) and with the power to take 'me' *captive* (7.23). Both points stand under the summarizing idea that the I-person *finds* her- or himself in a certain situation and that he or she sees certain things happening to, or rather *in*, her- or himself. That is crucially important. For it brings out particularly clearly the element of dissociation in the acratic experience described by Paul, its almost schizophrenic character. It is the ever clearer recognition of a fundamental and *unbridgeable* split *within oneself* that is so carefully brought out by Paul in the three steps we have identified. What, then, has this to do with the Law?

We saw that the meaning of Paul's use of the term *nomos* in the three verses is hotly contested. Here I shall start out from the overwhelming likelihood that Paul employs the term *nomos* all through to stand for the Mosaic Law. Surely, if a reading can at all be given that makes sufficient sense on that presupposition, the whole set-up of 7.7-25 within its context provides a very strong argument for taking that interpretive option.

First, let us construe *ton nomon* in 7.21 as an adverbial accusative of respect on the formal analogy of *ton kairon* in *Kai touto eidotes ton kairon hoti*…later in the letter (13.11).[22] Thus Paul will not be saying that he 'finds a law to the effect that…', but rather that 'as regards the Law, I find that…' Next let us consider the use of *nomos* in 7.22-23 on the supposition that Paul is speaking of the Mosaic Law throughout. We may begin by noting that the four cases of *nomos* in these two verses fall into two sets of pairs. There is God's law that the I-person takes delight in his inner person. This without any doubt stands for the Mosaic Law. But why is it called *God's* law? Answer: because that is how the I-person sees it in his 'inner person'. He or she precisely delights in the Mosaic Law *as* God's law. Corresponding with God's law to be understood in this particular way, there is 'the law of my mind' (7.23). It seems impossible not to take this as an expression of the very same thing that Paul has highlighted in 7.22, namely the Mosaic Law as seen by the I-person, and here by his or her 'mind' (*nous*). That, then, is one pair, as it were on the good side: an

---

22. Nobody, it sems, has made this particular comparison. It is not, of course, exact. But it is sufficiently close to provide excellent support for a reading of *ton nomon* here that others have already adopted (e.g. Meyer, 'The Worm', p. 79).

'external', good entity (ExG), namely the Mosaic Law, which is of course also *objectively* God's law, and an 'internal', good entity (InG), namely the Mosaic Law *as* assented to by the I-person's mind. But then there also is another pair. Paul first speaks of 'another law' that the I-person notices 'in my limbs' (7.23). This is clearly an internal entity on the bad side (InB). One would therefore expect this to correspond to an external entity on the bad side (ExB). In fact, Paul also speaks (7.23) of 'the law of sin', but also explicitly identifies this as being identical with the other bad law, the internal one (InB).[23] Thus here it is not even quite clear that there is an external entity at all. That should make us think.

Superficially, then, it looks as if there are two pairs involved: two laws on the good side (ExG and InG) and two laws on the bad side (ExB and InB)—and two external laws (ExG and ExB) and two internal ones (InG and InB). In fact, however, we have seen that on the bad side there is no clear distinction between external and internal. Or rather, it is the internal character that is in focus. Correspondingly, even though the Mosaic Law (on the good side—for as we remember, the Law *is* holy, just and good, 7.12) is an external entity, it is introduced (as God's law) in the form in which it is seen from the internal perspective. So here too it is this perspective that is the important one.

What all this points to is the following provisional conclusion: the 'two' laws (for 'two' cf. the reference in 7.23 to 'another' law in the limbs) that are spoken of in 7.22-23—one good and one bad—are basically *identified in terms of* the two parts of the I-person that are also introduced: the mind and the limbs. Or differently put, the 'two' laws are whatever they are—*as seen by*, or from the *perspective of*, those other two anthropological parts of the I-person. We shall push on in a moment to ask what that may mean. First we should notice the obvious fact that on such a reading Paul is directly engaged in combining whatever he aims to say of 'law' with the other aim of identifying two anthropological parts of the I-person and describing their (fundamentally disharmonious) interrelationship as part of *the same* person.[24]

23. It seems impossible to understand *tōi onti* in any other way than as implying an identification of the two laws.

24. Paul Meyer is right on target when he concludes that 'not only the "law of God" (b. 22) but also this "different law" (v. 23) is the Mosaic law!' ('The Worm', p. 79). But we should disagree when he also claims this: 'In sum, 7.13-25 culminates with a "cleavage", but it is in the *law* [Meyer's emphasis] and not in the self' ('The Worm', p. 78). The point is precisely that these two things—Law and self—go together.

So can we make sense of what Paul says of 'law' in the two verses on the supposition that he is all through speaking of the Mosaic Law? First of all, we have seen that he is not in fact just speaking of the Mosaic Law (God's law) and *another* law. Instead, he speaks of the Mosaic Law as seen from the perspective of the I-person's mind, namely as God's (own) law, and 'another' law in the sense of the same, Mosaic Law as seen from the perspective of the I-person's 'limbs'. We may get at the meaning of this by noting how Paul describes the activity of that 'second' law: it *wages war* on the Law as seen from the perspective of the I-person's mind and takes 'me' *captive* in the law of sin in my limbs. By contrast, in 8.2 the 'law' that is connected with the spirit, Christ, and life sets the person *free* from that same 'law of sin and death'. Now we can see what Paul has in mind. The Mosaic Law as seen from the perspective of the I-person's limbs is a law that *subdues* those living under it because (or to the extent that) they do *not* delight in it as God's law but instead have something in them (the limbs) that even wages war against it. As long as there is something in them that fights against the Law (even as this is assented to by the I-person's mind), so long the Law will retain its subduing character and thus hold 'me' (the I-whole) captive under it. It will be (felt as) a *tyrannical* law even though, as we know, it is in fact God's own law and is recognized as such and willingly assented to by the I-person's mind.

But can it be right to equate 'the law of sin that is present in my limbs' with the Mosaic Law as this *functions* in relation *to* 'my limbs'? Why should Paul, as it were, put the Mosaic Law *into* the limbs? After all, it can hardly be the Mosaic Law that wages war on itself, can it? The objection is well taken—and quite helpful for clarifying the reading that is being proposed here. It may serve to pinpoint what Paul is trying to say. He is *not* just speaking of the (Mosaic) Law for itself. He is speaking of the Law *as it functions or acts on* the I-person whose experience *with* the Law he is aiming to identify. And what he wishes to say on this question are two things. The first we already know: that the experience of *akrasia* is one in which the I-person sees her- or himself as being schizophrenically split between an I-part with which she or he identifies and another part which is both seen as a genuine part of the I-whole (oneself) and *also*—and at the same time (*that* is what makes it so schizophrenic)—*just* 'found' to be there, 'seen' from the outside to be there in a manner that makes it completely impossible for the I-person to *integrate* it within her- or himself. The second thing, however, is new: not only is the experience of *akrasia* of *that* kind; but the acratic experience of a split *extends* to the (Mosaic) Law itself, which is *itself* experienced as being split between being God's own law, to which one assents with one's mind, and 'another' law of sin in one's limbs, that is, the same Mosaic Law as it is experienced from the perspective of one's limbs. But although this idea is new, it is in fact quite straightforward and a logical conclusion to the whole line of thought that began in 7.7. In *akrasia* in relation to the Law, the Law too undergoes a split between being seen by the person in question as God's holy, just and good law, which one wills, and being seen by the person as a law (but of course we are still talking of the very same Law) which has a subduing force in so far as (in his or her limbs) the person does *not* will it.[25]

The upshot is this. Paul aims to describe the experience of *akrasia* in relation to the Mosaic Law (to which one basically assents) in three steps that gradually make that experience come out as being more and more unbearable. What makes it unbearable is the recognition of a fundamental, apparently unreconcilable split within the person described. In the first step, two elements in the experience of *akrasia* are identified: willing the Mosaic Law and a sense of perplexity when one acts against it. In the second step, this is spelled out with far greater precision. The I-person recognizes that there are two opposed parts in him- or herself, identifies strongly with one of those parts (the I-part) and dissociates him- or herself from the other part—while also allowing that the latter *is* a part of the I-whole that one oneself is. In the third step, Paul finally extends the split into the Law itself. Not only is there a split in the self: the Law too undergoes a split between being seen from the perspective of the I-person's mind *as* God's own law and being also seen now from the

25. It is reassuring to note that some scholars have grasped the essence of Paul's daring move here. E.g. van der Osten-Sacken, *Römer 8*, p. 210, who rightly states: 'Ist das "Gesetz meines Sinnes" der Nomos, sofern ihm das Ego...zustimmt, so ist das mit dem "anderen Gesetz" identische "Gesetz der Sünde" dasselbe Gesetz, sofern es vom Ego als (begehrendem und damit) unter die Sünde verkauftem in Brauch genommen ist... Das "Gesetz meines Sinnes" und das "Gesetz der Sünde" sind ein und dasselbe Gesetz Gottes, *das nach seinen beiden das Ego betreffenden Seiten hin ausgelegt wird* ...' (my italics). Theissen too is excellent (*Psychologische Aspekte*, pp. 192-3): 'Das Gesetz spaltet sich auf in ein 'Gesetz' in meinen Gliedern und ein anderes Gesetz, dem der Mensch mit seiner Vernunft dient' and 'Geschildert wird die Aufspaltung von "Gesetz" *und* "Ich"'. (my italics). Finally, Dunn, *Romans*, pp. 392-93 and 395, rightly speaks of a 'two-sidedness of the [Jewish] law'; and concerning the 'other', or 'different', law he notes that 'the "difference"' could be simply the differing way in which the law was experienced when it was used by sin (vv. 8, 11, 13), so different from the law acknowledged as good (vv. 16, 22)'. Comment on 'could be simply': it *is*—and it is no simple matter.

perspective of the I-person's limbs *as* a 'law of sin'.[26] That extension is quite bold but also entirely possible for Paul since from 7.14 onwards his theme has not been the Law itself, but rather the Law as seen from the anthropological side 'upwards'—*as* it relates to the different sides of the I-person.

7.24-25: Paul Glossing Himself

It will be immediately clear that the exasperated cry of 7.24a serves exceedingly well to give expression to the acratic experience as Paul has developed it in 7.15-23. For it captures the whole, basic situation of recognizing something in oneself from which one feels strongly dissociated and which one is nevertheless forced to allow as a genuine part of oneself.

It is also worth pointing out how well the notorious v. 25b will serve as a summary of the picture Paul has developed in 7.21-23—if it is in fact placed, as has been suggested many times, just before 7.24.[27] There are three points. First, the strategy of speaking of the Mosaic Law *through* the two anthropological sides to the I-person is very clearly maintained here: *with* my mind I serve God's law, and *with* my flesh the law of sin. Second, the use of 'serve' or 'slave for' (*douleuein*) is curiously apposite. It of course fits immediately into the picture painted in 7.23 when Paul speaks of slaving with *the flesh* to the law of *sin*. But also the idea of 'slaving' with one's mind to God's law is wholly apposite. For even the kind of 'delighting in' God's law that he has described in 7.22 is a 'servitude', though certainly of a different kind from that of the flesh. It is *willing* what one sees that God *demands*. Third, Paul's statement that 'I myself' (*autos egō*) serve, and so on, is a wholly apposite summary of a central point in 7.21-23: that the I-person is forced to recognize the two irreconcilable

---

26. For further clarification: In this function the Law is a 'law *of* sin' (*nomos tēs hamartias*) in the sense that it is the Mosaic Law as *connected with* sin, namely as working to keep it down—but unfortunately ineffectually and therefore also as having the actual function spelled out in 7.7-14 of generating *recognition* of sin. (Exactly the same idea is implied in Gal. 5.18-19, when Paul contrasts being led by the spirit with 'being under the Law' and then immediately begins to speak of the 'works of the flesh' (namely the acts explicitly *forbidden*, but *not prevented*, by the Law.)

27. For discussion and references see, e.g., Wilckens, *Der Brief*, pp. 96-97. Wilckens himself finds that the sentence is out of tune with the rest of the text due to its double use of the idea of 'servitude'. He therefore takes it as a gloss made by somebody who had misunderstood Paul. This gloss then crept into the text at a stage before the whole manuscript tradition.

parts *as* parts of her- or himself.[28] Indeed, one is tempted to say that the person who wrote the *autos egō* in 7.25b understood so well what Paul had been saying in 7.21-23 that it can only have been Paul himself (as opposed to some later commentator), whose gloss on his own argument may then have crept into the text in the wrong place.

Romans 7.7-25 and the Graeco-Roman Discussion of Akrasia
This ends my analysis of Paul's argument in the whole passage. What has it to do with *akrasia* and hence with the Graeco-Roman treatment of that phenomenon? Answer: Everything. We may show this by bringing in, at long last, a few references to that treatment, in particular as part of Graeco-Roman moral philosophy. The point lies in coming to see that the ancient philosophers' discussion of *akrasia* was focused on a single issue that is also *the* basic issue in Paul's account in Rom. 7.7-25: how can one *understand* that a person, S (1) wishes, all things considered, to do A, in other words *prefers* A-ing to anything else; (2) is aware of this at the very moment of action; (3) and then does B? It is well known that this was felt to be such a problem by Plato's Socrates that, in the *Protagoras* (352B-358D), he argued that one could not understand it and hence that in fact there was no problem of weakness of will in the form in which this was normally construed. This set the scene for Plato's successors. Thus what the philosophers did was to try to construct an account of what went into an apparently weak-willed action that would remove the apparent *paradox* of having 1, 2 and 3 together. For as it stands, so the philosophers rightly felt, that paradox amounts to a *crux* for thought. In relation to Paul, then, the point is that what he does in Rom. 7.7-25 is precisely to develop, spell out and almost 'celebrate' that crux for thought in its most emphatic and impressive form: in the recognition of a schizophrenic split in the mind of a person who basically sees the Mosaic Law as God's own law, a split that has such proportions that it even generates a kind of split in the Law itself. It is the *paradoxical*, schizophrenic character of weakness of will—so paradoxical that the philosophers did their utmost to 'resolve' it by explaining it away—that lies directly behind Paul's celebration of the split.[29]

28. Byrne's idea that the *autos egō* is intended to refer to 'the "I" left to its own merely human resources' misses the point and basically appears to reflect a form of piety one does not find in Paul (Byrne, *Romans*, p. 230).

29. In a paper published in 1985 ('Romans 7.14-25 and the Problem of *akrasia*', *Religious Studies* 21, pp. 495-515), A. van den Beld discusses Rom. 7.14-25 in close connection with philosophical analyses of *akrasia* both ancient (Plato, Aristotle) and

Commentators who do see that Paul belongs within the ancient tradition of reflection on the phenomenon of *akrasia* often provide a mixture of material deriving from a broader, more popular (or literary) branch of that tradition—beginning with Euripides and extending down to Ovid and Seneca's tragedies—and a more specific and technical branch, which is that of professional moral philosophy.[30] That is fair enough. And it is certainly appropriate to connect Paul with the broader tradition too and to see, for example the anguished exclamation in 7.24 as more or less a quotation from somebody's Medea.[31] But it is even more important to bring in the distinctly philosophical branch of the tradition. Some commentators do this, but appear to miss the basic point. It is true that there are two rather different proposals in the philosophical tradition for how to understand the phenomenon of *akrasia*. Thus where Aristotle had attempted to provide an account drawing on the idea of two different psychic faculties (a cognitive —that is, perceptual or rational—one and a desiderative or affective one), the Stoics were famous for having tried to account for every psychic phenomenon—*akrasia* included—in cognitive terms alone. This difference is in fact important for Paul too, but not directly in connection with his account of *akrasia*.[32] For here it is what is common to Aristotle and the

modern (Donald Davidson, R.M. Hare, Anthony Kenny). Although the paper is not intended as strictly exegetical, New Testament scholars would do well to consult it for its information concerning the issues involved in these analyses. As I see it, however, van den Beld misses the point of Paul's account when like the rest of the philosophers he attempts to find a philosophical explanation of the apparent paradox of *akrasia* that will also cover Paul. By contrast, Paul himself presupposes that kind of philosophical attempt, but employs the philosophers' initial development of the apparent paradox— to celebrate it!

30. E.g. Theissen, *Psychologische Aspekte*, pp. 214-21. Also S.K. Stowers, *A Rereading of Romans: Justice, Jews, and Gentiles* (New Haven: Yale University Press, 1994), pp. 260-64. In general, Stowers's book is the one that is most sensitive to Paul's close and serious interaction with his Jewish/Gentile context.

31. Cf. Stowers, *A Rereading*, pp. 271-72.

32. Where it matters is in relation to the question of how Paul thought that the state he has described in Rom. 7.7-25 of a constant risk of *akrasia* could eventually and finally be *overcome*. Paul's answer, as implied in Rom. 8.1-13, is: by the Christ event or rather, by a person's *experience* of it, an experience that has then precisely been triggered by God *through* the Christ event. Is that experience, then, a cognitive phenomenon or an 'affective', that is, basically desiderative one? It is cognitive—and hence 'Stoic'. Scholars who take the difference between the Aristotelian and the Stoics traditions to matter for Rom. 7.7-25 (wrongly, to my mind) include Theissen, *Psychologische Aspekte*, p. 221, and S. Vollenweider, *Freiheit als neue Schöpfung: Eine*

Stoics that matters: that both schools in a sense attempted to *explain away* (though in different ways) the phenomenon of *akrasia*, just as Plato's Socrates had famously denied its possibility.[33] What this shows is that the philosophers were keenly aware of the genuinely paradoxical character of the phenomenon and, as we saw, it is precisely that feature of it that Paul draws on extensively when he develops the overpowering, truly 'deadly' experience of seemingly finding oneself in the state of schizophrenic dissociation that is *akrasia*—as it were *before* the philosophers set out to find a way of domesticating the phenomenon. As experienced, *akrasia* does constitute a 'death', namely a crux for thought. That is what the philosophers realized and Paul with them. But he, of course, did not share, in Rom. 7.7-25, their interest in trying to 'solve' the problem itself. On the contrary, he aimed to develop it to make it stand out as being *as unresolvable as possible*—*for* the person to whom the 'good' side consisted in adherence to the Mosaic Law. As will by now be clear, the whole point of Rom. 7.7-25 is right from the start to work towards the startlingly strong description of the experience of *akrasia* that is given in 7.21-23 and is then given literary voice in 7.24. But Paul would not have been able to provide that kind of detailed, analytical description had he not been familiar in one way or another with the intense attempt in Graeco-Roman philosophy to find ways of overcoming the crux for thought that Paul—for strategic reasons of his own—celebrates.

Conclusion

More could be said in order to show the importance of situating the Paul of Rom. 7.7-25 within his Graeco-Roman context. In particular there is this point. If the passage serves as a negative foil for the positive account given in 8.1-13 of what, by contrast, the Christ event means for law-like behaviour on the part of Christ-believers, then here too Paul will belong within the context of Graeco-Roman moral philosophy. For there too *akrasia* was contrasted with another state of mind, which is that of the person who always and only does what is good, the truly virtuous person, the Aristote-

Untersuchung zur Eleutheria bei Paulus und in seiner Umwelt (FRLANT, 147; Göttingen: Vandenhoeck & Ruprecht, 1989), p. 352.

33. For Aristotle's attempt at a solution see in particular *Nicn. Eth.* 7.3.9-11, 1147a24-b5. For the Stoics see, e.g., Plutarch, *De Vir. Mor.* 446F-447A (also in *Stoicorum Veterum Fragmenta*, III (ed.) Hans von Arnim; Lipsiae: J.C. Hinrichs, 1903, p. 459).

lian *phronimos* and the Stoic Sage. If in Rom. 8.1-13 Paul is in a similar way working towards bringing in that type of state of mind, then we are obviously deeply involved in traditional theological issues concerning Christ-believing, genuine sinlessness, the relationship between 'indicative' and 'imperative', and more. But that is precisely the point. Paul belongs, with those interests and concerns of his that are reflected in the traditional theological issues, squarely within the Graeco-Roman ethical tradition. It is in this way that Graeco-Roman culture has been 'received' in this central New Testament figure.

THE RECEPTION OF THE PARABLES OF JESUS IN THE SYNOPTIC GOSPELS

Renate Banschbach Eggen

Reception theory in the interpretation of texts is based on the perception that the content of a text is not a fixed, invariable quantity, but rather is the result of the interaction between text and recipient and therefore differs from recipient to recipient.

This essay addresses the process of reception, focusing on the components in the reception process and result that are particular to individual recipients. The analysis will emphasize at which points and in which ways the understanding of the parables of Jesus presented in the Synoptic Gospels is influenced by the evangelists and their historical situation.

Parable research from Adolf Jülicher onwards can be divided into approaches that consider parables as figurative texts;[1] approaches that reject the distinction between image ('Bild') and subject ('Sache');[2] and

---

1. E.g. Adolf Jülicher, *Die Gleichnisreden Jesu* (Tübingen: J.B.C. Mohr [Paul Siebeck], 1899, 1910); C.H. Dodd, *The Parables of the Kingdom* (London: Nisbet & Co., 3rd edn, 1936); Joachim Jeremias, *The Parables of Jesus* (trans. S.H. Hooke; London: SCM Press, 3rd rev. edn, 1972), and in more recent approaches Bernard Brandon Scott, *Hear Then the Parable: A Commentary on the Parables of Jesus* (Minneapolis: Augsburg–Fortress, 1990); Craig. L. Blomberg, *Interpreting the Parables* (Leicester: Apollos, 1990) and John W. Sider, *Interpreting the Parables: A Hermeneutical Guide to their Meaning* (Studies in Contemporary Interpretation; Grand Rapids: Zondervan, 1995).

2. These approaches are generally termed 'New Hermeneutics'. They consider parables not as texts which tell us something about the kingdom of God which should be intellectually understood, but as language events which create new reality. Confronted with this new reality the listener of a parable is compelled to make a decision. Such approaches are found in Ernst Fuchs, *Hermeneutik* (Tübingen: J.C.B. Mohr [Paul Siebeck], 4th rev. edn, 1970); Eberhard Jüngel, *Paulus und Jesus: Eine Untersuchung zur Präzisierung der Frage nach dem Ursprung der Christologie* (Hermeneutische Untersuchungen zur Theologie, 2; Tübingen: J.C.B. Mohr [Paul Siebeck], 4th. edn, 1972); John Dominic Crossan, *In Parables: The Challenge of the Historical Jesus* (Sonoma, CA: Polebridge Press, 1994); Wolfgang Harnisch, *Die Gleichniserzählungen*

approaches that place the narrative character of Jesus' parables at the centre of attention.[3] This essay is based on the position that parables are figurative texts. This means that parables are considered as texts, which communicate their message by using images.

The narrative that constitutes the image of a parable (from now on: *image-text*) usually consists of a text that tells us something about a certain domain of everyday life, as for example farming, the work in a vineyard, a shepherd's behaviour, or the relationship between an employer and his employees. In order to analyse which message the parable is meant to communicate about the kingdom of God,[4] a particular process of interpretation is required. The result of this process is a text which conveys an explicit message about the kingdom of God in mainly non-figurative language. This non-figurative text about the actual subject of Jesus' preaching will in the following be referred to as the *subject-text* of a parable.

In the Gospels many of the parables of Jesus are supplied with such subject-texts. The process of interpretation leading up to these subject-texts is explicitly presented in the interpretation of the parable of the Sower (Mk 4.14-20 and par). In this interpretation people and artefacts in the image-text, which belong to the domain of everyday life (from now on *image-elements*), are equated with people and artefacts which belong to the domain of the relationship between God and man and are part of the subject-text (from now on *subject-elements*). In Mk 4.14-20 these equations are: seed = word; sower = the one who preaches the word; birds = Satan; different types of soil = different types of people.[5] In the subject-

Jesu: Eine hermeneutische Einführung (UTB für Wissenschaft: Uni-Taschenbücher, 1343; Göttingen: Vandenhoeck & Ruprecht, 1985); Hans Weder, *Die Gleichnisse Jesu als Metaphern: Traditions-und redaktionsgeschichtliche Analysen und Interpretationen* (FRLANT, 120; Göttingen: Vanderboek & Ruprecht, 3rd edn, 1984).

3.　E.g. Dan Otto Via, Jr, *The Parables: Their Literary and Existential Dimension* (Philadelphia: Fortress Press, 1974); Eckhard Rau, *Reden in Vollmacht: Hintergrund, Form und Anliegen der Gleichnisse Jesu* (FRLANT, 149; Göttingen: Vandenhoeck & Ruprecht, 1990) and Charles W. Hedrick, *Parables as Poetic Fictions: The Creative Voice of Jesus* (Peabody, MA: Hendrickson, 1994).

4.　In this article the term 'kingdom of God' is used as a collective name for the content of Jesus' preaching. It refers to the special relationship between God and man. Jesus taught the conditions for partaking in this relationship and the rewards which await those who take active part in this relationship.

5.　From a strictly linguistic viewpoint it is not the different types of soil that are assigned to different types of people, but what is sown into the different types of soil.

text the image-elements are substituted with the corresponding subject-elements. The relationship between the elements, however, which is mainly expressed by the verbs, remains the same in the subject-text as in the image-text. This may be demonstrated by the following formulation which combines both texts:

> The *seed* = *word* **is scattered**. The *soil* = *human beings* **receive** the scattered *seed* = *word.* Wherever the *soil* = *human beings* **do(es) not genuinely receive** the *seed* = *word, the birds* = *Satan* **take(s) away** the *seed* = *word.* The outcome **depends on the quality** *of* the *soil* = *human beings.*

The method used in the Gospels for the interpretation of Jesus' parables consists of assigning certain subject-elements to certain image-elements, transferring the relationship between these elements from the image-text to the subject-text and substituting the image-elements with the subject-elements.

Besides these *technical* steps, the process of interpretation requires making decisions concerning *content*, such as deciding which image-elements are to be taken into account and which subject-elements are to be assigned to which image-elements.

Both the technical method and the decisions concerning content are essential components of the process of interpreting the parables of Jesus. In this article these two components are kept clearly apart, and the question of reception will be considered separately for each one. The strict distinction between the technical method and the decisions on content as two separate components of the interpretation of Jesus' parables is one of the main topics of this article. I will demonstrate that the question of reception leads to different results when the evangelists' method of interpretation is kept separate from their decisions concerning content.

In the first part of the article the evangelists' method for interpreting Jesus' parables will be discussed. I will seek to demonstrate that the technical method of interpretation used by the evangelists does not constitute intervention by the evangelists, but that it is a natural way of proceeding, as long as the interpretation of a parable is meant to culminate in a concrete message about the kingdom of God. In contrast to the technical steps, the decisions on content in the evangelists' interpretations of Jesus' parables are clearly influenced by the evangelists' own historical situation.[6]

However, it is only the former alternative that makes sense within the interpretation of the parable as a whole.

    6.   Each time a component of the parables or their interpretation presented in the

This will be shown in the second part of the article. Finally, in the third and last part of the article, I will focus on the image-texts of the parables and discuss the problem of recognizing whether and how an image-text was modified by an evangelist.

The Technical Method of Interpretation
as a Component Independent of the Recipients

In 1886 Adolf Jülicher published the first part of his seminal work on the parables of Jesus *Die Gleichnisreden Jesu*.[7] There he claimed that the evangelists treated the parables of Jesus as allegories and not as parables.[8] He was convinced that the way the parables of Jesus were interpreted in Mk 4.14-20 imparted an air of secrecy to the parables. This was his main reason for rejecting the method of interpretation used by the evangelists:

> We now know why the parables are so dark and 'in need of an interpretation': because all of their main terms (ἀκουόμενα) have to be understood in a completely different way from their usual meaning, because in order to achieve the σύνεσις the listeners have to put other terms (νοούμενα) in their place, which are somehow similar but yet belong to a different domain.[9]

Here it is obvious that Jülicher is referring to the technical method of interpretation. Even though some scholars soon began to question many parts of Jülicher's work, his rejection of the method of interpretation presented in the Gospels has been widely accepted.[10] It provided the

Gospels is characterized as being influenced by the evangelists, one should of course consider if it is not instead the influence of earlier collectors of the sayings of Jesus which is evident there. However, this question cannot be discussed within the framework of this article.

7.   This part was revised and together with part two edited as one volume in 1899 but retains seperate pagination. This book was reprinted in 1910.

8.   Cf. Jülicher, *Die Gleichnisreden Jesu*, I, pp. 49-52.

9.   Adolf Jülicher, *Die Gleichnisreden Jesu,* I, p. 47. My translation of: 'Wir wissen nun, weshalb die Parabeln so dunkel und einer "Deutung bedürftig" sind: weil sämtliche Hauptbegriffe in ihnen statt in ihrer gewöhnlichen Bedeutung in ganz anderm Sinne verstanden werden wollen, weil der Hörer, um zur σύνεσις zu gelangen, an Stelle der ἀκουόμενα andere, zwar irgendwie ähnliche aber doch einem andern Gebiete zugehörige Begriffe (νοούμενα) einsetzen muss.'

10.   Cf. Kurt Erlemann, 'Adolf Jülicher in der Gleichnisforschung des 20. Jahrhunderts', in Ulrich Mell (ed.), *Die Gleichnisreden Jesu 1899–1999: Beiträge zum Dialog mit Adolf Jülicher* (BZNW, 103; Berlin: W. de Gruyter, 1999), pp. 5-37 (33), and John R. Donahue, *The Gospel in Parable* (Philadelphia: Fortress Press, 1990), p. 8. Both

foundation on which later theories of interpretation were built. By declaring the only method of interpreting the parables of Jesus handed down to us by the Gospels to be wrong, Jülicher opened up for development new theories on how the parables of Jesus are to be interpreted 'in the right way'. Jülicher himself replaced the method of interpretation presented in the Gospels by his own method of 'the single point'. He maintained that the correct way of interpreting the parables is to find the single point of similitude between the half that illustrates (image-text) and the half that is illustrated (subject-text).[11]

This method of interpretation, however, presents some problems. In order to be able to find the single point of similitude, the interpreter must be presented not only with the image-text, but also with an explicit subject-text. The problem is that Jülicher necessarily rejected the subject-texts presented in the Gospels since he considered them to be results of the allegorical interpretation, which he considered to be an incorrect way of interpreting Jesus' parables. Another problem with Jülicher's theory was first clearly pointed out by Charles H. Dodd: 'Those who follow Jülicher's method tend to make the process of interpretation end with a generalization'.[12] The points of similitude that Jülicher deduces from Jesus' parables are ethical

---

Harnisch and Weder clearly express their agreement with Jülicher (cf. Harnisch, *Die Gleichniserzählungen Jesu*, p. 42, and Weder, *Die Gleichnisse Jesu als Metaphern*, p. 11). Fiebig argued quite early against Jülicher's rejection of allegory (cf. Paul Fiebig, *Die Gleichnisreden Jesu im Lichte der rabbinischen Gleichnisse des neutestamentlichen Zeitalters: Ein Beitrag zum Streit um die 'Christusmythe' und eine Widerlegung der Gleichnistheorie Jülichers* [Tübingen: J.C.B. Mohr (Paul Siebeck), 1912], pp. 119-32). However, his studies had little effect on the further development of parable research. Only in more recent studies has Jülicher's rejection of the 'allegorical' interpretation of Jesus' parables again been questioned, as, e.g., in Madeleine Boucher, *The Mysterious Parable: A Literary Study* (CBQMS, 6; Washington: Catholic Biblical Association, 1977); Hans-Josef Klauck, *Allegorie und Allegorese in synoptischen Gleichnistexten* (NTAbh, NS 13; Münster: Aschendorff, 1978); and Sider, *Interpreting the Parables*. Scott agrees with Jülicher that the interpretations of Jesus' parables presented in the Gospels are secondary. What Scott considers as being secondary, however, is not the method of interpretation but the decisions concerning content: 'the abiding significance of Jülicher's work is the demonstration that these allegories represent the situation (*Sitz im Leben*) of the early church and not that of Jesus. The problem with allegory in the parables is not allegory per se, but the ideological reading of the parables with an ideology that is manifestly later' (*Hear Then the Parable* p. 44).

11. Cf. Jülicher, *Die Gleichnisreden Jesu*, I, p. 70.
12. Dodd, *The Parables of the Kingdom*, p. 24.

commonplaces. Thus, using Jülicher's method of interpretation the parables of Jesus do not say anything concrete about the kingdom of God. Instead they have become illustrations of moral principles.

Joachim Jeremias made this problem the starting point of his own study of the parables of Jesus. According to Jeremias, 'Jülicher left the work half done';[13] 'The main task still remains to be done: the attempt must be made to recover the original meaning of the parables'.[14] In order to recover the original meaning of the parables, the original historical setting of the parables in the life of Jesus has to be discovered. By placing the parables of Jesus in their original settings Jeremias recovers their original message. These settings are mostly situations that raise problems or questions to which the parables provide the answers. Consequently, the subject-texts achieved in this way deal with concrete aspects of the relationship between God and man.

Examining Jeremias's interpretations, one finds the same technical method of interpretation which is presented in Mk 4.14-20. His interpretation of the parable of the Seed Growing Secretly (or the parable of the Patient Husbandman as he prefers to call it) usefully illustrates this. According to Jeremias, the message about the kingdom of God that Jesus originally wanted to convey by telling this parable reads as follows:

> Thus it is with the Kingdom of God; thus with the same certainty as the harvest comes for the husbandman after his long waiting, does God when his hour has come, when the eschatological term is complete, bring in the Last Judgement and the Kingdom. Man can do nothing with regard to it; he can only wait with the patience of the husbandman (James 5.7).[15]

Comparing this subject-text with the image-text given in Mk 4.26b-29, one finds that Jeremias substitutes the husbandman—who does not know how the seed sprouts and grows—with man in general, and the harvest with the last judgment and the kingdom. This means he proceeds in the same technical way as presented in Mk 4.14-20: there the word is assigned to the seed; and different groups of people who show different attitudes towards the word are assigned to the different types of soil.

Jeremias's interpretation of the parable of the Seed Growing Secretly is far from being methodologically exceptional. This becomes clear in those parts of Jeremias's study where he compares a parable's message provided in the Gospels with its recovered 'original' message. Such a comparison of

13. Jeremias, *The Parables of Jesus*, p. 19.
14. Jeremias, *The Parables of Jesus*, p. 19.
15. Jeremias, *The Parables of Jesus*, pp. 151-52.

the different messages conveyed in the parable of the Labourers in the Vineyard is found in his chapter entitled 'The Change of Audience'. According to Jeremias, the parable's 'original' message can be formulated as follows:

> The parable is clearly addressed to those who resembled the murmurers, those who criticized and opposed the good news, Pharisees for example. Jesus was minded to show them how unjustified, hateful, loveless and unmerciful was their criticism. Such, said he, is God's goodness, and since God is so good, so too am I.[16]

In order to understand this message, the original recipients of Jesus' parables had to put themselves in the place of the grumbling workers and God in the place of the landowner. The same procedure is found in the interpretation of the Early Church, with the only difference being that 'the tradition underwent an alteration or restriction of the audience'.[17] That is to say, it is no longer the original recipients of Jesus' parables, but the members of the Christian community in the time of the Early Church, who put themselves in the place of the grumbling workers:

> As the context in Matthew (the question of Peter in 19.27) shows, the primitive Church related the parable to the disciples of Jesus, and thus applied it to the Christian community. That is easy to understand, since they were in the same position as the Church today when it preaches about the Pharisee-stories of the Gospels: it has to apply to the community words which were addressed to opponents.[18]

It is clear that Jeremias uses the same method of interpretation as the evangelists. This contradicts Jeremias's claim that he explicitly agrees with Jülicher in rejecting just this method of interpretation: 'the interpretation of the parable of the Sower is a product of the primitive Church which regarded the parable as an allegory, and interpreted each detail in it allegorically'.[19] There is no doubt that Jeremias considers Jülicher's 'final discarding of the allegorical method of interpretation'[20] as one of the essential advances in the history of the interpretation of parables.

That discrepancy between theory and practice, which can be found in many of the studies that adopted Jülicher's rejection of the Gospels' method of interpreting the parables of Jesus, is evident in Hans Weder's book *Die*

---

16. Jeremias, *The Parables of Jesus*, p. 38.
17. Jeremias, *The Parables of Jesus*, p. 38.
18. Jeremias, *The Parables of Jesus*, p. 38.
19. Jeremias, *The Parables of Jesus*, p. 79.
20. Jeremias, *The Parables of Jesus*, p. 18.

Gleichnisse Jesu als Metaphern. In the second part of his book, Weder offers his own interpretations of the parables of Jesus. There he presents the message of each parable both in a Jesus-version (*Jesusstufe*) and a church-version (*Gemeindestufe*). Both these versions of a parable's message are in many cases formulated in such a way that it is possible to compare them very closely. This comparison is made possible because both versions were arrived at by using the same method of interpretation. This can be illustrated by Weder's interpretation of the parable of the Seed Growing Secretly. Weder presents the Jesus-version of this parable as follows:

> As the farmer does not contribute anything to the ripening of the seed after having sowed and the harvest nevertheless will certainly come about, so Jesus does nothing other than bring on the kingdom of God (in word and action). The *fulfilment* of the kingdom is not his business; it will be the wonderful deed of God.[21]

According to Weder, the church-version differs from the Jesus-version in one specific respect: v. 28 was not originally part of the parable but was added during the period of the Early Church. According to Weder, the message that the members of the Early Church derived from the parable reads as follows:

> With this version, it is also certain that nothing has to be done to bring about the fulfilment. According to v. 28b, this is valid even if the fulfilment is long in coming. So the congregation looks back to the time of sowing, when Jesus acted, as itself being within the time of inscrutable growth, and looks forward to the time of the harvest, when God will act (v. 29).[22]

How did Weder get from the image-text in Mk 4.26b-29 to this message about the relationship between God and man, if not by substituting the sowing farmer with Jesus; the ignorant and inactive farmer with the church-members; and the farmer at the time of harvest with God? This procedure

---

21. Weder, *Die Gleichnisse Jesu als Metaphern*, p. 118. My translation of: 'Wie der Bauer nach der Aussaat zur Reifung des Samens nichts mehr tut und doch die Ernte gewiß kommen wird, so tut auch Jesus nichts mehr als daß er die Gottesherrschaft (in Wort und Werk) nahebringt. Die *Vollendung* der Basileia ist nicht seine Sache, sie wird vielmehr Gottes wunderbare Tat sein.'

22. Weder, *Die Gleichnisse Jesu als Metaphern*, p. 119. My translation of: 'Fest steht auch für diese Stufe, daß zur Vollendung nichts getan werden muß. Nach V. 28b gilt dies auch dann, wenn die Vollendung auf sich warten läßt. Die Gemeinde blickt also zurück auf die Zeit der Aussaat, wo Jesus handelte, sie selbst befindet sich in der Zeit des unbegreiflichen Wachstums, und sie schaut voraus auf die Zeit der Ernte, in der Gott handeln wird (V. 29)'.

corresponds with the procedure in Mk 4.14-20, and it should not be criticized since it is the interpretation of the Early Church we are presented with
here. Analysing the procedure leading to the message of the Jesus-version,
however, we find just the same method of interpretation: in order to arrive at
this message Weder had to substitute the sowing farmer with Jesus; and the
farmer, who becomes active at the time of the harvest, with God. Otherwise
it is difficult to explain how Weder can start with a text about the cultivation
of grain and end up with a text about Jesus and God.

   This analysis shows that the method of interpretation used by Weder is
the same as the one presented in Mk 4.14-20. This method does not
conform to Weder's theoretical reflections on the process of interpretation
presented in the first part of his book. There he claims that a distinction
should not be made between the image-half and the subject-half of a
parable.[23] Weder explicitly demands: 'The *content* being expressed in the
parables must *not* be separated from the *form* in which it is expressed'.[24]
Consequently, according to Weder's theory, it is impossible to formulate a
subject-text, such as the Jesus-version of the message conveyed in the
parable of the Seed Growing Secretly, which Weder himself formulates.
This discrepancy between theory and practice is also apparent within
Weder's theoretical explanations: even though Weder's parable-theory is
thoroughly based on Ricoeur's understanding of metaphor,[25] Weder uses
the traditional understanding of metaphor as well:

> That does *not*, however, imply that each detail in the parable must be
> understood as exclusively *literal*. Rather it is possible that they carry
> *metaphorical* meanings that are important for the understanding of the
> whole. It has long been acknowledged that words such as 'father', 'king',
> 'landlord' and the like refer also in a parable *to* God, without the parable
> becoming an allegory because of that. The same goes for other narrative
> elements, such as for example the employing of workers in the vineyard
> (metaphor for God's claim on man) or the paying off of one day's wages
> (metaphor for man's being rewarded by God).[26]

   23. Cf. Weder, *Die Gleichnisse Jesu als Metaphern*, p. 64.
   24. Weder, *Die Gleichnisse Jesu als Metaphern*, p. 64. My translation of: 'Der in
den Gleichnissen zur Sprache kommende *Inhalt* darf also *nicht* von der *Form*, in
welcher er ausgesagt wird, getrennt werden'.
   25. Weder refers mainly to Paul Ricoeur, 'Stellung und Funktion der Metapher in
der biblischen Sprache', in Paul Ricoeur and Eberhard Jüngel (eds.), *Metapher: Zur
Hermeneutik religiöser Sprache. Mit einer Einführung von Pierre Gisel* (Evangelische
Theologie, Sonderheft; Munich: Chr. Kaiser Verlag, 1974), pp. 45-70.
   26. Weder, *Die Gleichnisse Jesu als Metaphern*, p. 70. My translation of: 'Das

Here Weder quite clearly states that words in the image-text have to be understood as references to subject-elements. That is exactly what is done in Mk 4.14-20 as well: the seed is understood as referring to the word of God and the soil in its different qualities as referring to human beings and their differing receptiveness to, and engagement with, the word of God.

The analyses of both Weder's and Jeremias's interpretations reveal the same method of interpretation as the one presented in Mk 4.14-20. Both Weder and Jeremias arrive at messages about the kingdom of God by substituting image-elements with elements belonging to the domain of the kingdom of God, while the relations between those elements are transferred from the image-text to the subject-text without the meaning being substantially affected. This leads us to conclude that, where the interpretations of the parables of Jesus are meant to result in concrete messages about the kingdom of God, this is achieved by following the method presented in Mk 4.14-20 and parallels. Within the framework of this article it is not possible to produce sufficient proof for this assertion.[27] The analyses presented so far provide a basis for claiming that the evangelists' method of interpreting the parables of Jesus is not a product of their personal intervention or misunderstanding, but that it is a natural component of the process of interpreting parables. The following discussion will be based on this claim.

The Influence of the Evangelists on Decisions Regarding Content in the Interpretation Process

Despite using the same method of interpretation different interpreters may arrive at different results. Otherwise it would be difficult to explain why a parable can transmit different messages in different Gospels, as is the case

besagt allerdings *nicht*, daß alle Einzelzüge im Gleichnis ausschließlich *wörtlich* zu verstehen sind. Vielmehr können sie für das Verständnis des Ganzen wichtige *metaphorische* Bedeutungen mit sich tragen. Schon lange ist erkannt worden, daß Wörter wie "Vater", "König", "Hausherr" udgl auch in einem Gleichnis metaphorisch *auf Gott* verweisen, ohne daß das Gleichnis dadurch zur Allegorie würde. Dasselbe gilt auch für andere Erzählelemente, wie zB das Anstellen von Arbeitern in den Weinberg (Metapher für die Inanspruchnahme des Menschen durch Gott) oder die Auszahlung eines Taglohnes (Metapher für die Belohnung des Menschen durch Gott).'

27. A more complete discussion is to be found in my forthcoming doctoral thesis. There Jülicher's theory is thoroughly analysed and the reception of Jülicher's interpretative theory within New Testament scholarship is discussed. In the second part of my thesis numerous interpretations of different scholars are analysed with respect to their method of interpretation.

with the parable of the Lost Sheep, which is presented both in the Gospel of Matthew (18.12-14) and in the Gospel of Luke (15.4-7). In what follows, I will first focus on this parable. Its two different interpretations will serve to illustrate at what point in the interpretative process the specific decisions of individual evangelists influence the result of the interpretation.

The Parable of the Lost Sheep

The message to be derived about the relationship between God and man from the parable of the Lost Sheep is different in the Gospel of Matthew than in the Gospel of Luke. The applications added in Mt. 18.14 and Lk. 15.7 show clearly which message is extracted in each of the two Gospels. In Matthew this message reads: 'In the same way, it is not your heavenly Father's will that one of these little ones should be lost' (Mt. 18.14).[28] But Luke has: 'In the same way, I tell you, there will be greater joy in heaven over one sinner who repents than over ninety-nine righteous people who do not need to repent' (Lk. 15.7). Both interpretations are based on the method of interpretation discussed above, as can easily be shown: in the image-text the relation between the shepherd and the one sheep lies in the fact that the one sheep gets lost. In Mt. 18.14 the same relationship is to be found between God and one of 'these little ones':[29] God does not want one of 'these little ones' to get lost. Obviously, the message presented in v. 14 can be derived from the image-text by transferring the relationship between the shepherd and the one sheep described in the image-text into the subject-text by replacing the single sheep with 'one of these little ones' and the shepherd with God. The same steps lead up to Lk. 15.7. Here, too, the relationship between the shepherd and the one sheep is transferred to the subject text. The shepherd's joy in being able to count the one sheep, which had been lost, as one of his own again, corresponds to the great joy God takes in being able to count a sinner as a righteous person again.

In both Gospels the interpretation of the parable of the Lost Sheep is clearly based on the same technical method. In spite of this the interpretative conclusions are drawn differently in Matthew and Luke. The reason

28. Biblical quotations are from the *Revised English Bible* (Oxford: Oxford University Press, 1989).

29. Within the Gospel of Matthew, the expression 'these little ones' (οἱ μικροὶ οὗτοι) occurs (in addition to here, Mt. 18.6, 10, 14) only in Mt. 10.42. It clearly refers to Christians, but it is difficult to decide if it refers to a specific group of Christians (cf. Ulrich Luz, *Das Evangelium nach Matthäus*, III [EKKNT, 1; Zürich: Benziger Verlag, 1997], pp. 20-21).

for this can be found in the fact that the process of interpretation not only includes technical steps, but also decisions concerning content. Whereas the technical method is the same independent of the evangelists, the decisions concerning content are not necessarily the same in different Gospels.

One of these decisions concerning content is the choice of which subject-elements are to replace the image-elements. Here we find a clear difference between the interpretation in the Gospel of Matthew and the one in the Gospel of Luke: in Mt. 18.14 the one sheep is replaced by 'one of these little ones'; in Lk. 15.7 it is replaced by a sinner.

Another difference between the two interpretations lies in what is emphasized in the image-text, and how this placement of emphasis affects content. In Lk. 15.7 the focus is on the shepherd's great joy over the one sheep which was found again, whereas in Mt. 18.14 the weight of focus is on the value of the individual sheep itself.

Both sorts of decisions—both the choice of subject-element and the choice of where to place emphasis—lead to different results in Matthew and Luke. The reason for this has to do with the fact that the parable of the Lost Sheep is to be found in different literary contexts in Matthew and Luke. Within both Matthew 18 and Luke 15 the parable is presented as a reaction or answer to a concrete problem. Which subject-elements should be chosen and where the emphasis should be placed are determined by this context.

Matthew 18.6 and 10 tell us something about 'these little ones'. In both verses it is obvious that they are given a special value in the relationship between God and man. Since the parable of the Lost Sheep directly follows v. 10,[30] it is quite clear that this parable also deals with 'these little ones'. The literal context also implies that the joy of the shepherd serves to accentuate the value of the one sheep. Consequently, when formulating the parable's message about the relationship between God and man, one substitutes the one sheep with 'one of these little ones'. The value of the individual becomes the main point.

Jesus' positive attitude towards tax collectors and sinners, which outrages the Pharisees and scribes, is clearly the main subject in Luke 15. In this context, the parable of the Lost Sheep functions as an answer to the reaction of the Pharisees and scribes. Consequently the message transmitted in the parable deals with tax collectors, sinners and their relationship to God, and the emphasis is on the joy, which clearly expresses a positive attitude towards the sinner.

---

30. Based on text criticism, v. 11 is generally considered to be a later addition (cf. Luz, *Das Evangelium nach Matthäus*, III, pp. 24-25. n. 1).

Each evangelist presents the parable of the Lost Sheep in a different literary context. That leads to different decisions with regard to the content. As a result different messages about the kingdom of God emerge, or more precisely different aspects or problems in the relationship between God and man are discussed. In this example the choice of context appears to depend on the individual decision of the evangelists.

So far my observations have been on the parable of the Lost Sheep. In what follows another parable shall serve as an example: the parable of the Seed Growing Secretly. This parable is unique to Mark. This means there are no competing interpretations of this parable to be found in the Gospels, which might thus be compared. New Testament studies, however, provide several different interpretations of this parable. The interpretations of various scholars have resulted in diverse 'original' messages about the kingdom of God. The significant discrepancies between these interpretations suggest that the results are influenced by the individual decisions of the interpreters. A comparison of different interpretations of the same parable may therefore reveal at which points in the process of interpretation the specific decisions of the individual interpreter have influenced the results of the interpretation. This is the case both for the decisions made by the evangelists and those made by modern interpreters.

The Parable of the Seed Growing Secretly
The image-text of the parable of the Seed Growing Secretly (Mk 4.26b-29) reads:

> A man scatters seed on the ground; he goes to bed at night and gets up in the morning, and meanwhile the seed sprouts and grows—how, he does not know. The ground produces a crop by itself, first the blade, then the ear, then full grain in the ear; but as soon as the crop is ripe, he starts reaping, because harvest time has come.

The evangelist presents only the image-text of this parable. He fails to supply either an explicit subject-text or a brief application. However, the parable's context within the Gospel of Mark provides a clear set of guidelines for understanding this parable. Mark 4.14-20, the explicit interpretation of the preceding parable of the Sower, contains clear instructions about which elements from the subject-domain have to be assigned to which elements in the image-text. The word of God must be equated with the seed. Different types of people must be equated with the different qualities of the soil. In addition, it is quite clear that Jesus must be equated with the sower, since he is the one who spreads the word of God. If the same set of equations is used for the parable in Mk 4.26b-29 and the relations between the elements in the image-text are transferred to the subject-text, the following message about the relationship between God and man is arrived at:

> Jesus spreads the word of God. He does not contribute to its further development. Human beings themselves have to make sure that the word develops and brings forth the right result. At the end of this process, Jesus again goes into action.

In order to find the main emphasis with regard to the content, one must look at the literary context in which the parable is to be found. In ch. 4 of the Gospel of Mark, three parables (4.3-8; 4.26-29; 4.31-32.) are presented. The image-texts of all three parables deal with growth. The parable of the Seed Growing Secretly is the second one of these three parables. Seed and soil are elements which are common to all three image-texts. If the same key of interpretation is used for all three parables, their messages about the relationship between God and man reveal a clear consistency: Mk 4.3-8 shows that the preaching of Jesus does not have the same effect on everyone. The result depends on the attitude and the degree of engagement of the individual. In Mk 4.26-29 one is told that the interval between Jesus being active and his eschatological return is the time during which everything depends on man's own activity and engagement. The emphasis with regard to the content is to be found here in the centre of the image-text, in which the activity of the soil is described. Mark 4.31-32 show what the proper result should be: the content of Jesus' preaching should become more important than anything else in a person's life.

Within the context provided by the other two parables of growth, the parable of the Seed Growing Secretly conveys a message about man's responsibility during the interval after Jesus was present on earth preaching the coming of God's kingdom and before his return at the end of time. Joachim Jeremias derives quite a different message from this parable, however, as has already been seen previously:

> Thus it is with the Kingdom of God; thus with the same certainty as the harvest comes for the husbandman after his long waiting, does God when his hour has come, when the eschatological term is complete, bring in the Last Judgement and the Kingdom. Man can do nothing with regard to it; he can only wait with the patience of the husbandman (James 5.7).[31]

---

31. Jeremias, *The Parables of Jesus*, pp. 151-52. The same quotation is referred to earlier (see n. 15).

This message differs clearly from the one to be derived from the literal context in Mark 4. The relationship between the farmer, the soil and the seed which is described in the image-text is also transferred into the subject-text in Jeremias's interpretation. The image-elements, however, are not substituted with the same subject-elements as in the context of Mark: the soil is substituted with God, and the sower who does not contribute to the growth is substituted with man. The choice of these subject-elements is determined by the context in which Jeremias places the parable:

> It has often been conjectured that this parable was intended as a contrast to the efforts of the Zealots to bring in the Messianic deliverance by a forcible throwing off of the Roman yoke: and here it must be remembered that ex-Zealots too belonged to the circle of the disciples. Why did Jesus not act when action was what the hour demanded? Why did he not take vigorous steps to purge out the sinners and establish the purified community...? Was not this refusal of Jesus a denial of the claim of his mission? Once again it is a contrast-parable by which Jesus replied to the doubts about his mission, and to frustrated hopes.[32]

From this historical context which Jeremias outlines for the parable, it follows quite logically that the idle farmer must be seen as an equivalent to the Zealots—and not the soil as would be natural within the literary context of Mark. In Jeremias's interpretation the weight of emphasis is also determined by this historical context. Since the parable is read as an answer to the doubts of the Zealots, the certainty of growth and development is automatically emphasized.

A quite different historical context is outlined by Heinrich Baltensweiler. In his interpretation of the parable of the Seed Growing Secretly he proposes the following:

> The parable Jesus tells refers to the many disciples who were with him in the beginning, who probably also passed on the word, but then suddenly turned away from him and fell back into infidelity... We have to imagine that only a few disciples remained with Jesus. For them the others' break with the faith and their infidelity occasioned an inclination to doubt. How is it with the kingdom of God when such a thing happens?[33]

---

32. Jeremias, *The Parables of Jesus*, p. 152.

33. Heinrich Baltensweiler, 'Das Gleichnis von der selbstwachsenden Saat (Mk 4.26-29) und die theologische Konzeption des Markusevangelisten', in F. Christ (ed.) *Oikonomia: Heilsgeschichte als Thema der Theologie* (Festschrift Oscar Cullmann; Hamburg: Herbert Reich Evang. Verlag, 1967), pp. 69-75 (72). My translation of: 'Jesus sagt das Gleichnis in bezug auf die vielen Jünger, die anfänglich bei ihm waren,

Here Baltensweiler sketches a concrete problem which the parable is meant to answer. It is therefore natural that the group most affected by this problem is to be found in the subject-text of the parable. Consequently Baltensweiler substitutes the sowing farmer with the disciples in general. He substitutes the idle farmer with those disciples who again break faith ('The not-knowing is an expression for the farmer's disbelief'[34]). The result is the following interpretation:

> Jesus answers this question with the parable of the Unbelieving Husband-man. This husbandman throws seed on the ground, but he does not believe it capable of anything. Without him knowing it, however, the seed grows by itself, and it bears fruit. Inevitably the harvest comes! Jesus comforts his disciples. He knows that in him, with the preaching of the Word, the king-dom of God is now present. He sends his disciples out to preach the beginning of the kingdom (Mt. 10.7 and parallel). In spite of the later infidelity of so many disciples, nothing alters the fact that the spread word takes effect and that the fulfilment of the time of salvation is as certain as its beginning.[35]

Craig Blomberg assumes a historical context for the parable which is quite similar to Baltensweiler's:

> The parable's message fits in well with a setting in Jesus' ministry. Not long after his ministry was underway, his disciples came to see that his mission was turning in unanticipated directions, so that some decided to leave him (Jn 6:66). Jesus teaches that the kingdom will eventually come in triumph but first he must follow the way of the cross.[36]

---

wohl auch das Wort weitersagten, aber sich dann plötzlich von ihm abwandten und in den Unglauben zurückfielen... Wir müssen uns vorstellen, daß nur wenige Jünger bei Jesus blieben. Für diese war der Abfall und der Unglaube der andern eine Anfechtung. Wie steht es mit dem Reich Gottes, wenn solches geschieht?'

34. Baltensweiler, 'Das Gleichnis von der selbstwachsenden Saat', p. 72. My translation of: 'Das Nicht-Wissen ist Ausdruck für den Unglauben des Landmannes'.

35. Heinrich Baltensweiler, 'Das Gleichnis von der selbstwachsenden Saat', pp. 72-73. My translation of: 'Auf diese Frage antwortet Jesus mit dem Gleichnis vom un-gläubigen Landmann. Dieser wirft den Samen auf das Land, er traut ihm nichts zu. Ohne daß er es weiß, wächst aber die Saat von selbst, und sie bringt Frucht. Unausweichlich kommt die Ernte! Jesus tröstet seine Jünger. Er weiß, daß jetzt in ihm, mit der Predigt des Wortes, das Reich Gottes da ist. Er sendet seine Jünger aus, um den Anbruch des Reiches zu verkünden (Mt. 10.7 par). Trotz des nachträglichen Unglaubens so vieler Jünger ändert sich gar nichts an der Tatsache, daß das ausgestreute Wort wirkt, und daß die Vollendung der Heilszeit ebenso sicher ist wie ihr Beginn.'

36. Blomberg, *Interpreting the Parables*, pp. 265-66.

Consequently he arrives at a quite similar interpretation:

> The one main point of comparison in verses 27-28 teaches merely that as
> the grain does ripen despite all of the forces working against it, so also
> God's kingdom will grow into all he intends for it, despite the uncertainties
> of human existence which might cast doubt over its staying power.[37]

Once again it is quite clear that the choice of context has a decisive influence on the result of the interpretation.

The comparison of different interpretations of the parable of the Seed
Growing Secretly confirms what we have already seen with regard to the
parable of the Lost Sheep: in the interpretation of parables conclusions
concerning content are dependent on the context which is assumed for the
parable. The context determines which aspect of the kingdom of God,
which question or problem in the relationship between God and man, a
parable tells us something about. That again determines which elements in
the relationship between God and man replace which elements in the
image-text.

The Recipients' Influence on the Choice of Context
If one assumes that the original context of Jesus' parables has been lost
during the process of tradition, the choice of context necessarily depends
on decisions made by later recipients. The evangelists place the parables
of Jesus into a context of interpretation by putting them in certain places
within their Gospels.

In Mark the parable of the Seed Growing Secretly is given during a
speech by Jesus, which, among other things, contains three parables dealing with growth. This speech by Jesus—and especially the two other parables of growth—provides the immediate literary context for the parable
of the Seed Growing Secretly. Within this literary context the parable of
the Seed Growing Secretly tells us something about the time after the
presence of Jesus on earth and his return at the end of time. Even though
the delay of the Parousia is not a major concern, it represents an essential
basis for the message of the parable. The delay of Parousia is a problem
that first came to attention during the Early Church. Thus, within the context of Mark 4 the message of the parable of the Seed Growing Secretly
clearly reflects a historical situation which is to be assumed as of primary
importance for the original addressees of the Gospel of Mark. It therefore
seems likely that the evangelist had in mind the historical situation of his

37. Blomberg, *Interpreting the Parables*, p. 264.

own addressees as a context for the parable and thus related its message to this situation.

These conjectures are borne out by the seventh of Jeremias's laws of transformation. According to this law of transformation the Early Church related the parables of Jesus 'to its own actual situation, whose chief features were the missionary motive and the delay of the Parousia'.[38] The literary context of the parable of the Seed Growing Secretly would therefore seem to be secondary. Consequently, the question of its 'original' context must always be decided by the scholar who interprets the parable. The fact that different New Testament scholars recover different, but allegedly original, historical settings shows that the choice of context depends on the theological basis and theoretical concepts of the interpreter, even in the case of modern recipients.

The contexts in which the parable of the Lost Sheep is situated within the Gospels of Matthew and Luke cannot clearly be related to characteristic problems or questions during the period of the Early Church. Therefore, there is always the possibility of one of these contexts being identical with the original historical setting of the parable. The different opinions about the original setting of the parable of the Lost Sheep which can be found in New Testament scholarship show that this question is difficult to answer. For example Rudolf Bultmann considers Matthew's presentation of the parable as the original one.[39] Joachim Jeremias, however, is convinced that the parable's context in Matthew shows that 'the primitive Church related the parable to the disciples of Jesus, and thus applied it to the Christian community'.[40] Consequently, he regards Luke's presentation of the parable as being equivalent to the original one. Recently, Eberhard Rau claimed that the debate with the Pharisees about Jesus' attitude towards sinners can easily be assigned to Jesus himself. Consequently, according to Rau, the parable's context in Luke can reasonably be considered as its original historical setting.[41] Even though the 'original' context may appear in one of the Gospels, the choice of the 'original' historical context for the parable of the Lost Sheep depends, after all, on decisions made by the scholar who interprets it.

38. Jeremias, *The Parables of Jesus*, p. 113.
39. Cf. Rudolf Bultmann, *Die Geschichte der synoptischen Tradition* (FRLANT, 29; Göttingen: Vandenhoeck & Ruprecht, 9th edn, 1997), p. 184.
40. Jeremias, *The Parables of Jesus*, p. 38.
41. Cf. Eckhard Rau, 'Jesu Auseinandersetzung mit Pharisäern über seine Zuwendung zu Sünderinnen und Sündern: Lk 15.11-32 und Lk 18.10-14a als Worte des historischen Jesus', *ZNW* 89 (1998), pp. 5-29 (9-13 and 28-29).

As shown above, the choice of context has a decisive influence on choices with regard to content. Thus any interpretation of Jesus' parables depends a great deal on the decisions of the actual interpreter. This raises the question if the parables of Jesus are adequate vehicles for conveying the original message of Jesus. The question can be answered in the affirmative as long as it can be assumed that the image-texts were transmitted without being substantially altered. This is because an image-text's semantic structure essentially restricts the choice of subject-elements. As will be shown in the following, the image-texts see to it that the messages of Jesus' parables are dependent on the actual recipient to a lesser degree than is suggested by the reflections above.

If one accepts that the image-texts do have a controlling function, the supposition that the image-texts presented in the Gospels have been changed by the evangelists appears to be quite problematic. As soon as an interpreter assumes that a parable's image-text has been changed by the evangelist and therefore bases his interpretation on an 'original' image-text recovered by herself or himself, the image-text's controlling function is eliminated. This will be illustrated by the parable of the Seed Growing Secretly and its different interpretations.

The Problem of the Recipients' Influence on the Image-Text

The image-text of the parable of the Lost Sheep depicts the relationship between a shepherd and his sheep. This relationship is characterized by the fact that the sheep are dependent on the shepherd. Undoubtedly, a shepherd cares for and protects his herd. It is evident from this that God or Jesus is meant to be indicated by the figure of the shepherd when interpreting the parable, and that what is said about the shepherd and his sheep is meant to be applied to the relationship between God and man. Thus it is predetermined that the parable of the Lost Sheep should tell us something about God's or Jesus' caring for human beings as individuals. It is not determined, however, whether a special group is being addressed, and which group it might be. In this regard, the choice of subject-elements depends on the context chosen by the recipient. Consequently, different solutions are to be found in Luke and Matthew.

The clear hierarchy of relations between a shepherd and his sheep, a king and his servants, a landowner and his workers or a father and his sons, is reflected in the relationship between God and man or between Jesus and man. Thus, in these cases it is clear from the outset that the person who has the greatest authority in the image-text has to be substituted with God or Jesus in the subject-text. Similarly, in parables whose image-texts deal with seed and growth it is natural to replace the seed with the word of the kingdom of God or with the kingdom of God itself. Seed is spread, develops and bears fruit. The relationship between the seed, the sower (spreading the seed), the soil and the fruit, is considered by interpreters to be equivalent to the relationship between the word of the kingdom of God, the preacher (spreading the word), the people who receive it, and the fulfilment brought by the kingdom of God. That is explicitly expressed by Adolf Jülicher in his interpretation of the parable of the Seed Growing Secretly: 'where *nothing but fruit-bearing* is in question, where a costly harvest *has to* be the goal of it, there he has dealt with the kingdom of God'.[42]

That the semantic relations in the image-text have a decisive bearing on choosing which image-element should be substituted with which subject-element, is also obvious at another point in Jülicher's interpretation. Considering the question of which subject-element should be assigned to the idle sower, Jülicher states:

> This feature of the 'not- knowing how' alone cannot possibly be meant to refer to the builder of the kingdom of God, since the νύκτα καὶ ἡμέραν after καθ. καὶ ἐγείρ. makes it impossible to interpret it as reference to single events. And could the relationship between Christ and his congregation or his kingdom be described in a more miserable way than by using the image of a man sowing during winter and harvesting in summer and in the meantime leaving the field to itself?[43]

On the basis of his knowledge about the domain of the relationship between God and man, Jülicher considers the ignorance and passivity which are attributed to the sower in the image-text as not being compatible with Jesus.

These examples show that the image-text's semantic structure, or more precisely, the relations between the elements in the image-text, place clear

---

42. Jülicher, *Die Gleichnisreden Jesu*, II, p. 543. My translation of: 'wo *nichts als Fruchtbringen* in Frage kommt, wo eine köstliche Ernte das Ende sein *muss*, da hat er vom Reich Gottes gehandelt'.

43. Jülicher, *Die Gleichnisreden Jesu*, II, p. 542. My translation of 'Allein dieser Zug von dem "nicht wissen wie" ist unmöglich auf den Sohn Gottes, den Erbauer des Gottesreichs gemünzt, das νύκτα καὶ ἡμέραν bei καθ. καὶ ἐγείρ. schliesst die Deutung auf einmalige Ereignisse aus, und könnte man überhaupt das Verhältnis Christi zu seiner Gemeinde oder zu seinem Reich elender darstellen als unter dem Bilde eines Mannes, der im Winter sät und im Sommer erntet und in der Zwischenzeit den Acker schlechthin sich selber überlässt?'

limitations on the kinds of interpretations which can be made. First, the relations are transferred from the image-text to the subject-text without being changed in any essential way, as was explained in the first part of the article. Second, these relations are decisive with regard to the choice of subject-elements. Thus, the context's influence on the outcome of an interpretation is considerably reduced.[44] This controlling function of the image-text's semantic structure is only valid as long as the image-texts of Jesus' parables are accepted *in the form presented in the Gospels*.

Most of the Early Church's influence on the parables of Jesus claimed by Joachim Jeremias in his book *The Parables of Jesus*, result in direct or indirect changes to the image-texts. Jeremias, and many scholars after him, have identified such changes in the image-texts of Jesus' parables and consequently based their own interpretations on 'original' image-texts which they themselves have recovered. Even though one admits the plausibility of what Jeremias has to say, it has to be wondered if changes made to the image-texts can be identified precisely enough in order for them to be reversed and the original texts regained.[45] Such doubts tend to suggest themselves especially when scholars propose quite different 'original' image-texts for the same parable, as in the case of the parable of the Seed Growing Secretly. Jeremias, Baltensweiler and Blomberg accept the image-text presented in Mk 4.26-29, whereas Jülicher considers v. 29 to be partly or completely secondary. However, the 'original' image-text recovered by Weder does not contain v. 28.

A historical overview of the parable of the Seed Growing Secretly and its interpretations is presented by Gerd Theissen in his article 'Der Bauer und die von selbst Frucht bringende Erde'. There he divides the interpretations to be found in New Testament studies into 'dialectical' and 'hermeneutic' ones. However, when he states that '[w]ithout omitting v. 29 the "dialectical" interpretation can hardly be made'[46] he makes it clear that the

---

44. Similarly Klaus Berger, *Theologiegeschichte des Urchristentums: Theologie des Neuen Testaments* (UNI-Taschenbücher für Wissenschaft: Grosse Reihe; Tübingen: Francke, 1994), p. 595. Berger also states that the choice of context depends on a recipient's decision. At the same time he makes it clear that the structure of the image-text limits the alternatives for this choice.

45. A view which criticizes attempts to recover the original sayings of Jesus is expressed by Jens Schröter, 'Markus, Q und der historische Jesus: Methodische und exegetische Erwägungen zu den Anfängen der Rezeption der Verkündigung Jesu', *ZNW* 89 (1998), pp. 173-200 (178-82).

46. Theissen, 'Der Bauer und die von selbst Frucht bringende Erde: Naiver Syner-

different 'original' image-texts, to some degree, are due to the interpreters' different theological positions.

Theissen's own interpretation of the parable again shows that the image-text's semantic structure determines which subject-element can replace which image-element:

> According to the inner structure of the parable's picture, its main aim is to pinpoint a cooperation between sower and soil, in which one side has to rely wholly on the 'self-effectiveness' of the other. However, concerning the subject, what is meant? If one takes into account the simple rule of interpretation that parables offer the listener points of identification (the so-called meeting-points ['Verschränkungen']), so that rather than being incomprehensible allegories they can be understood directly, then there are two possible interpretations. The listener can identify with the sower. This sower represents man's position. He is given the courage and confidence that the seed really will spread and bear fruit. Behind the self-efficacy of the seed then stands hidden the work of God... However, the farmer at the end of the parable is the same as the sower at the beginning. If one would want to understand the parable homogeneously, the sower would transparently represent God from the beginning: When realizing his kingdom God acts like someone who entrusts the 'soil' with his seed so that it will bear fruit by itself.[47]

The relations between the elements in the image-text limit the possibilities for the interpretation considerably. Thus, as long as the image-texts have not been essentially altered, it is to a certain extent safe to say that the parables can convey the messages Jesus originally meant to convey.

gismus in Mk 4.26-29?', *ZNW* 85 (1994), pp. 167-82 (171). My translation of: 'Ohne Streichung von V. 29 läßt sich die 'dialektische' Deutung also kaum durchführen'.

47. Theissen, 'Der Bauer und die von selbst Frucht bringende Erde', pp. 178-79. My translation of: 'Nach der inneren Struktur des Gleichnisbildes zielt seine Pointe auf eine Kooperation zwischen Sämann und Erde, bei der die eine Seite ganz auf die "Selbstwirksamkeit" der anderen vertrauen muß! Was aber ist sachlich gemeint? Wenn man die schlichte Interpretationsregel berücksichtigt, daß Gleichnisse in Einzelelementen Identifikationsangebote für die Hörer enthalten (die sogenannten "Verschränkungen"), ohne unverständliche Allegorien zu sein, sondern um unmittelbar verstanden zu werden, dann gibt es zwei mögliche Deutungen. Der Hörer kann sich mit dem Sämann identifizieren. Dieser vertritt die Seite des Menschen. Ihm wird Mut und Vertrauen zugesprochen, daß die Saat wirklich aufgeht und Frucht bringt. Hinter der Selbstwirksamkeit der Saat steht dann verborgen Gottes Wirken... Nun ist der Bauer am Ende des Gleichnisses derselbe wie der Sämann am Anfang. Will man das Gleichnis daher einheitlich verstehen, so wäre der Sämann von vornherein für Gott transparent: Gott verhält sich bei der Verwirklichung seiner Herrschaft wie jemand, der seinen Samen der "Erde" anvertraut, damit diese von selbst Frucht bringt.'

However, as soon as parts of the image-text are considered as not original, the controlling function of the image-text is eliminated. The same is the case when the semantic structure of the image-text is disregarded. Theissen's remark that 'If one would want to understand the parable homogeneously...' indicates that he does not accept the image-text's semantic structure as authoritative. In his conclusion he tries to combine two interpretations without showing any consideration for the fact that those two interpretations are based on different semantic structures in the image-text.

Most of the New Testament scholars who interpret the parable of the Seed Growing Secretly obviously do not accept the semantic structure of its image-text as being authoritative. This is the main reason for the fact that several quite different interpretations of this parable are to be found in New Testament scholarship. In the image-text Mk 4.26b-29, it is the same person who sows, harvests and does not know how the seed sprouts and grows. It therefore seems quite clear that Jülicher does not take the image-text seriously when he states: 'At no point is the narrator intent on stating the gradualness, the slowness (?) of the growth, which matters to him as little as that the sleeping and rising, ignorant man should be just the sower.'[48]

Yet even Jeremias, Baltensweiler and Blomberg divide the figure of the sower into different persons in the same way: the sower, who goes to bed and gets up and does not know how the seed sprouts and grows, is substituted by all three interpreters with a different subject-element than the sower who sows and harvests. Jeremias and Blomberg replace the former with human beings in general: the latter, however, they replace with God or Jesus.[49] Baltensweiler even divides the sower into three different persons: the sowing one is substituted with Jesus and his disciples, the idle one with those disciples who fall back into infidelity, and within Baltensweiler's interpretation the one harvesting can only be substituted with Jesus or God.

Given the different ways in which the image-text is manipulated, it is not surprising that the interpreters derive quite different messages from the same parable.

48. Jülicher, *Die Gleichnisreden Jesu*, II, p. 544. My translation of: 'Die Allmählichkeit, die Langsamkeit (?) des Wachstums zu konstatieren, hat dem Erzähler nirgend angelegen, so wenig wie ihm daran liegt, dass der schlafende und aufstehende, der nicht wissende Mann gerade der Säemann ist'.

49. Similarly Jürgen Becker, *Jesus von Nazareth* (Berlin: W. de Gruyter, 1996), pp. 153-54.

The question which arises is if the parable of the Seed Growing Secretly can be interpreted differently from what is suggested by the context in Mark 4. As long as the semantic structure of the parable's image-text is accepted as being authoritative, many of the interpretations which can be found in New Testament studies must be considered inadequate. However, if one is willing to accept essential changes in the semantic structure of the image-text, quite a number of different messages about the relationship between God and man can be transmitted by the same parable. As soon as the controlling function of the image-text is suspended, the individual recipient's decisions regarding context have a maximum impact on the interpretation.

Summary

For many of Jesus' parables the evangelists not only present the image-texts but also provide more or less complete formulations of the message about the kingdom of God conveyed by them. These formulations represent a process of interpretation which is shown in Mk 4.14-20 and parallels. This process includes both a technical method and decisions regarding content. In this essay the question of reception and its influence on the parables of Jesus in the Synoptic Gospels is addressed separately with regard to the technical method and decisions concerning content.

In the first part of the article the technical method of interpretation is discussed. This discussion suggests that the technical method of interpretation presented in Mk 4.14-20 and parallels is not a result of decisions made by the evangelists themselves, but represents the logical way of proceeding whenever a concrete message about the kingdom of God is derived from a parable of Jesus. Jülicher's rejection of this method as allegorical and therefore an inadequate way of interpreting Jesus' parables has been accepted by many New Testament scholars. Analyses of interpretations of the parables of Jesus which result in concrete messages about the kingdom of God done by the same scholars, however, show the same method of interpretation as in Mk 4.14-20 and parallels. The technical method of interpretation presented in the Synoptic Gospels therefore appears to be independent of the recipients.

The recipients' influence on the outcome of the interpretations is to be found in the decisions regarding content. Which image-element is replaced with which subject-element when formulating a parable's message about the kingdom of God is largely determined by the *context* in which the parable is placed. If it is assumed that the original historical settings of the parables of Jesus have been lost during the process of transmission, then the choice of context necessarily depends on the recipient. This is the case not only for those interpretations presented in the Gospels but also for interpretations performed by New Testament scholars today. Their choice of context has essential influence on their decisions regarding content and thereby on the outcome of their interpretation of a parable.

As shown in the last part of the article, the choice of context is, however, decisively limited by the semantic structure of the image-text. It therefore appears rather problematic to regard parts of a parable's image-text as secondary and to change the semantic structure of the image-text in order to regain the 'original' parable. A modern interpreter who believes that he or she eliminates the evangelists' subjective influence on the parables of Jesus, increases the possibility that his or her own decisions will have a disproportionate influence on the outcome of the interpretation. The different messages which different scholars have derived from the parable of the Seed Growing Secretly offer persuasive evidence of this.

JESUS AS MESSIANIC TEACHER IN THE GOSPEL ACCORDING TO MATTHEW: TRADITION HISTORY AND/OR NARRATIVE CHRISTOLOGY

Samuel Byrskog

Defining the Problem

The author of the Gospel according to Matthew begins his narrative by defining Jesus as the anointed one, the Messiah. The very first verse, which might be programmatic for the entire story,[1] conveys a clear messianic description of the main character, βίβλος γενέσεως Ἰησοῦ Χριστοῦ υἱοῦ Δαυὶδ υἱοῦ Ἀβραάμ ('book of descent of Jesus the Messiah, the Son of David, the Son of Abraham') (1.1). The subsequent genealogy keeps to the Davidic line and concludes in vv. 16, 17 by again defining Jesus as Χριστός. The same term recurs in v. 18a, which functions as a headline of 1.18b–2.23.

In 23.10 this Χριστός has become the only instructor of the disciples. As in 1.17, the term Χριστός is now employed by itself, not together with Ἰησοῦς, and carries the characteristics of a proper messianic title. Jesus' teaching to the disciples concerning their status as brothers and his position as their only teacher leads, quite surprisingly, to an explicit reference to the messianic identity of this didactic figure, καθηγητὴς ὑμῶν ἐστιν εἷς ὁ Χριστός ('one is your teacher, the Messiah'). The Messiah has become a teacher!

How is this possible? What has happened during the course of the story? *How are we to explain this peculiar connection between the messianic and the didactic role of Jesus in Matthew?* There are two alternatives to be considered here. The first one approaches the problem from the perspective of *tradition history*,[2] suggesting that as the tradition evolved the

---

1. So, e.g., D. Dormeyer, 'Mt 1.1 als Überschrift zur Gattung und Christologie des Matthäus-Evangeliums', in C.M. Tuckett, G. Van Belle and J. Verheyden (eds.), *The Four Gospels 1992* (Festschrift F. Neirynck; 3 vols.; BETL, 100A-C; Leuven: Leuven University Press, 1992), II, pp. 1361-63.

2. I am aware that the expression 'tradition history' is problematic in view of the

messianic label became linked with didactic categories with which the author was familiar and which he applied. An *a priori* assumption speaking in favour of this alternative is that the author elsewhere proves himself to be thoroughly familiar with a number of Jewish beliefs. The second alternative proposes that the author employed the *narrative* of the story as a means to modify the messianic label, adding new didactic characteristics to it. An *a priori* assumption speaking in favour of this alternative is that the author evidently did, in the end, create a coherent narrative with its own temporal and causal order of events. To be sure, these two alternatives do not necessarily exclude each other, *but they imply two rather different ways of approaching what we normally call christology: one in which the Christology is very much linked to the tradition history of the Christological labels, and one in which the narrative itself develops and determines the Christology.*[3]

---

different ways of using the term 'tradition'. It does not here denote a definable block of transmitted material in the narrow, technical sense, but comes close to what we sometimes call 'motif', that is, tradition as a definable ideological construct.

3. The former approach has dominated scholarship for quite some time. Prominent representatives are O. Cullmann, *Die Christologie des Neuen Testaments* (Tübingen: Mohr Siebeck, 5th edn, 1975), and F. Hahn, *Christologische Hoheitstitel: Ihre Geschichte im frühen Christentum* (FRLANT, 83; Göttingen: Vandenhoeck & Ruprecht, 4th edn, 1974). As regards Matthew, one notices the focus on titles and designations in J.D. Kingsbury's influential book *Matthew: Structure, Christology, Kingdom* (Minneapolis: Fortress Press, 2nd edn, 1989). The same tendency is to be seen in H. Geist, *Menschensohn und Gemeinde: Eine redaktionskritische Untersuchung zur Menschensohnprädikation im Matthäusevangelium* (FzB, 57; Würzburg: Echter Verlag, 1986). Already L.E. Keck warned against focusing too much on christological titles as one tries to comprehend the identity and signficance of Jesus, 'Toward a Renewal of New Testament Christology', *NTS* 32 (1986), pp. 362-77. Today Kingsbury stresses very much the christological importance of the narrative, in, e.g., *Matthew as Story* (Philadelphia: Fortress Press, 2nd edn, 1988). A development towards a narrative Christology in Matthew can be seen in the works of U. Luz, e.g., 'Eine thetische Skizze der matthäischen Christologie', in C. Breytenbach and H. Paulsen (eds.), *Anfänge der Christologie* (Festschrift F. Hahn; Göttingen: Vandenhoeck & Ruprecht, 1991), pp. 221-235; 'The Son of Man in Matthew: Heavenly Judge or Human Christ', *JSNT* 48 (1992), pp. 3-21. For further literature, cf. the survey by M. Müller, 'The Theological Interpretation of the Figure of Jesus in the Gospel of Matthew: Some Principal Features in Matthean Christology', *NTS* 45 (1999), pp. 157-73 (160-65). For the Gospel of Mark, cf. recently E.K. Broadhead, *Naming Jesus: Titular Christology in the Gospel of Mark* (JSNTSup, 175; Sheffield: Sheffield Academic Press, 1999).

The Messiah as Teacher in the History of Tradition

What didactic traits were attributed to the Messiah in the tradition? Psalm 2 and Isaiah 11 were important messianic texts. One finds no explicit didactic role ascribed to the expected figure in these texts.[4] Isaiah 11.2, however, implies a certain connection to some didactic notions. The spirit of wisdom and understanding (רוח חכמה ובינה / πνεῦμα σοφίας καὶ συνέσεως) shall rest on the shoot that comes out from the stump of Jesse. We find similar categories within the book of Isaiah only in relation to God's servant. He will bring forth justice (משפט / κρίσιν), he has a torah, a teaching (תורה),[5] which the coastlands wait for (Isa. 42.3-4).

In Qumran the didactic categories were of course primarily tied to the priestly Messiah. CD 6.11 portrays him as the one who teaches righteousness (יורה הצדק), CD 7.18 and 1QFlor. 1.11 as someone who studies the torah (דורש התורה). The *Testament of Levi* 18.2-7 indicates that the didactic traits attributed to the priestly Messiah were not unheard of elsewhere: the Lord will raise up a new priest to whom all the words of the Lord will be revealed, the light of knowledge (φῶς γνώσεως) will kindle, the spirit of understanding and sanctification (πνεῦμα συνέσεως καὶ ἁγιασμοῦ) shall rest upon him. Perhaps the didactic traits of the eschatological high priest in Qumran were accentuated in order to reduce the disappointment and cognitive dissonance which occurred when the Righteous Teacher—whom the Qumranites interpreted in priestly categories—died without the eschaton having come to its final fulfilment.[6]

The Davidic Messiah is not a didactic character to the same extent in the Dead Sea Scrolls. We find, as in Isaiah 11, that one uses wisdom terminol-

---

4. God himself, by contrast, is depicted as a teacher in the Old Testament. Cf. Isa. 2.3 (= Mic. 4.2); 28.26; 30.20 (with the singular construction); 48.17; 51.4. See E. Schawe, 'Gott als Lehrer im Alten Testament. Eine semantisch-theologische Studie' (PhD Diss., University of Fribourg, 1979). The metaphor of rain in Hos. 10.12 and Joel 2.23 was later understood to imply teaching (text in G. Dalman, *Arbeit und Sitte in Palästina* [7 vols.; BFCT; Gütersloh: C. Bertelsmann, 1928–42], I, p. 122). These two texts might have influenced the use of the label מורה הצדק in the Dead Sea Scrolls. *Targ. Neb. Joel* 2.23 refers explicitly to an authoritative eschatological teacher. See S. Byrskog, *Jesus the Only Teacher: Didactic Authority and Transmission in Ancient Israel, Ancient Judaism and the Matthean Community* (ConBNT, 24; Stockholm: Almqvist & Wiksell, 1994), pp. 117-18.

5. LXX of Isa. 42.4 translates/replaces לתורתו of the MT with ἐπὶ τῷ ὀνόματι αὐτοῦ.

6. I have developed this hypothesis in *Jesus the Only Teacher*, pp. 126-30, 191-93.

ogy to describe him—or David, his ancestor, to be more precise. The clearest evidence of this is perhaps 11QPs[a] Dav Comp 27.2-5: 'And David, the son of Jesse, was wise [חכם], and a light like the light of the sun, and literate [סופר], and discerning [נבון]... And the Lord gave him a discerning and enlightened spirit [רוח נבונה ואורה]. And he wrote 3,600 psalms ...'. Although we cannot be sure that 11QPs[a] actually originated within the Qumran community, there is nothing to suggest that it was entirely at odds with its messianology. The Davidic Messiah carries the traits of wisdom and discernment,[7] like a scribe.[8] Other texts might point in the same direction.[9]

The messianic notions within early pious groups, with clear allusions to Isaiah 11, become visible in the hymns of *Psalms of Solomon* 17 and 18. The Messiah is here portrayed as a person of great wisdom (17.23, 29, 35, 37; 18.7). The didactic traits are accentuated and go beyond what is said in Isaiah 11. According to *Pss.Sol.* 17.42-43 the messianic figure performs the activity of 'discipline', 'education', *paideia*. Rainer Riesner has shown that we are dealing with an interpretation going back to the Greek translation of Isa. 50.4 and 53.5.[10] The expression למודים לשון, 'the tongue of a teacher' (NRSV), literally, 'a tongue of those who are taught', in 50.4 is translated γλῶσσαν παιδείας ('tongue of instruction'); and מוסר שלומינו עליו, 'upon him was the punishment that made us whole' (NRSV), literally, 'discipline was upon him for our peace', in 53.5 is rendered εἰρήνης

---

7. For a broader assessment of the Qumran wisdom texts, cf. D.J. Harrington, *Wisdom Texts from Qumran* (London: Routledge, 1996).

8. J.A. Sanders, the editor of 11QPs[a], made the following comment on Dav Comp: 'At Qumrân David was thought of not only as a musical composer and author of the Psalter under prophetic inspiration, but also as a *lakham*, capable of the kind of thinking elsewhere attributed to the great Wisdom teacher Ben Sira' (*The Psalms Scroll of Qumrân Cave 11* [DJD, 4; Oxford: Clarendon Press, 1965], p. 92).

9. Cf. the notion of God's chosen one in 4QMess.ar. (4Q534), with allusions to Isa. 42.1-6. The herald, or the anointed one, in 11QMelch 18-20 is probably to be identified with Melchizedek, which indicates a priestly connotation attached to the didactic role. The new texts that have become available in recent years do not—to my knowledge—provide any further material to the issue under consideration. For a general discussion, cf. J.J. Collins, *The Scepter and the Star: The Messiahs of the Dead Sea Scrolls and Other Ancient Literature* (New York: Doubleday, 1995); J. Zimmermann, *Messianische Texte aus Qumran: Königliche, priesterliche und prophetische Messiasvorstellungen in den Schriftfunden von Qumran* (WUNT, 2.104; Tübingen: Mohr Siebeck, 1998).

10. R. Riesner, *Jesus als Lehrer: Eine Untersuchung zum Ursprung der Evangelien-Überlieferung* (WUNT, 2.7; Tübingen: Mohr Siebeck, 3rd edn, 1988).

ἡμῶν ἐπ’ αὐτόν. *Psalms of Solomon* 17.42-43 is apparently part of this interpretative line of tradition. Thus we detect how some pious groups accentuated the didactic traits of the messianic figure through a subtle development of certain characteristics that the book of Isaiah associated with the servant. Already Isa. 42.3-4 indicates, as we saw, the didactic function of the servant. God's servant becomes the model of the Messiah as teacher.

The *Targum of Isaiah* confirms this didactic and messianic development of the notion of the servant. Isaiah 11.1-2 is related directly to the Messiah, as is 42.1-6 with its didactic characteristics. To be sure, to my knowledge we still do not possess any text which clearly points to a messianic interpretation of Isa. 50.4.[11] Yet, one notices that the Targum of this verse depicts the servant as a teacher. He now receives 'the tongue of those who teach', literally, 'a tongue of teachers' (ל יֹשֵׁן דמלפּין), being able to teach with wisdom the righteous who faint for the words of God's law. *Targ. Neb. Isa.* 53.5 is messianic, however. The didactic traits of the servant/the Messiah are also enhanced.[12] 'By his teaching' (בְּאלפּנֵיה), it is said, 'his peace will increase upon us, and in that we attach ourselves to his words [לפתלמוהי] our sins will be forgiven us'. *These scattered pieces of information suggest that some pre-Christian pious circles and people related to the synagogue employed the image of God's servant in Second Isaiah to strengthen and develop the didactic function of the Davidic Messiah.*

As we move on to the rabbinic literature, we come across a significant 'rabbinization' of the messianic figure. Towards the end of the third century CE, as far as we can judge, the messianic dreams began to flourish (again). Moreover, the Messiah now becomes an authoritative Torah teacher.[13] He is רבי ומרי, 'my teacher and my lord' (*b. Sanh.* 98a). *Targ.*

---

11. Cf. already P. Seidelin, 'Der Ebed Jahwe und die Messiasgestalt im Jesajatargum', *ZAW* 35 (1936), pp. 194-231 (204, 219).

12. Cf. B.D. Chilton, *The Isaiah Targum: Introduction, Translation, Apparatus and Notes* (The Aramaic Bible, 11; Edinburgh: T. & T. Clark, 1987), p. xvii.

13. The texts are plenty and of varying character. See, e.g., *Midr. Ps.* 2 (§ 9); 21 (§ 1); 110 (§ 4). According to R. Hanin, Isa. 11.10 suggests that the Messiah should be only the teacher of the Gentiles, since God was the sole teacher of the Jewish people (*Gen. R.* 98 [§ 9]). This opinion remained, however, a minority view. M. Hengel regards it as an expression of anti-Christian polemics, 'Jesus als messianischer Lehrer der Weisheit und die Anfänge der Christologie', in *Sagesse et religion: Colloque de Strasbourg* (Bibliothèque des centres d'études supérieures spécialisés; Paris: Presses universitaires de France, 1979), pp. 147-88 (172).

Neb. Isa. 12.3 speaks of a 'new teaching' (אולפן חדת) in the messianic age. According to the rabbis the Messiah will bring a 'new Torah' (תורה חדשה),[14] the 'Torah of the Messiah' (תורה של משיח).[15] The Torah that came forth from Sinai is not replaced but receives its final and complete interpretation and application.[16] It seems the didactic identity of the rabbis was projected onto the awaited messianic figure of the future. To summarize, a few basic patterns have emerged:

1   The image of the Davidic Messiah did not, to begin with, contain any significant didactic traits. The characteristics that come closest to the didactic ones are wisdom and understanding, but the Messiah is not portrayed as a person performing actual teaching.

2   The didactic understanding of the Messiah was nurtured within a group that identified itself in priestly and didactic categories. The notions of the teaching activity of the priestly Messiah were therefore not transferred to the Davidic Messiah. In Qumran, wisdom and understanding continued to be the basic didactic traits of the Messiah of David.

3   The more elaborated didactic traits of the Davidic Messiah emerge via the figure of the servant in Second Isaiah. Isaiah 42.1-6; 50.4; and 53.5 are important texts. They contain potentials of a messianic and/or didactic interpretation, which are developed in the *Psalms of Solomon* and the *Targum of Isaiah*.

The rabbis eventually enhanced the didactic traits of the Messiah by portraying him as an authoritative rabbi whose teaching will provide the final and decisive interpretation of the Torah. This development is not, however, anchored within a definable tradition history. Rather, it indicates how the group's own self-understanding affected and strengthened certain characteristics in the image of the Messiah. The didactic labels that were tied to the notion of God's servant fade into the background, being replaced with images that are grounded on the didactic identity of the rabbis themselves.

14. *Lev. R.* 13 (§ 3).
15. *Eccl. R.* 11.8.
16. W.D. Davies, *The Setting of the Sermon on the Mount* (Cambridge: Cambridge University Press, 1964), pp. 109-190; P. Schäfer, 'Die Torah der messianischen Zeit', *ZNW* 65 (1974), pp. 27-42.

The Messianic Tradition in the Gospel According to Matthew

As a second step I ask how the picture of the Messiah and the picture of Jesus as teacher are related to each other in the Gospel according to Matthew. We have seen that Mt. 23.10 connects the two, describing Jesus as καθηγητής and as Χριστός; the instructor is explicitly defined as the Messiah. Is this connection to be explained by reference to the tradition history outlined above?

The author uses the term Χριστός 15 or 16 times in reference to Jesus.[17] The various conceptions that are linked to it on other occasions, besides 23.10, have to do with the birth of Jesus (chs. 1–2), his deeds (11.2), Peter's confession (16.16, 20), the question about David's son (22.42), the notion that Jesus is the Son of God (16.16; 26.63) or a prophet (26.68), and the issue of whom the crowd thinks should be crucified (27.17, 22). The term does not recur after the account of the crucifixion.

It is indeed very difficult to detect a clear didactic connotation. The expression τὰ ἔργα τοῦ Χριστοῦ ('the works of the Messiah') in 11.2 comes perhaps closest to such a connotation, because it follows after the author has summarized Jesus' activity by telling the hearers/readers of his teaching and preaching in the cities. But on the other hand, the answer given to the question of whether he is the one who is to come refers to other activities, to therapeutic and kerygmatic ones (11.5).

We receive the same impression as we look at the use of the expression υἱὸς Δαυίδ ('son of David'). It occurs 10 times in reference to Jesus, within varying grammatical constructions. As is well known, the author relates it primarily to Jesus' therapeutic activity (9.27; 12.23; 15.22; 20.30, 31)—perhaps a reflection of the author's acquaintance with certain notions concerning Solomon.[18] The rest of the occurrences appear as the crowds and the children cry 'Hosanna' (21.9, 15) and, subsequently, as Jesus discusses with the Pharisees the matter of whose son the Messiah is (22.42, 45). After the cryptic question of how the Messiah can be the son of David,

17. Only a few mss of 16.21 use the term.

18. The most important text is Josephus, *Ant.* 8.45-49. For discussion, with references to sources and literature, see L. Novakovic, 'Jesus as the Davidic Messiah in Matthew', *HBT* 19 (1997), pp. 148-91. In this article the author develops insights from her ThM thesis, 'Jesus as the Son of David within Matthew's Narrative' (Rüschlikon [CH]: The International Baptist Theological Seminary, 1995). In addition, cf. K. Paffenroth, 'Jesus as Anointed and Healing Son of David in the Gospel of Matthew', *Bib* 80 (1999), pp. 547-54.

the expression strangely disappears from the narrative. Despite this peculiar narrative closure of the issue, it is evident that the son of David is not a teacher in Matthew; he is primarily a healer.

Did the author incorporate a didactic understanding of the Messiah via the notion of God's servant? Several scholars have pointed to the vital importance of this notion in the Matthean portrayal of Jesus.[19] From the Markan narrative the author took over and incorporated the allusion to God's servant in connection with the baptism (Mk 1.11/Mt. 3.17), the transfiguration (Mk 9.7/Mt. 17.5), the saying concerning giving one's life as a ransom for many (Mk 10.45/Mt. 20.28), and probably also in connection with several texts dealing with the suffering and death of Jesus.

In addition, two of the important fulfilment quotations are taken from the servant songs, those in 8.16-17 and 12.18-21. While the former relates the notion of the servant directly to Jesus' therapeutic activity, 12.18-21 betrays an interesting combination of various ideas. The quotation is taken from Isa. 42.1-4, which, as we have seen, some Jewish circles had already interpreted in a didactic fashion. The therapeutic ministry is still central; it surrounds the entire quotation. At the same time the opposition towards Jesus has increased (v. 14). In the immediate context of the quotation, Jesus silently avoids confrontation and exhorts the crowds not to tell anyone who he really is. But there is more to the quotation than the humble attitude of the servant. The servant is also the one who will proclaim justice to the nations (v. 18);[20] his name will give them hope (v. 21). The author carefully incorporates a didactic trait into the notion of the servant, thus subtly preparing the hearers/readers for the fuller commission of the disciples. In their mission to the nations, as it is initiated by the Resurrected

---

19. B. Gerhardsson, 'Gottes Sohn als Diener Gottes: Messias, Agape und Himmelsherrschaft nach dem Matthäusevangelium', *ST* 27 (1973), pp. 73-106; *idem*, 'Sacrificial Service and Atonement in the Gospel of Matthew', in R.J. Banks (ed.), *Reconciliation and Hope: New Testament Essays on Atonement and Eschatology* (Festschrift L.L. Morris; Exeter: Paternoster Press, 1974), pp. 25-35; D. Hill, 'Son and Servant: An Essay on Matthean Christology', *JSNT* 6 (1980), pp. 2-16; R. Schnackenburg, "Siehe da mein Knecht, den ich erwählt habe…" (Mt 12.18): Zur Heiltätigkeit Jesu im Matthäusevangelium', in L. Oberlinner and P. Fiedler (eds.), *Salz der Erde— Licht der Welt: Exegetische Studien zum Matthäusevangelium* (Festschrift W. Vögtle; Stuttgart: Katholisches Bibelwerk, 1991), pp. 203-222.

20. For the importance of the concept of justice in this context, see R. Beaton, 'Messiah and Justice: A Key to Matthew's Use of Isaiah 42.1-4?', *JSNT* 75 (1999), pp. 5-23. Beaton does not, however, pay attention to the nations as the object of the proclamation of justice, failing to detect the subtle connection to 28.19-20.

One in 28.19-20, the mission of Jesus the servant will find its concrete manifestation. *The notion of the servant, with its tradition history, thus serves as a 'cognitive matrix' for the fusion of the therapeutic activity with the didactic activity, which finally turns out to be the mission that the disciples are commanded to take over and carry on.*

Perhaps it is possible to accentuate further this connection between servant and teacher by noticing how the therapeutic activity sometimes functions as a kind of teaching elsewhere in the Matthean narrative. While Mk 1.39 connects healing with preaching, the crucial summaries in Mt. 4.23 and 9.35 relate it also to teaching. The two activities actually go hand in hand on several occasions in Matthew. In 4.24 Jesus cures all the sick ones that are brought to him, and these persons are subsequently present at the teaching on the mountain (5.1; 7.28-8.1). Second, the author collects a number of episodes concerning Jesus' therapeutic activity in chs. 8–9, and twice he inserts into this context a didactic category in reference to Jesus (8.19; 9.11). Third, just as the teaching in the Sermon on the Mount is described as words, λόγοι (7.24, 26, 28), so the λόγος of Jesus accomplishes the healing (8.8, 16). As Heinz Joachim Held and others have shown, the author usually concentrates the episodes concerning Jesus' miracles around dialogues and Jesus-sayings.[21] Fourth, the people of Jesus' hometown react strongly against his teaching, and as a consequence he does not perform many miracles there (13.54-58). Finally, according to 21.14-16 Jesus performs a miracle and awakens the anger of the opponents, but subsequently it is Jesus' teaching in the temple that causes the opponents to question his authority (21.23).

These are just a few examples. The healing is a kind of teaching. When the image of the servant is related to one of these activities, the other is therefore also implied. Perhaps we see here the traces of how the author had picked up and elaborated one spectrum of the tradition history. In the notion of the Messiah as God's servant he could relate Jesus' therapeutic and didactic activity in a meaningful way.

---

21. H.J. Held, 'Matthew as Interpreter of the Miracle Stories', in G. Bornkamm, G. Barth and H.J. Held (eds.), *Tradition and Interpretation in Matthew* (trans. P. Scott; London: SCM, 2nd edn, 1982), pp. 165-299 (168-211, 233-37). Cf. also K. Gatzweiler, 'Les récits de miracles dans l'Évangile selon saint Matthieu', in M. Didier (ed.), *L'Évangile selon Matthieu: Rédaction et théologie* (BETL, 29; Gembloux: Duculot, 1972), pp. 209-220 (212-13); B. Gerhardsson, *The Mighty Acts of Jesus according to Matthew* (trans. R. Dewsnap; Scripta Minora, 1978-79.5; Lund: C.W.K. Gleerup, 1979), pp. 40-41, 46-47, 53.

However, this tradition history is certainly not to be found on the surface of the story. It is difficult to detect and remains hypothetical. Possibly we are dealing with a multidimensional interaction of different inter-texts which indirectly shaped the author's understanding of Jesus as the Messiah. *We have discovered a thin thread, a tiny glimpse, but we cannot speak of a significant christological trait.* It is necessary, therefore, to turn to an analysis which takes as its direct point of departure the didactic categories used in the Matthean narrative, in order to see if and how the author's narrative ambitions bring out the image that is made explicit in Mt. 23.10, καθηγητὴς ὑμῶν ἐστιν εἷς ὁ Χριστός.

The Didactic Christology in the Gospel According to Matthew

To begin with, let us make a comparison. The three Synoptic Gospels give a somewhat diverse picture of Jesus as teacher. Noticing the use of only the most common didactic terms (διδάσκαλος ['teacher'], διδάσκειν ['teach'], διδαχή ['teaching'], διδασκαλία ['teaching']), we find 35 occurrences in Mark and Luke respectively, and 30 in Matthew. In Mark, 33 of these instances refer to Jesus and his activity; in Luke, 32; in Matthew, 25. In addition, the Markan narrative employs ῥαββί ('rabbi') and ῥαββουνί four times in addressing Jesus (Mk 9.5; 10.51; 11.21; 14.45); the Matthean narrative also uses it four times, but only twice for Jesus (26.25, 49). The Lukan narrative does not use this term at all, but betrays a certain preference for ἐπιστάτα ('Master') (Lk. 5.5; 8.24, 45; 9.33, 49; 17.13).

To the extent that the Christology of a Gospel has to do with how the characters of the story address Jesus and thus express a relationship to him, it is essential to notice that Matthew never puts a didactic address of Jesus on the lips of the disciples; here Matthew differs significantly from both Mark and Luke. Does this imply that the author of the Matthean narrative was purposely reserved towards regarding Jesus as a teacher? Yes and no! This feature of the Matthean narrative has, paradoxically enough, to do with an ambition to portray Jesus as a teacher who is unlike any other teacher. There are two observations pointing in this direction.

First, in 26.25, 49 Judas uses the term ῥαββί to address Jesus. It appears that in 26.25 the Matthean author added this designation himself, thus developing what he found in Mk 14.45 and later reproduced in 26.49. At an earlier point in the narrative, Jesus had explained that the scribes and the Pharisees love to have people call them rabbi, urging the disciples therefore to avoid using this designation among themselves (23.7-8). As the author still puts it on the lips of Judas as he greets Jesus, he subtly points to Judas's erroneous understanding of who Jesus really is. *To Judas, the betrayer, Jesus was merely one teacher among many. He had not really grasped the greatness of Jesus as teacher*, the author implies.

Second, it is noteworthy that the other disciples and the people who show trust in Jesus' therapeutic capability use the term κύριε ('Lord'). The contrast to other characters in the story, and their use of other labels, is clearly illustrated on two occasions: in 8.19 a scribe addresses Jesus with διδάσκαλε, while in 8.21 one of the disciples uses κύριε; and in 26.22 the disciples ask one after the other μήτι ἐγώ εἰμι, κύριε ('surely it is not me, Lord'), while in 26.25 Judas employs the expression μήτι ἐγώ εἰμι, ῥαββί 'surely it is not me, rabbi'. The same pattern appears when we compare the other Synoptics. Three times Matthew alone uses κύριε where both Mark and Luke have διδάσκαλε, ῥαββί ('surely it is not me, rabbi') or—in Luke—ἐπιστάτα ('Master').[22] Jack D. Kingsbury has shown that κύριος as used for Jesus does not function as a fixed christological title of majesty in Matthew, but as a relational term validating the superior status of Jesus in a general manner.[23] The use of this rather vague label is suitable in order not to nullify the didactic portrayal of Jesus. It is thus important to notice that *the author does not replace the didactic address with a christological title redefining entirely the didactic role of Jesus.* Jesus does not, so to say, cease to be a teacher just because he is called κύριος. On the contrary, *by addressing Jesus with the term κύριε, the disciples and the believing people attribute an extraordinary status to him as teacher*. As teacher he is their lord!

This impression, gained in part from a comparison with the other Synoptics, is reinforced when we hear/read the Gospel as a coherent narrative. As we all know, the Christology of a narrative is much more than the mere accumulation of certain titles and labels. The story of the narrative develops step by step a Christology in which words, actions, and episodes placed in a certain relation to each other all have a role to play. In Matthew this kind of christology includes a narrative use of the didactic terms. I thus turn to a brief study of how these terms are integrated into the narrative structure of the story, to what we may call the didactic storyline of Matthew.

22. Mt. 8.25/Mk 4.38/Lk. 8.24; Mt. 17.4/Mk 9.5/Lk. 9.33; Mt. 17.15/Mk 9.17/Lk. 9.38. Once Matthew and Luke both have κύριε where Mark has ῥαββουνί (Mt. 20.33[cf. 9.28]/Mk 10.51/Lk. 18.41).

23. Kingsbury, *Matthew*, pp. 103-113.

The first thing notice is that the beginning of the story, which is so important for determining the hearers'/readers' disposition to what follows subsequently,[24] contains no didactic categories. This initial observation makes is clear that the story concerns basically someone who is much more than, and very different from, any ordinary teacher. As we have seen, the story begins with an explicit messianic definition of its main character: it is the story about 'Jesus the Messiah, the son of David, the son of Abraham' (1.1).

The narrator introduces, somewhat abruptly, the didactic terms as this Messiah is to begin his active ministry. We detect two important structural markers. First, Jesus' teaching is mentioned as an essential part of the author's first summary of his activity (4.23). It receives the first position within the first triad of teaching, preaching and healing. The author later repeats this summary in whole (9.35) or in part (11.1b) and thereby regularly reminds the hearers/readers about how to understand what this 'Jesus the Messiah, the son of David, the son of Abraham' said and did. Second, the story receives a further didactic dimension as Jesus for the first time is to give a speech. At this point the narrator's comments play a minor role and are subordinated to the words of the main character, and the only comment of the narrator indicates the didactic identity of the speaker (5.1-2; 7.28-29). Hence, as Jesus for the first time in the story raises his voice to speak more extensively, he speaks as a teacher. The hearers/readers begin to realize that the person who at the beginning was presented in messianic terms is in fact a teacher.

The subsequent narrative provides several 'didactic events',[25] accentuating and developing the didactic storyline. As we just noticed, the narrator several times reminds the hearers/readers of Jesus' teaching activity (9.35; 11.1; 13.54); and before 16.21, after which the narrative moves towards Jesus' suffering, death and resurrection, it presents him five times as διδάσκαλος.[26] The most frequent use of the didactic terms appears after Peter, in 16.13-20, has confessed Jesus as the Messiah, the son of the

---

24. For an overview of this debate among literary theorists, cf. M.C. Parsons, 'Reading a Beginning/Beginning a Reading: Tracing Literary Theory in Narrative Openings', *Semeia* 52 (1990), pp. 11-31.

25. I understand the 'events' of a story as consisting of several actions and happenings arranged in a particular temporal and causal sequence. See S. Chatman, *Story and Discourse: Narrative Structure in Fiction and Film* (Ithaca, NY: Cornell University Press, 1978), pp. 43-95. Cf. also M. Powell, *What is Narrative Criticism? A New Approach to the Bible* (London: SPCK, 1993), pp. 35-42.

26. 8.19; 9.11; 10.24, 25; 12.38.

living God.[27] Now the author reveals step by step the central importance of the didactic storyline, educating the disciples—and thus the hearers/readers—to be faithful to Jesus as teacher and thus eventually to carry on his teaching activity in their own mission of making disciples (28.19-20).

The narrative strategy of the didactic storyline after 16.21 is seen clearly in the use of the term διkάσκαλος in 23.8-10 and 26.18. In 23.8 Jesus employs this term for himself, giving the didactic label a kind of normative legitimation. This didactic climax of the story has, in addition, been prepared in a sophisticated way at previous points during the same phase of the narrative. The term is used in 17.24 and 19.16, but by people who are not close to Jesus. As Jesus subsequently enters Jerusalem, the centre of opposition and rejection, it occurs on the lips of the opponents addressing Jesus (22.16, 24, 36). Also the crowds, according to the narrator, are astounded at his διδαχή. The 'didactic events' of the story are thus becoming more and more frequent. At 23.8-10 we have therefore reached a decisive point of the didactic storyline. Now, after the opponents and the crowds have understood him as a teacher, Jesus himself speaks of his didactic role and stresses that he is in fact a teacher; yes, he is *the* Teacher, the only teacher of the disciples, the messianic teacher.

The decisive point at 23.8-10 is confirmed in 26.18. Jesus here tells his disciples to refer to him merely as ὁ διδάσκαλος, without any further comments concerning his identity. This is the first and the only time that this designation is employed with the definite article and without any further qualification, without adding, for instance, αὐτοῦ or ὑμῶν (his or yours). The fact that the author, in this case, was influenced by the Gospel tradition (cf. Mk 14.14; Lk. 22.11) does not diminish the significance of the narrative location in Matthew. At 23.8-10 the hearers/readers were educated to understand the didactic label correctly. The teacher is the Messiah, they were taught. No further comments from the narrator or the actors are therefore necessary. At this point they can themselves fill out the 'empty gaps' of ὁ διδάσκαλος with the proper connotations. They know that the teacher is, in fact, the very person who spoke of himself as the only messianic teacher and instructor of the disciples. They are fully educated in this regard; and accordingly, no further instances of the designation appear.

The didactic storyline has thus defined Jesus as the messianic teacher. What remains is to guide the disciples to carry on faithfully Jesus' teaching activity in their own mission. Their commissioning in 28.16-20 forms

---

27.   17.24; 19.16; 21.23; 22.16, 24, 33, 36; 23.8; 26.18, 55; 28.20.

the climax of the entire Matthean story.[28] Just as the beginning of a story is important, so is the end. The implications of the choices previously made between different possibilities in the narrative become evident and are given their final interpretation. At this point in the Matthean narrative, the didactic storyline reaches its culmination and goal.[29] Just as Jesus taught his disciples when he spoke to them for the first time in the narrative, so he now commissions them to make disciples by, among other things, teaching the nations to obey everything that he has commanded them (28.19-20). The didactic part of the commission links back to 5.19, where Jesus exhorted the disciples not to annul even the least of the commandments (of Jesus) as they teach others.[30] Throughout the ensuing narrative they have followed their teacher, seen and heard him performing his active ministry; and now, at the very end of the narrative, after his death and resurrection, they have been reunited with him and are qualified to carry on his teaching in a way that does not annul even the least of the commandments.

We have noticed the storyline that emerges through a close analysis of the didactic terms used in the narrative. This line is clear enough to be visible on the surface of the narrative structure. Along this line the author has intertwined other markers that further, and in a different way, define and enhance Jesus as teacher. In a previous study I paid attention to the equal status of Jesus' teaching and God's commandments in Matthew; to the correlation between Jesus' emphatic ἐγὼ δὲ λέγω ('but I tell you') and the *passivum divinum*, ἐρρέθη ('it is said'), in the so-called Antitheses; to the threefold εἷς of Mt. 23.8-10 and its allusion to the threefold confession of the one God in the *Shema'* (Deut. 6.4-5); and to the Wisdom categories in 8.19-20; 11.19, 25-30; 12.42; and 13.54, suggesting that Jesus assumed functions similar to the divine Wisdom.[31] Together they form a kind of *didactic Christology*, serving as labels that establish and validate

28. S. Byrskog, 'Slutet gott, allting gott: Matteus 28.16–20 i narrativt perspektiv', in B. Olsson, S. Byrskog and W. Übelacker (eds.), *Matteus och hans läsare—förr och nu: Matteussymposiet i Lund den 27–28 april 1996* (Religio, 48; Lund: Teologiska institutionen, 1997), pp. 85-98.

29. Cf. A.T. Lincoln, 'Matthew—A Story for Teachers?', in D.J.A. Clines, S.E. Fowl and S.E. Porter (eds.), *The Bible in Three Dimensions: Essays in Celebration of Forty Years of Biblical Studies in the University of Sheffield* (JSNTSup, 87; Sheffield: JSOT Press, 1990), pp. 103-125.

30. For a more extensive analysis, see S. Byrskog, 'Matthew 5.17-18 in the Argumentation of the Context', *RB* 104 (1997), pp. 557-71.

31. Byrskog, *Jesus the Only Teacher*, pp. 290-306.

Jesus' didactic *exousia* as it appears in 7.29; 21.23-27; and 28.18.[32] *In this way the author has created an image of the teacher which at the end goes beyond the tradition-historical connection between the therapeutic and didactic activity of the messianic servant.*

The History behind the Story

What is then, after all, the background of this elevated didactic Christology in Matthew? The picture of Jesus in the Gospel tradition has of course been influential. The author usually betrays a rather close dependence upon previously formulated material—the Markan narrative in particular —and we must therefore assume that his portrait of Jesus as teacher was not done in isolation from characterizations he had encountered elsewhere. But these considerations do not explain the significant changes he made to the Gospel tradition and the consistent narrative strategies he used, all in order to create a coherent didactic storyline.

We noticed above that the rabbis projected part of their own situation and identity onto their messianic expectations. Perhaps the author of the Gospel according to Matthew, and the group around him, similarly projected their own situation onto 'Jesus the Messiah, the son of David, the son of Abraham', thus legitimizing their own didactic identity. The hypothesis emerging in this essay is that *the tradition-historical background was shaped in ways that are explicable in terms of sociology of knowledge and that affected, perhaps even determined, the development of the didactic storyline of the Matthean narrative.*

One indication of this process is the distinction between the terms ῥαββί and διδάσκαλος in Matthew. As we have seen, the author avoids using ῥαββί for Jesus, except on the lips of Judas. The term ῥαββί has a decisively negative connotation in the story. This is evident not only from the fact that only the traitor uses it to address Jesus, but also from the accusations in 23.7-8. It is a title that the Jewish teachers love to have applied to themselves. By contrast, in 23.8a Jesus exhorts the disciples not to use it for themselves. Afterwards, in 23.8b, as he speaks of himself as a teacher he changes to διδάσκαλος. The semantic synonymity of the two terms is broken; independently of the previous Gospel tradition, the author introduces a sharp distinction between their connotations.[33]

---

32. See now also Müller, 'The Theological Interpretation', pp. 164, 170-72.

33. This distinction is not present in Mark, where ῥαββί/ῥαββουνί and διδάσκαλος carry similar didactic connotations. I do not agree with B.T. Viviano's sugges-

It is improbable that ῥαββί means only 'my teacher', 'my great one', at this time.[34] Its function as a proper title is indicated by the fact that the text does not portray a close relationship between two persons, where expressions such as 'my teacher' or 'my great one' would be natural. The text indicates a very general way of addressing teachers. Moreover, in 23.8 ῥαββί is given in the singular, whereas Jesus addresses several people and uses the plural καθηγηταί ('teachers') in the parallel statement at 23.10a. The author evidently reacts against ῥαββί as a proper title, not simply as a respectful way of addressing the Jewish teachers.

Looking more closely at how the term רבי ('rabbi') is used in some rabbinic texts, we discover a development from its function as an expression of quality or relation to its function as a proper title with the suffix having no real pronominal significance.[35] A letter written by R. Sherira (c. 906–1006), the Gaon of the Pumbedithan academy, to the North African community at Kairouan, mentions Johanan b. Zakkai as the first one to carry the title.[36] Johanan died, as far as we know, around 80 CE. Other rabbinic sources, to be dated before the letter, confirm R. Sherira's view. In these sources the term is usually not prefixed to the name of the old sages. We find it used as a proper title during the first generation of tannas: R. Zadok, R. Eliezer b. Jacob, R. Hanina b. Dosa. The letter also relates the title to the ordination; and another text, in *b. B. Meṣ.* 85a, takes for granted that the gold-trimmed cloak put on the one ordained at the ceremony of ordination was a token closely related to the bestowal of the title 'Rabbi'.[37] R. Ba (c. 270 CE)—or R. Abba b. Zabda—says in *y. Sanh.* 19a that Johanan b. Zakkai was the first one to practise ordination.

tion that ῥαββί/ῥαββουνί has no didactic connotation in Mark but is roughly equivalent to κύριος ('Rabbouni and Mark 9.5', *RB* 97 [1990], pp. 207-218). For arguments against Viviano, see Byrskog, *Jesus the Only Teacher*, p. 285.

34. Differently Riesner, *Jesus als Lehrer*, p. 271; A.F. Zimmermann, *Die urchristlichen Lehrer: Studien zum Tradentenkreis der διδάσκαλοι im frühen Urchristentum* (WUNT, 2.12; Tübingen: Mohr Siebeck, 2nd edn, 1988), pp. 172-73.

35. For a fuller treatment, with references to sources and literature, see Byrskog, *Jesus the Only Teacher*, pp. 93-96.

36. The letter is dated to 987 CE. An English translation of the relevant text portion is given by H. Shanks, 'Is the Title "Rabbi" Anachronistic in the Gospels', *JQR* 53 (1962/63), pp. 337-45 (338). For further information concerning the letter, see H.L. Strack and G. Stemberger, *Introduction to the Talmud and Midrash* (Edinburgh: T. & T. Clark, 1991), p. 7.

37. Cf. also *b. Sanh.* 13b. For further discussion, see J. Newman, *Semikhah (Ordination): A Study of its Origin, History and Function in Rabbinic Literature* (Manchester: Manchester University Press, 1950), pp. 117-18; E. Lohse, *Die Ordination im*

As it seems, shortly after 70 CE there was a need for consolidation and legitimation among the Jewish teachers. This process expressed itself in various ways, as we all know. Apparently one element had to do with the attempt to legitimize the teachers by giving them a proper didactic title. If we agree with the majority of scholars dating the Gospel according to Matthew after 70—perhaps some time during the 80s—and hear/read the narrative in the context of an intense discussion with concurrent Jewish leaders, we may detect the background of the negative connotation attached to ῥαββί as well as of the sophisticated narrative technique by which the author creates a 'didactic Christology' and enhances Jesus to the only teacher of the disciples. *The author of Matthew and the group around him needed to establish their own identity and withdrew therefore from the contemporary attempts to legitimize the authority of the Jewish teachers by means of a didactic title; they refused to use the same title for themselves and for Jesus, instead confessing Jesus as by every measure a unique teacher and instructor.*

Conclusion

I conclude that the Christology of the Gospel according to Matthew, at least as far as the notion of Jesus as messianic teacher goes, was created at the intersection of tradition history and narrative strategies. This Christology cannot be grasped solely by reference to exact Jewish notions; by the same token, it does not emerge independently of these. The process I have detected has to do with how a person and a group have shaped and re-shaped traditional images according to the needs of consolidation and identity that were awakened in relation to other persons and groups. The story lives from and within the tension arising when old convictions of previous times were confronted with the author's 'now'.[38] A one-sided focus on either tradition history or narrative Christology provides therefore only a partial and incomplete account of how Jesus was understood.

Once this has been said, we also need to take seriously the fact that the author to a large extent abandoned the tradition-historical background as

Spätjudentum und im Neuen Testament (Göttingen: Vandenhoeck & Ruprecht, 1951), p. 52; K. Hruby, 'La notion d'ordination dans la tradition juive', *Maison Dieu* 102 (1970), pp. 30-56 (36-37).

38. I explore this tension from a broader and somewhat different perspective in S. Byrskog, *Story as History—History as Story: The Gospel Tradition in the Context of Ancient Oral History* (WUNT, 123; Tübingen: Mohr Siebeck, 2000). The discussion of the present essay is not included in the book.

he created his narrative. History becomes story; the narrative world invades, takes over and captures history, redefining the messianic categories. The author indeed might have received impulses from the tradition history for connecting Jesus the teacher with Jesus the Messiah in 23.10, but within the narrative world of the story this connection has less to do with the notion of God's servant and more to do with the narrative progression whereby words, actions and episodes build up and lead to the decisive didactic climax. To speak paradigmatically of Jesus as the messianic teacher—or to speak similarly with other christological labels, for that matter—neglects the insight that the Christology is always 'happening' in the story. Just as the 'Gospel' comes to us in the form of a story, so the Christology remains conditioned by the narrative. The narrative Jesus is always, so to say, 'im Werden' ('in becoming').

THE RECEPTION OF PAUL IN THE ACTS OF THE APOSTLES

Niels Hyldahl

Paul in the Acts of the Apostles: A Complex of Questions and Problems

From a receptionist point of view it would make good sense, on the occasion of his 250th anniversary, to discuss Goethe's reception in Scandinavia, thereby understanding the literary effect of his works and their appropriation. As to the light thrown upon Goethe's *own* works by such an investigation nothing much could be hoped for, but the understanding of Scandinavian literature itself, however, would be greatly enhanced. Goethe's own works are all—some more than others—reflected in Scandinavian poetry, and always in such a way that a literary comparison is directly possible. Something similar could be said about the reception of, for example, Shakespare's literary work.

But when it comes to the reception of Paul in the Acts of the Apostles it must be admitted that it is quite uncertain what kind of a reception one should be speaking of. For despite the most energetic efforts spent on the issue, no one so far has succeeded in convincing anybody, or even proving, that the author of Acts knew and used (at least some of) Paul's letters. The difficulty is compounded by the fact that authors of antiquity seldom use explicit or verbal quotations (apart, of course, from quotations from the Old Testament or the Greek poets). This is evident in Luke's use of the Gospel of Mark[1]—and it is only because we are in possession of Mark that we can see both *that* and *how* Luke made use of Mark, but even so it must be admitted that no proof, in the strict sense of the word, has as yet been produced to show that Luke actually knew and used Mark; it has only been assumed that this was probably the case. A comparable or similar use of the letters of Paul in the second half of the same authorship, Acts, has so

---

1.   Gitte Rasmussen, 'Den rigtige rækkefølge: Et indblik i Lukas-skrifternes redaktionelle tilblivelse' [The Correct Sequence: An Insight into the Redactional Origin of Luke–Acts], in Lone Fatum and Mogens Müller (eds.), *Tro og historie* (FBE, 7; Copenhagen: Museum Tusculanums Forlag, 1996), pp. 206-214, esp. 206-208.

far not actually been proved—the less so as, in this case, two very different literary genres are involved: letters opposed to historical relation.
Without any *proof* that the Pauline letters were actually used by the author
of Acts it cannot convincingly be claimed that the author of Acts knew the
letters of Paul—for without documented use the hypothesis of knowledge
remains purely speculative.

The result is confusing. The reception of Paul in Acts is, to use an
expression from modern nuclear theory, an *Unbestimmtheitsrelation*
('relation of indefiniteness'). If Acts is an early writing it is not to be
expected that the author knew the Pauline letters. But if Acts is a late writing it must be expected that at least some of the letters may have been
used—and, therefore, also known—by the author. In order to avoid this
difficult dilemma or alternative most interpreters have chosen to claim that
Acts is neither early nor late and that the author did not make use of the
letters, but only referred to the Pauline tradition.

This compromise solution is, however, not without its problems. Even a
cautious dating of Acts to c. 80–100 CE will make it extremely difficult to
claim that the author was ignorant of the existence of Pauline letters—the
Roman congregation, from which came *1 Clement* to the Corinthian congregation in the 90s, knows about 1 Corinthians and refers to the contents
of this Pauline letter. The position that most interpreters of Acts hold is,
indeed, purely speculative: they claim that the author knew (several of) the
letters of Paul, but that he deliberately chose not to use them. Against this
position two objections can be raised: (1) If it is not proved that the author
used at least some of the letters, then—as already said—it cannot reasonably be claimed that he knew them; it is meaningless to claim that the
author knew the letters if it cannot be proved that he used them; and (2) a
knowledge of (at least some of) the letters cannot be suppressed in the
sense that the author should have ignored them—partly because this would
seem to be psychologically improbable, partly because it would be difficult to understand why the author, whose sympathy for Paul is evident,
should consciously have chosen to ignore the letters.

From this follows the untenability of another position. As is well known,
in post-apostolic times the letters of Paul had become the object partly of
cautious criticism (cf. 2 Pet. 3.16: 'they [the letters of Paul] contain some
obscure passages, which the ignorant and unstable misinterpret to their
own ruin, as they do the other scriptures'), and partly of direct and hereti-
cal misuse (Marcion; cf. 1 Tim. 6.20). It is then claimed that such allegations were the reason why the letters were passed over in silence by the
author of Acts. But if the letters of Paul at the time when Acts was written

had become the object of either criticism or misuse, or both, it is difficult to explain why Paul's person and his work should have escaped attention, and it is precisely Paul and his work that are praised highly in Acts, whereas his letters are not mentioned at all, neither positively nor negatively. In other words: no inconsistency is to be detected in Acts between the person and the work of Paul on the one hand and his letters on the other, exactly because the letters are not mentioned with a single word.

A fundamental, but somehow understandable, difference between the letters of Paul and the portrait of Paul in Acts is apparent from the fact that the letters are addressed to *already established congregations*, in particular congregations founded by Paul himself (in Thessalonica, Philippi, Corinth, and so on), whereas those parts of the text of Acts which are 'covered' by the Pauline letters themselves have to do with the establishment of these congregations (in Philippi, Thessalonica, Corinth, etc.). Only in one single case does Acts refer to the situation in an already established congregation, namely the farewell discourse of Paul to the Ephesian elders (Acts 20.18-35), and precisely in this speech signs have been detected which show a possible dependence upon themes touched upon in the Pauline letters.[2] Another text of Acts has also been interpreted to show that the author used Paul's letters: the rumour about Paul's allegedly law-critical teaching of the Diaspora Jews (Acts 21.20-21) which, as it seems, had in no way been anticipated in the earlier parts of Acts and was also immediately afterwards denied through his payment for the four poor Nazirites' offerings in the Temple (Acts 21.26).[3] However, this rumour has its origin in Pauline tradition rather than in the letters themselves (*in casu*: Galatians) and does *not* indicate that the letters had been used; as it is formulated, it is in fact contradicted by the text of the letters. The rumour and its no less explicit denial is presumably best understood as a characteristic feature in the portrait of Paul which the author of Acts wishes to communicate; I shall return to this below.

There is no getting around the fact that, in the representation of Paul in Acts, one has to reckon with a Pauline tradition of some measure—no matter whether the author used the letters or not. A few details will soon

---

2. Lars Aejmelaeus, *Die Rezeption der Paulusbriefe in der Miletrede (Apg 20.18-35)* (Annales Academiæ Scientiarum Fennicæ, B/232; Helsinki: Suomalainen Tiedeakatemia, 1987); with hesitation Andreas Lindemann, *Paulus im ältesten Christentum: Das Bild des Apostels und die Rezeption der paulinischen Theologie in der frühchristlichen Literatur bis Marcion* (BHT, 58; Tübingen: J.C.B. Mohr, 1979), p. 169.

3. Lindemann, *Paulus im ältesten Christentum*, pp. 169-70.

show that the author did in fact use a Pauline tradition which cannot be referred to the letters. First, there is the information that Paul was a Roman citizen (Acts 16.37-38; 22.25-29; 23.27)—this bit of information is not found in the letters, and could not be expected to be found there; the doubt that has been raised about the correctness of this information[4] is probably without any foundation.[5] Secondly, the information that Paul was from Tarsus in Cilicia (Acts 9.11, 30; 11.25; 21.39; 22.3; 23.34), which is no doubt correct, is not found in the letters and must therefore be referred to the Pauline tradition.

I am fully aware that the letters are the only sources of a lot of details about Paul, and that these details may be signified as events.[6] To these details belong Paul's imprisonment in Ephesus which only the letters tell us about, whereas Acts is completely silent about it; and the references to several persons only mentioned in the letters, especially Titus. Nevertheless it must be admitted that Acts also contains several details not mentioned in the letters which—precisely because they do not reveal any clear tendencies—should be taken seriously. They are about the foundation of certain of the Pauline congregations. Here we have the information about Jason in connection with the foundation of the congregation in Thessalonica (Acts 17.5, 6, 7, 9): he was a Thessalonian and the owner of a house in the city where the new community met; possibly he was of Jewish origin, or else he belonged to the godfearing Gentiles. And why should the information about Dionysius, a member of the council of the Areopagus, and Damaris (17.34) not be correct? That Paul, accompanied by Timothy, had actually visited Athens is a fact (1 Thess. 3.1-2), even if the details about Timothy's movements are not quite correctly rendered in the story of Acts. In connection with the foundation of the congregation in Corinth certain details are told which the letters do not fully report. Titius Justus, who like Jason owned a house and was a godfearing Gentile (Acts 18.7), is not mentioned by Paul in his letters, and although we hear of Crispus and

4. Wolfgang Stegemann, 'War der Apostel Paulus ein römischer Bürger?', *ZNW* 78 (1987), pp. 200-29; John Clayton Lentz, Jr, *Luke's Portrait of Paul* (SNTSMS, 77; Cambridge: Cambridge University Press, 1993), esp. pp. 43-51: 'Paul, the Roman Citizen'.

5. Rainer Riesner, *Die Frühzeit des Apostels Paulus: Studien zur Chronologie, Missionsstrategie und Theologie* (WUNT, 71; Tübingen: J.C.B. Mohr, 1994), pp. 129-39: 'Exkurs I: Das römische Bürgerrecht des Paulus'; Peter van Minnen, 'Paul the Roman Citizen', *JSNT* 56 (1994), pp. 43-52.

6. Cf. the extensive list in John Coolidge Hurd, *The Origin of I Corinthians* (London: SPCK, 1965 [rep.; Macon, GA: Mercer University Press, 1983]), pp. 24-25.

Sosthenes in the letters of Paul (1 Cor. 1.1, 14), it is not said that they had been presidents of the synagogue (Acts 18.8, 17) and therefore were Jews by origin. Only Acts tells us that Paul stayed in Corinth one and a half years (18.11). As to Ephesus, valuable information is found in Acts: for two full years Paul was teaching at Tyrannus's school in Ephesus and thus became the teacher of the whole population of Asia, both Jews and Greeks (19.9-10—unfortunately we do not know who this Tyrannus was, but he seems to have been a parallel figure to Jason in Thessalonica and Titius Justus in Corinth); and the total length of Paul's stay in Ephesus was three years (19.8, 10; 20.31). To this may be added the list of the seven persons who accompanied Paul on his last travel to Jerusalem: Sopater from Beroea; Aristarchus and Secundus from Thessalonica; Gaius from Derbe; Timothy, and Tychicus and Trophimus from Asia (20.4; cf. 19.29 about Aristarchus and Gaius; 21.29 about Trophimus; and 27.2 about Aristarchus —Sopater, Secundus and Trophimus are not mentioned in the genuine letters of Paul). Outside the Pauline congregations Philip the Evangelist, one of the seven overseers (6.5), is mentioned as living in Caesarea by the Sea together with his four prophesying daughters (21.8-9; cf. 8.40); mention is made also of Mnason from Cyprus, probably a Christian of Jewish origin, who lived in or near Jerusalem (21.16). And whence should we know that Paul had a sister, and she again a son, in Jerusalem if not from Acts (23.16)? The author of Acts, therefore, did in fact draw on a Pauline tradition which must have been quite extensive.

We have also noted that at a certain point Acts reveals its knowledge of a *rumour* about Paul which could not have come from the letters, but from the Pauline tradition—a rumour which the author of Acts considers false and therefore denies (Acts 21.20-21, 26). This means that the author of Acts not only transmits the contents of a Pauline tradition which he is familiar with, but also is anxious to correct this tradition in order to produce a better understanding of Paul than that expressed in the existing tradition. This is confirmed by later statements in Acts where the author similarly refers to and reproduces rumours about Paul which he then corrects. In the Temple precincts Paul is accused by the Jews of having taught against the people and against the law and against the Temple, and of having profaned the sanctuary, by bringing Greeks into the Temple— this last accusation referred to Trophimus from Ephesus whom they had seen together with Paul in the city (21.28-29). In Tertullus's accusation before the procurator Felix, Paul is charged with being a pest and promoting disorder among the Diaspora Jews all over the world; with being the ringleader of the sect of the Nazarenes; and with having tried to profane the Temple (24.5-6)—according to Paul's ensuing defence these were evidently groundless accusations. Later, when questioned by Festus, the successor of Felix, Paul denies the allegations of having offended against the law of the Jews, against the Temple, and against the emperor (25.7-8). And lastly, in his words to the most prominent of the Roman Jews whom he had called together, Paul states that he has done nothing against the people or the customs of their forefathers (28.17).

The total picture is easily sketched: Is there knowledge of (some of) the letters of Paul? Perhaps, but this is uncertain. Is there knowledge of the Pauline tradition? Yes. Has there been a correction of (part of) this tradition? Yes.

Taking into consideration the great inconsistencies between the story about Paul as told in Acts and the Pauline letters themselves it would be tempting to conclude that the only basis which the author of Acts had for his story about Paul was indeed the Pauline tradition itself—not any of the letters. None of the textual coincidences often referred to between the letters and Acts (πορθέω: Acts 9.21; Gal. 1.13, 23; ταράσσω: Acts 15.24; Gal. 1.7; 5.10; εἰς διαταγὰς ἀγγέλων / διαταγεὶς δι' ἀγγέλων: Acts 7.53; Gal. 3.19) is sufficient proof that the author of Acts used (some of) the letters of Paul (in this case, Galatians), as the basis of his account.

The origin of the Pauline tradition as used and partly corrected by the author of Acts remains uncertain. Only very simplistically can it be said that the letters form the basis of the tradition (Pauline letters → Pauline tradition) and that this tradition formed the basis of the account in Acts (Pauline tradition → Acts). Such a simplification overlooks the fact that the Pauline tradition cannot possibly be explained simply by reference to the letters of Paul and that the account in Acts aims at more than simply retelling the story—it wants to correct the tradition.

Olof Linton has tried to throw light upon the Pauline tradition as displayed in Acts. On the basis of Galations 1–2 he reconstructs a 'Galatian' version of Paul's interaction with Jerusalem and claims that this 'Galatian' version is identical with or at least related to the account in Acts 9 and 15.[7] The weaknesses of this hypothesis are evident: (1) It is not possible to claim the existence of a 'Galatian' version and reconstruct it on the basis of Galations 1–2 simply by turning Paul's account upside down in some kind of mirror reading; (2) besides, the 'Galatian' version does not after all coincide fully with the account in Acts 9 and 15.

7.   Olof Linton, 'The Third Aspect: A Neglected Point of View. A Study in Gal. i-ii and Acts ix and xv', *ST* 3 (1949), pp. 79-95 (originally Swedish, from 1947).

Gerd Lüdemann has claimed that if only the account of Paul in Acts is critically analysed, and redaction and tradition carefully separated, then the tradition will be found to coincide with the picture of Paul as reconstructed solely on the basis of the letters.[8] But also in this case the weaknesses are clear: (1) The 'result', that is, the portrayal of Paul as reconstructed solely on the basis of the letters, is already known before any analysis of Acts is attempted, and it is therefore relatively easy to make the analysis of Acts fit the 'result'; (2) the analysis of Acts does not result in any real understanding of or insight into Acts as a theological and literary work, but serves only to establish the agreement between the tradition contained in Acts and the contents of the letters of Paul.

It should be emphasized that both Linton and Lüdemann deny the possibility that the author of Acts made use of the letters of Paul or some of them. In this respect they represent the common view of the twentieth century, contrary to the view held by most interpreters of the nineteenth century, that the author of Acts did in fact know and use the Pauline letters.

Paul and the Jews According to Acts

In order not to complicate further the relation between the letters of Paul, the story about Paul in Acts and the Pauline tradition used by the author of Acts, I should prefer to try shedding some light on the view which the author of Acts intends to convey to his readers on the relation between Paul and the Jews. We are here evidently at the kernel of the matter and the very heart of what the author of Acts wishes to communicate. A clarification of this subject will therefore also throw light upon the reception of Paul in Acts.

In advance it can briefly be stated that on the other hand, in Acts, Jews *en bloc* represent the adversaries of Christ and Christianity, while on the other hand Paul as a follower of the Way is an eminent example of genuine and law-abiding Judaism, faithful to the writings and, from a Jewish point of view, not to be blamed for anything. In other words: on the other hand *Jewish accusations against Paul are false, while on the other hand the essence of Christianity is identical with that of Judaism in so far as Judaism is not judged according to its empirical, aggressive appearance, but according to its true essence.*

8. Gerd Lüdemann, *Das frühe Christentum nach den Traditionen der Apostelgeschichte: Ein Kommentar* (Göttingen: Vandenhoeck & Ruprecht, 1988).

The question is this: Where is the *Sitz im Leben* of such an understanding of the relation between Judaism and Christianity to be found, and how do we best account for the explanation which the author wishes to impart to us of this relation?

In order to answer this question it will be necessary, at least briefly, to contemplate the other parts of the authorship, that is, Luke and the parts of Acts not directly concerned with Paul. It will then appear that the view of the Jews is not limited to the Pauline parts of Acts alone, but is common to the authorship as such.

In Luke several details should be observed. First and foremost we have the double story of the birth and childhood with its impressive Temple piety and law-abidingness; the priest Zechariah; the circumcision of John the Baptist and Jesus on the eighth day (Lk. 1.59; 2.21); the presentation of Jesus in the Temple (2.22-24); Jesus as a boy in the Temple—but also the old Simeon's words to Mary: 'This child is destined to be a sign that will be rejected; and you will be pierced to the heart; many in Israel will stand or fall because of him' (2.34-35). The expectation of 'the restoration of Israel', 'the liberation of Jerusalem' and 'the hope of Israel' is strong here, as in the rest of the authorship (Lk. 2.25, 38; 23.51; 24.21; Acts 1.6; 28.20). Therefore, Christianity brings what the pious among the Jews are hoping for and expecting. There is also the centurion of Capernaum whose servant was dying and about whom the elders among the Jews said to Jesus: 'He deserves this favour from you, for he is a friend of our nation and it is he who built us our synagogue' (Lk. 7.4-5). Finally, there is the Passion narrative which differs in one significant respect from the other evangelists' narratives: the Jews not only demanded that Jesus be crucified, but they also were the actors who crucified him when he was handed over to them—at least this is the impression conveyed to the readers (23.26 ff.; 24.20). This is confirmed several times in Acts where the Jews are unambiguously charged with having crucified Jesus (Acts 2.23, 36; 3.13-15; 4.10; 7.52; 10.39; 13.28-29).[9] Therefore, *the hardened among the Jews—that is, the majority of the people—are themselves responsible for the delay of the liberation of Israel.*

In Acts there is first the impressive prelude to the story, represented by the day of Pentecost (Acts 2.1-41). Exclusively Jews (and their proselytes)

---

9. Cf. Mark Harding, 'On the Historicity of Acts: Comparing Acts 9.23-5 with 2 Corinthians 11.32-3', *NTS* 39 (1993), pp. 518-38, esp. 524-29.

are present, Jews from every nation under heaven (2.5), that is, Jews both from the Diaspora and from Palestine, and at that only pious, non-aggressive Jews. Of these pious Jews no less than 3000 repented after having heard Peter's sermon and they were baptized on the very day of Pentecost (2.41).

Next there is the Christians' daily attendance at the Temple in Jerusalem: 'One and all they kept up their daily attendance at the temple' (2.46; cf. 3.1-10; 5.12, 20)—an attendance that continued even during Paul's last visit to Jerusalem (21.27-30; 24.17-18; cf. 22.17-21). And we are told that many of the priests at the Temple adhered to the faith (6.7). Whether the Christians also kept up the offerings in the Temple is perhaps less clear, although it should not be forgotten that offerings in the Temple are spoken of both in the birth and childhood narratives (Lk. 2.24) and in the account about Paul's purification and his and the four Nazirites' vows (Acts 18.18, 22; 21.24, 26; 24.17).[10] The Christians' Temple piety should not be disregarded.

There is further the *quasi-* or pro-Christian attitude of Gamaliel, the Pharisee and respected teacher of the law (Acts 5.33-42). On his advice the apostles are discharged, and the explicit change from *casus eventualis* to *casus realis* in his speech (ἐὰν ᾖ ἐξ ἀνθρώπων...εἰ δὲ ἐκ θεοῦ ἐστιν ('if this comes from men...but if it comes from God'): 5.38-39) can best be explained as indicating that the author of Acts pictures Gamaliel as in favour of the Christ believers.[11] In other words: sensible, non-aggressive Jews were well aware that Jews who believed in Christ were sincere and respectable people—at any rate they were not rebels like Judas the Galilean or Theudas (5.36-37) or, in the case of Paul, like the Egyptian who led 4000 terrorists into the desert (21.38).

In the Jewish accusations against Stephen (6.8-15) we meet for the first time in Acts accusations similar to those later raised against Paul, and like

---

10. Acts 18.22 implies a visit to Jerusalem: 'On landing in Caesarea, he [Paul] went up [to Jerusalem] and greeted the church; and then he went down to Antioch'.

11. How Gamaliel's pro-Christian attitude may be reconciled with the information that he was the teacher of Paul at the time when Paul persecuted the Christians (Acts 22.3) is not to be answered here. Also the question of the divergence between the picture of the Pharisees in Luke—not least in the parable about the Pharisee and the tax-collector (Lk. 18.10-13)—and in Acts is left unanswered; in Acts the Pharisees generally seem to be pictured positively (Acts 5.33-39; 23.6-9), if not unconditionally (see Acts 15.5, where Christians of Pharisaic observance demanded circumcision and law-abidingness from the Gentile Christians—a request that was *not* complied with at the apostolic conference).

these the accusations against Stephen also turn out to be false rumours which can be dismissed by the author of Acts. Stephen was accused of having spoken blasphemously against Moses (the law) and against God. In the Council the accusers (Hellenists, or Jews from the Diaspora) could only produce *false* witnesses who claimed that Stephen had been speaking against this holy place (the Temple) and against the law; for these allegations they referred to what they said they had heard from Stephen—that Jesus himself would destroy this place (the Temple) and alter the customs handed down to the Jews from Moses.

Two details in these Jewish accusations against Stephen are remarkable. (1) The accusations are false, because they have been raised by false witnesses and they are denied in Stephen's subsequent speech. The speech shows Stephen as the great storyteller of the Bible: not least in the tradition about Moses who 'received the living utterances of God to pass on to us', i.e. the law (Acts 7.38), about David who 'begged leave to provide a dwelling place for the God of Jacob' as a replacement for the Tent which had been brought into the promised land carefully, and about Solomon who realized this plan (7.44-50)—even though the author of Acts is perfectly aware of what the prophet (Isa. 66.1-2) says, that the Most High does not live in houses made by men (cf. Paul in the Areopagus speech, Acts 17.24). Stephen's law- and Temple abidingness is documented throughout the speech and the charges against him are therefore denied. It is not possible to find in the speech any basis whatsoever for the traditional allegation that Stephen's attitude to the Temple and the law should have been critical—which, if proven, would have been really surprising, all things considered, since Stephen would then have admitted the justice of the accusers' charges against him.[12] (2) The accusations are based

---

12. This against, e.g., Geert Hallbäck, *Apostlenes Gerninger* (Det Danske Bibelselskabs Kommentarserie; Copenhagen: Det Danske Bibelselskab, 1993), pp. 63-74, with his otherwise excellent analysis of Stephen's speech. Hallbäck claims that both the literary source of the speech and the speech itself are orientated to Diaspora Judaism and contain both a law—and Temple-critical attitude towards Palestinian Judaism. *But a purely literary approach to the speech does not allow any such conclusions!* Only when looked upon as a kind of transparency behind which the 'historical' reality—known from the outset—is believed to be seen, does it seem possible to detect this law- and Temple-critical attitude (cf. Hallbäck, *Apostlenes Eerninger*, p. 65: 'A universalistic, "Hellenistic" preaching of Christ, such as Stephen's probably was, may very easily—and correctly!—have been understood as a preaching against the Temple and the law' [my trans.]). It is astounding that a historian who has never expressed himself about the possible background of the speech has to remind a literary scholar about this...

on what Jesus is supposed to have said: that he would destroy the Temple and alter (or abolish) the customs handed down from Moses. Since these accusations are only rumours which false witnesses have brought forward and at that only secondary (false witnesses → Stephen → Jesus) they are of no value and may be dismissed—the more so as, according to Luke, Jesus has said nothing of the kind. According to Mt. 26.61 and Mk 14.58, false witnesses had indeed accused Jesus of having said that he would destroy the Temple and build another in three days, and according to Jn 2.19 Jesus had explicitly said so. But not according to Luke! All references to the destruction of the Temple are postponed until the Stephen story in Acts and there emptied of their substance.[13] Neither Jesus nor Stephen has in any way expressed himself against the Temple or against the law. It is only false rumours brought about by aggressive Jews who might be able to convince some people.

Something similar can be said in the case of Paul: only false, ungrounded rumours spread by aggressive Jews have led to the assumption that he had spoken against the law and the Temple.

This is further confirmed when Paul's missionary method is taken into consideration. He always addresses himself first to the Jews wherever he arrives, and only when disagreement arises and the Jews reject his preaching does he turn to the local non-Jews. This procedure—which in all probability does not accord with the actual procedure followed by Paul according to his letters (cf., e.g., 1 Thess. 1.9-10)—is very obvious in the programmatic words to the Jews in Antioch in Pisidia: 'It was necessary that the word of God should be declared to you first [πρῶτον, cf. Acts 3.26; Rom. 1.16; 2.9, 10]. But since you reject it und judge yourselves unworthy of eternal life, we now turn to the Gentiles' (Acts 13.46). The objection that Christianity is un-Jewish and consequently illegitimate because of its obscure origin is untenable. Paul—and the apostles and Barnabas—have done all they possibly could in order first and foremost to let the Jews hear the word of God. When they reject it the blame is upon themselves. Gentiles who adhered to the Christian faith may, in spite of the Jews' general rejection of it and because of its Old Testament and Jewish origin, be assured of the theological legitimacy of Christianity. In other words: *Christianity is not the work of man, but of God.*

---

13. A similar 'postponement' occurs at Acts 23.2-5 with the dialogue between Paul and the high priest Ananias, corresponding to the dialogue between Jesus and the high priest Annas in Jn 18.19-24.

This obligingness towards the Jews comes into appearance several times in Acts. The first time is in connection with the vision Peter had in Simon the tanner's house in Joppa. Peter sees something like a great sheet coming down from heaven to the earth, and in the sheet were all kinds of animals, clean and unclean. In spite of an order from heaven to kill and eat, Peter refuses to obey, three times, and at last the sheet is removed while he is still hungry (Acts 10.9-16; cf. 11.4-10). Thus the most prominent of the apostles was law-abiding and obliging towards the Jews to such a degree that *he refused to do what even the heavenly Lord commanded him to do!* Only at the intervention of the Holy Spirit does Peter give in and has Cornelius and his house baptized (10.44-48; cf. 11.15-17).

The next time we meet this obligingness and law-abidingness is at the apostolic conference in Jerusalem—precisely in the description of the agreement on the four points of the apostolic decree (15.20, 29; 21.25). As is well known, these are the rules of the Mosaic law applying to non-Jews living in Israel (Lev. 17.8, 10-16; 18.6-30).[14] The text of Acts explicitly refers, therefore, to the law itself: 'For Moses has never lacked spokesmen in every town for generations past; he is read in the synagogues sabbath by sabbath' (Acts 15.21). Indeed, the agreement on the apostolic decree and the decree itself are formally described as a concession on the part of the Jewish Christian towards the Gentile Christians to the effect that these are not obliged to keep all of the commandments of the Mosaic law, including the commandment of circumcision. But in reality the decree is to be understood as an obligingness on the part of the Gentile Christians towards the commandments of the law: 'Look, we keep the rules of the Mosaic law applying to non-Jews living together with Jews! *Thus* far we have gone in respect of law-abidingness and we do precisely what the law demands of non-Jews! What more would you expect us to do?' It is not a question of incomprehensible mildness on the part of Jews towards non-Jews or of non-Jews' failing ability to keep more than but a small part of the law, but on the contrary it is a question of the Gentile Christians' obligingness towards the relevant demands of the law. It goes without saying that with this understanding of the function of the apostolic decree there is no point in asking for its historicity. Even according to Acts its importance was limited to Gentile Christians in mixed congregations in Syria and Cilicia, including Syria's metropolis Antioch (Acts 15.23; see, however, also 16.4); in addition, the decree only had theoretical importance at the time

14. Cf. Hans Conzelmann, *Die Apostelgeschichte* (HNT, 7; Tübingen: J.C.B. Mohr, 1963), pp. 84-85.

when Acts was being written, and its possible spread is not easily tracked in the early history of the church.[15] It is characteristic that the decree is referred to during Paul's last meeting with James and the leaders of the Jerusalem congregation (Acts 21.25). James is not there to inform Paul of anything—Paul had himself been present and had taken part in the propagation of the decree. Neither is it a piece of information given by the author to his readers—they had already received this information. On the contrary the reference is to be understood from its context: just as there are no longer any problems with the Gentile Christians (they conform to the decree), so the Jewish Christians—represented by Paul—must show that there are no longer any problems with them. In other words: *the apostolic decree is the fictitious and learned invention of the author of Acts in order to demonstrate how obliging the Gentile Christians had been towards the Jews and the Mosaic law.*

The third time we meet this obligingness towards the Jews and the law is when Timothy is introduced (Acts 16.1, 3). He was the son of a believing Jewish woman and a Greek father. As Paul wished to make him his coworker on his travels he had him circumcised 'out of consideration for the Jews who lived in those parts', for they all knew that his father was a Gentile. Many interpreters understand this piece of information historically, concluding that even after his conversion Paul continued to 'preach circumcision' (Gal. 5.11). Or they refer to Titus who, like Timothy's father, was a Greek (Gal. 2.3) and who, although not compelled to be circumcised (Gal. 2.3), nevertheless—so it is supposed—underwent circumcision of his own free will.[16] I really do not know from where exegesis draws such myths about Paul and Timothy and Titus—*if not precisely from the story in Acts about Paul's having Timothy circumcised!* This story about the circumcision of Timothy does not, however, need to be based on 'historical' reality at all; its existence is rather exclusively due to the author's wish to portray Paul as being obliging to the Jews and as law-abiding as possible. The rumour that Paul taught 'all the Jews in the gentile world to turn their backs on Moses telling them not to have their children circumcised' (Acts 21.21) is—as the reader will understand—false and without any foundation.

The next incident occurs during Paul's last visit to Jerusalem (Acts

---

15. The signs of its spread (Rev. 2.14, 20; Justin, *Dial.* 34.8; Tertullian, *Apol.* 9.13; Eusebius, *Hist. Eccl.* 5.1.26 etc.; see Conzelmann, *Die Apostelgeschichte*, p. 85) are in reality casual and reveal knowledge and use of Acts rather than actual practice.

16. E.g. Linton, 'The Third Aspect', pp. 87-88.

21.18–23.30). James and the elders of the congregation in Jerusalem have heard Paul telling in detail all that God had done among the Gentiles by means of his ministry, and—we are explicitly told—when they heard this, they gave praise to God (21.20; cf. 11.18, 23-24; 14.27; 15.3, 12; cf. Gal. 1.24). Considering the joy caused by Paul's account it seems quite astounding that the congregation with James at its head immediately afterwards makes the observation that 'there are many thousands of believers among the Jews, all of them staunch upholders of the law' (21.20) and that all these aggressive Jewish Christians have heard false rumours about Paul's failing law-abidingness (21.21). How could the leadership of the Jerusalem congregation be *that* alien to the feelings of their own congregation? At any rate, James proposes that Paul publicly demonstrate his law-abidingness through purification and through payment for four poor Nazirites' offerings in the Temple, thereby contradicting the false rumours about him (21.23-24). Paul accepts the proposal and the procedure starts; but before it is finished Paul is attacked by Jews from Asia in the Temple precincts (21.26-27; cf. 24.17-21; 26.21).

What is surprising is not so much Paul's willingness to demonstrate that he keeps the law. In this case the information is perhaps even trustworthy, for when the redactional work of Acts is taken into consideration, it includes the information that Paul himself was a Nazirite (cf. Acts 18.18) and therefore like the four Nazirites whom James presented to him was compelled to bring the offerings prescribed in the law.[17] Whether Paul has thus far compromised his own standards is a question not to be answered here. But according to Acts his behaviour is clear: Paul demonstrates his obligingness towards the Jews, proves his law-abidingness and denies the rumours about him.

What is really surprising is that these allegations of Paul's anti-Jewish attitude, to which James refers, are brought about by Christian Jews all of whom are 'staunch upholders of the law': θεωρεῖς, ἀδελφέ, πόσαι μυριάδες εἰσὶν ἐν τοῖς Ἰουδαίοις τῶν πεπιστευκότων καὶ πάντες ζηλωταὶ τοῦ νόμου ὑπάρχουσιν ('you see, brother, how many thousands of converts we have among the Jews, all of them staunch upholders

---

17. That Paul's Nazirite vow in Acts 18.18 (cf. his visit in Jerusalem 18.22) in reality belongs to his *last* journey to Jerusalem, started at 20.3, I suggested as a possibility in *The History of Early Christianity* (Studies in the Religion and History of Early Christianity, 3; Frankfurt: Peter Lang, 1997), pp. 150-51 and 239, while Rasmussen, 'Den rigtige rækkefølge', pp. 210-13, has given convincing proof that it really is so.

of the Law' Acts 21.20). Undeniably it is tempting to follow the correction of the text which was proposed by both Baur and Munck: to delete the words τῶν πεπιστευκότων ('of converts') as erroneous—possibly they originate in the reference to 'the Gentiles who have come to faith' (περὶ δὲ τῶν πεπιστευκότων ἐθνῶν ['as for the gentile converts']) a little later in the text (Acts 21.25).[18] If this conjecture is correct there is no longer any reference to Jewish Christians in the text, but to aggressive, non-believing Jews—corresponding to those whom the 'historical' Paul had every reason to fear (cf. Rom. 15.31-32), who actually attacked him in the Temple precincts, and who believed the rumours corresponding to those recently referred to by James (Acts 21.28). There is no need to refer to the fact that elsewhere the author of Acts is anxious to show the great increase of Christian Jews in Palestine (1.15; 2.41; 4.4; 6.1, 7; 9.31), for in Acts the Christian Jews (and Gentiles!) are always pious, never aggressive; this is also true of the Hellenists and the Hebrews (6.1)—the struggle between them did not take place inside the Christian community, but outside (cf. the reference to the non-Christian Hellenists in 9.29).[19] The words τῶν πεπιστευκότων in Acts 21.20 are therefore to be deleted from the text.[20]

---

18. Cf. F.C. Baur, *Paulus, der Apostel Jesu Christi* (Stuttgart: Becher & Müller, 1845) pp. 199-200 [= 2nd ed., vol. I, Leipzig: Fues's Verlag, 1866]), pp. 227-228); Johannes Munck, *Paulus und die Heilsgeschichte* (Acta Jutlandica, 26.1; Copenhagen: Munksgaard, 1954), pp. 235-36. The proposal is accepted by Rasmussen, 'Den rigtige rækkefølge', pp. 210-11. See also my *The History of Early Christianity*, p. 150 with n. 40.

19. Cf. my *Udenfor og indenfor: Sociale og økonomiske aspekter i den ældste kristendom* [*Outside and Inside: Social and Economical Aspects of the Earliest Christianity*] (Tekst & Tolkning, 5; Monografier udgivet af Institut for Bibelsk Eksegese; Copenhagen: G.E.C. Gad, 1974), pp. 7-52; my *The History of Early Christianity*, pp. 166-76: 'Hellenists and Hebrews'. In Acts 11.20 the correct reading is of course Ἕλληνας, not—as in The Greek New Testament and Nestle-Aland—Ἑλληνιστάς.

20. I here correct myself; in *History of Early Christianity*, p. 150, I still rejected the proposal to amend the text. Holger Mosbech, *Sproglig Fortolkning til Apostlenes Gerninger* (Copenhagen: Gyldendal, 2nd ed, 1945), p. 215, who did not accept the proposal of Baur's, wrote: 'ἐν τοῖς Ἰουδαίοις [at Acts 21.20] stand…a little awkward (one should expect: τῶν ἐν τοῖς Ἰουδαίοις πεπιστευκότων or τῶν πεπιστευκότων [τῶν] ἐν τοῖς Ἰουδαίοις)'. Some MSS therefore omit these words, while other MSS correct to Ἰουδαίων, about which Mosbech wrote: 'this last text fits well: "that there are many thousands of Jews who have come to faith" (*Sproglig Fortolkning*, p. 215; my trans.). The original text, which corresponds to the conjecture proposed by Baur and Munck, would then be as follows: θεωρεῖς, ἀδελφέ, πόσαι μυριάδες εἰσὶν

They have done almost irreparable damage in establishing a sharpened contrast between Jewish and Gentile Christianity and alleging the nomistic character of Jewish Christianity.[21]

After this example of Paul's law-abidingness and Temple piety we meet him again, in a kind of flashback, in the Temple during his first visit to Jerusalem after his Damascus conversion: Acts 22.17-21 (cf. 2 Cor. 12.2-4). He sees and hears in the Temple the heavenly Lord who sends him 'to the Gentiles far away' (22.21). Next we experience almost an identification between Christianity and that kind of Judaism which keeps to the hope of Israel and the resurrection (23.6; 26.6-8, 23; 28.20). Paul declares that he is a Pharisee and believes in the resurrection of the dead and that he 'has belonged to the strictest group in our religion' (23.6; 26.5; cf. Phil. 3.5). Not least the dialogue between Paul and Agrippa is of particularly programmatic importance: "King Agrippa, do you believe in the prophets? I know you do". Agrippa said to Paul: "With a little more of your persuasion [πείθεις, perhaps better: 'conviction'] you will make a Christian of me". "Little or much", said Paul, "I wish to God that not only you, but all those who are listening to me today [the readers of Luke and Acts], might become what I am—apart from these chains!"' (Acts 26.27-29).[22]

Conclusion

In the attempt undertaken above to throw light upon the relation between Paul and the Jews it should not be overlooked that at least two apparently conflicting tendencies are involved. According to one of them, the author

---

Ἰουδαίων καὶ πάντες ζηλωταὶ τοῦ νόμου ὑπάρχουσιν. Indeed, here we have the original text!

21. E.g. Hallbäck, *Apostlenes Gerninger*, p. 191: '[Jerusalem] is no longer the place of the first successful Christian mission, but the place where the relation between Jewish and Gentile Christianity is most sharply drawn up', and p. 192: 'These Jewish Christians were a powerful factor in Jerusalem, and they are evidently sceptical of the recognition at the apostolic conference of Paul's Gentile mission' (my trans.). Cf. Lüdemann, *Das frühe Christentum*, p. 244, with his allegation of the nomistic character of the Jerusalem community in the 50's.

22. The characteristic σήμερον, 'today', is found also in Lk. 2.11; 4.21; 19.5, 9; 23.43, where it probably refers to the time of Jesus, in contrast to the similar expressions used by Paul in 2 Cor. 6.2; cf. Hans Conzelmann, *Die Mitte der Zeit: Studien zur Theologie des Lukas* (BHT, 17; Tübingen: J.C.B. Mohr, 5th edn, 1964), pp. 25-32. But in Acts 26.29 σήμερον seems rather to apply to the time of the readers of Luke and Acts. See, however, also 24.21.

of Acts underlines the concordance and continuity between Judaism and Christianity, between Israel and the new people of God (cf. Acts 15.14). In this light it would be possible to speak of a *coherence* in the history of salvation. The other tendency seems to point in the opposite direction. Here the author underlines the discontinuity and the missing concordance between Judaism and Christianity, and he does so by stressing the Jewish rejection of salvation, first and foremost exemplified in their execution of Jesus, in contrast to the Gentile acceptance of salvation, not least effected through Paul's preaching. Here it would be possible to speak of a *break* between Judaism and Christianity, between Jews and Christians.

How can this coherence and this break best be understood? It would be possible to see this doubleness as a kind of 'dialectic' strain, thus maintaining that this very doubleness is characteristic of the theology of the author of Luke–Acts.[23] Or one might emphasize the coherence, thereby reducing the Gentile Christians into a kind of 'god-fearing people' or 'proselytes' in relation to Israel and Judaism.[24] Or again, one might accentuate the break, understanding the Gentile Christians as representatives of the 'true' Israelites who rightly inherit the promises.[25]

Doubleness, coherence or break? Simply to choose between these three options is not advisable. For in speaking of a coherence between Israel and the new people of God, one must be aware that it is a question of a coherence with the pious, non-aggressive Israel—not simply with the Jews. And when speaking of a break, it is important to see that this break is not due to the Gentile Christians' refusal of the Jews, but, on the contrary, to the Jews' internal divisions and disagreement and their refusal of the Christian belief. At the time of the authorship this break was already a long established historical fact. The future seems to belong to the Gentiles alone (Acts 28.28!)—not in spite of, but because of the historical origin of Christianity. The fallen, but now rebuilt house of David includes indeed all the peoples whom the Lord has claimed as his own (Acts 15.16-17, quoting Amos 9.11-12). But since the Jews have refused the Christian

---

23. E.g. Conzelmann, *Die Apostelgeschichte*, p. 10, with reference to his *Die Mitte der Zeit*.

24. E.g. Jacob Jervell, 'Das gespaltene Israel und die Heidenvölker: Zur Motivierung der Heidenmission in der Apostelgeschichte', *ST* 19 (1965), pp. 68-96 (= 'The Divided People of God: The Restoration of Israel and Salvation for the Gentiles', in *idem, Luke and the People of God: A New Look at Luke–Acts* [Minneapolis: Augsburg, 1972], pp. 41-74). I do not know Jervell's commentary on Acts.

25. So most interpreters.

preaching, salvation seems now accessible to the Gentiles only. Israel has barred its own admittance to salvation.[26]

Luke–Acts is not entertaining, edifying literature (Ernst Haenchen),[27] but apologetics, through which Christianity seeks to find its political way into official recognition as a way of replacing the empirical, aggressive and obstinate Israel.

'Do you believe the prophets? I know you do.' The question that Paul asks King Agrippa and answers himself signifies Christianity as drawing its proof of truth from the Old Testament scriptures whose predictions are seen as fulfilled in the Jesus events and the expansion of Christianity. Or, as it is said in the parable of the rich man and Lazarus: 'If they do not listen to Moses and the prophets they will not be convinced [πεισθήσονται, cf. Acts 26.28] even if someone should rise from the dead' (Lk. 16.31). The preconditions of being able to produce this proof of truth are extensive studies of the Scriptures—in the case of Luke–Acts on the basis of Septuagint. From Moses, the prophets and the psalms it is shown that everything that has been predicted is fulfilled (Lk. 24.44-49; Acts 8.35; 17.2.11; 18.28; 28.23). A number of Old Testament texts are reviewed carefully and in detail in order to demonstrate that they are about Christ and his believers—not, for example, about David (Ps. 16.8-10 in Acts 2.25-36; cf. 13.35-36; Ps. 2.1-2 in Acts 4.25-30; Ps. 2.7 in Acts 13.33-34; Ps. 110.1 in Acts 2.32-35); words from the Scriptures about the Jewish rejection of the Christian belief are quoted (Hab. 1.5 in Acts 13.40-41; Isa. 6.9-10 in Acts 28.25-27) and, correspondingly, words about the Gentiles' acceptance of the belief (Isa. 49.6 in Acts 13.47; Amos 9.11-12 in Acts 15.15-18). The extensive proof from Scripture produced in Luke and, even more, in Acts, which deserves a fuller and more intensive study than can be provided here, is altogether an *apologetic enterprise*, the closest parallel to which is to be found not in the letters of Paul, but in the apologists, first and foremost in the writings of Justin from about 150.

With this determination of the apologetic and theological aim of the authorship the question about its readers also seems to be answered. From

26. It should be added that proselytes and godfearing Gentiles also belong here—both of which groups play important roles in Luke–Acts. In this respect the situation is similar to that of Justin's Dialogue with the Jew Trypho: Trypho is accompanied by potential proselytes and/or godfearing Gentiles ready, before meeting Justin, to convert to Judaism.

27. Ernst Haenchen, *Die Apostelgeschichte* (Kritisch-exegetischer Kommentar über das Neue Testament, 3; Göttingen: Vandenhoeck & Ruprecht, 13th edn, 1961) (= *idem*, *The Acts of the Apostles* [Philadelphia: Westminster Press, 1971]).

one point of view we are dealing with a Gospel writing (accompanied by an account of the apostolic time). But while the other Gospel writings—Matthew, Mark and John—presumably were meant for use in the Christian community, Luke–Acts differs significantly from these in being written as *a work for the public*. That this really is the case is seen in the preface of Luke (Lk. 1.1-4) and its dedication to 'Your Excellency [κράτιστε] Theophilus' (Lk. 1.3; cf. Acts 1.1)—the same way of addressing as is used in the story about Paul when the procurators Felix and Festus are addressed, both orally and in writing (Acts 23.26; 24.3; 26.25). Unfortunately we are not able to identify Theophilus. The name is known from literature, inscriptions and papyri as far back as the third century BCE, and is used of both Jews and non-Jews.[28] In Luke–Acts Theophilus was a person of high rank, presumably within the Roman administration and possibly of non-Jewish origin—a person who could 'recognize' himself in the persons of Felix and, no less, Festus. This is probably the closest we may come to an answer of this question. Decisive is the observation that through his dedication the author of *Ad Theophilum 1–2* has entered his writing into the apologetic literature of the time.[29]

28. W. Bauer and K. Aland, *Wörterbuch zum griechischen Neuen Testament* (Berlin: W. de Gruyter, 6th edn, 1988) That the name should have only a symbolic meaning is excluded through the address κράτιστε—the possibility is correctly left unmentioned by Bauer/Aland.

29. Cf. C.F. Evans, *Saint Luke* (TPI New Testament Commentaries; London: SCM Press; Philadelphia: Trinity Press International, 1990), pp. 104-111. I am not convinced that Loveday Alexander, *The Preface to Luke's Gospel: Literary Convention and Social Context in Luke 1.1-4 and Acts 1.1* (SNTSMS, 78; Cambridge: Cambridge University Press, 1993) has presented the final solution to the problems of the preface.

IN QUEST OF THE ELEVATED JESUS:
REFLECTIONS ON THE ANGELOMORPHIC CHRISTOLOGY
OF THE BOOK OF REVELATION WITHIN ITS JEWISH SETTING

Håkan Ulfgard

Within the general theme of this conference, the intention of my contribution is to discuss how some aspects of the Christology of the book of Revelation may reflect the ways in which the author has utilized and developed received concepts and imagery within his Jewish tradition. Christology is a most distinguishing feature of the Johannine Apocalypse within the context of the New Testament canon. Its elevated, heavenly Jesus figure has little in common with the earthly Jesus of the Gospels or with the Pauline risen Christ. In this paper I would like to explore a possible setting for this particular expression of early Christian confession of the resurrected Jesus and of his elevation to divine glory within its contemporary Jewish framework. As a result, it will become necessary to reflect further on the various forms of Judaism in which early Christologies were shaped.

While the notion of a special, transcendent fellowship between the human and angelic world has long been acknowledged as firmly established by the Qumran findings, the idea of an exaltation of certain divinely inspired or blessed human beings to angelic status is a more controversial subject. What is at stake is the picture of ancient Judaism as strictly monotheistic, and, in particular, the Christian confession of the risen Jesus as Lord and God. However, as recent scholarly discussion has pointed out—for example, within the framework of the on-line course on 'Mediator Figures' run by Prof. James R. Davila at the University of St Andrews, Scotland—there were possibilities already within ancient Judaism itself of ascribing angelic or divine functions or qualities to human beings without overstepping the bounds of traditional monotheistic belief. In the case of Jesus this seems to have worked as a first step towards later Christian confession of him as truly divine and truly human Lord, worthy of praise and glory and sharing the throne of God.

My ambition in this essay is to discuss how some aspects of the Christology of Revelation may be more adequately understood when seen within the context of Jewish angelology and messianology as these phenomena are witnessed in Qumranite and other extra-biblical texts. This will be effected by drawing attention to some significant scholarly contributions from recent years. Thus, for instance, I am far from alone in the association of Revelation with Qumran/Essene Judaism.[1] But how can it be that the Jesus figure of Revelation shows elements resembling contemporary Jewish angelology, at the same time as he is clearly distinct from and superior to all heavenly beings in his messianic roles as 'the Lamb' and 'the Root of David'? The wider issue concerned is the emergence—still within the bounds of Judaism—of a worship of Jesus as divine agent which comes close to transcending the restrictions of monotheism.

In his important study of the background for the development of early Christology, *Angel Veneration and Christology: A Study in Early Judaism and in the Christology of the Apocalypse of John*, Loren T. Stuckenbruck draws attention to the tension in Revelation between on the one hand an 'angelomorphic' Christology and on the other a consequent emphasis on the unique status of Jesus as the slaughtered Lamb, which gives him a decisive role in the drama of salvation depicted in the book, and which clearly demonstrates his superiority over all the celestial beings.[2] Despite this elevated status, which distinguishes Jesus from all other heavenly creatures, Stuckenbruck argues that the intention of the author has not been to transcend the bounds of Jewish monotheism. As the title of his book indicates, the background may be found in the tendency towards

---

1. As a recent example, cf. the claim by Stephen Goranson, 'Essene Polemic in the Apocalypse of John', in J. Kampen (ed.), *Legal Texts and Legal Issues: Proceedings of the Second Meeting of the International Organization for Qumran Studies Cambridge 1995* (Festschrift Joseph M. Baumgarten; Leiden: E.J. Brill, 1997), pp. 453-60: 'The Apocalypse of John shows influence of Essene thought, including Essene polemic. In other words, John, the author of the Apocalypse, shared much of the Essene worldview and may have been an Essene before he became a Christian' (p. 453). Cf. also the chapter on structural hermeneutical similarities between Revelation and the Qumran writings in Steve Moyise, *The Old Testament in the Book of Revelation* (JSNTSup, 115; Sheffield: Sheffield Academic Press, 1995), pp. 85-107.

2. WUNT, 70; Tübingen: J.C.B. Mohr (Paul Siebeck), 1995; see esp. pp. 209-245, 'Aspects of Angelology and Monotheism in the Christology of the Apocalypse of John', in which the introductory and judgment scenes of 1.12-20 and 14.6-20 are analysed. In particular, Stuckenbruck draws attention to the cosmic/angelic figures of Dan 7.9-14 and 10.5-6 as the biblical sources of inspiration for John's 'angelomorphic' Christology (pp. 211-21).

angel veneration within certain forms of ancient Judaism, not least as evinced by some of the Qumran texts. An implicit criticism of angel veneration may thus be detected in 19.10 and 22.8-9, where the angel refuses John's devotional attitude. No such refusal occurs when Jesus is portrayed in angelomorphic shape in the introductory vision (1.12-20).[3] By virtue of his role as the slaughtered Lamb and of his resurrection from the dead, after which he has been elevated to sharing God's throne (3.21), Jesus is truly worthy of glorification and worship. Without giving up his monotheism, the author of Revelation depicts a Jesus figure who through his elevation is so intimately united with God the Father that he may be accorded a share of the devotion of all worshippers—angelic or human.

Already the beginning of Revelation gives a hint of its particular Christology, with Jesus in a unique role, subordinated in relation to God but superior to all angelic beings. The whole book is a 'revelation of Jesus Christ' (subjective genitive),[4] but this is a revelation which has been given to him by God (Ἀποκάλυψις Ἰησοῦ Χριστοῦ ἣν ἔδωκεν αὐτῷ ὁ θεός). There must be no question that it is God the Father himself who is the ultimate source for the revelation of the divine judgment and salvation, with Jesus as the principal mediator figure. The identity of the messenger who brought the revelation to John (καὶ ἐσήμανεν ἀποστείλας διὰ τοῦ ἀγγέλου αὐτοῦ) is not clear, though, and the same uncertainty concerns the identity of the sender, namely the subject of ἐσήμανεν. Is God the sender, or is it Jesus? In both cases, John's role is to be the witness of a revelation which may be qualified in a double sense as 'the word of God' (ὁ λόγος τοῦ θεοῦ) and 'the testimony of Jesus Christ' (ἡ μαρτυρία Ἰησοῦ Χριστοῦ). The combined expression sends an important signal about the 'subordinate parallelism' of the message revealed to John: fundamentally, it comes from God, but it is mediated, and testified to, by Jesus.[5]

---

3.   Stuckenbruck, *Angel Veneration*, pp. 245-61, 269-73. Cf. the argument in Heb. 1–2 for the superiority of the Son over all angelic beings; see further pp. 119-39, on the significance of this text for understanding early Christian angelology and Christology.

4.   Cf., e.g., David E. Aune, *Revelation 1–5* (WBC, 52; Dallas: Word Books, 1997), p. 6.

5.   It is of great importance to be aware of the use of these designations in Revelation. When, as in 6.9-11, only the first formula appears, this indicates that the author has the 'martyr' souls of pre-Christian times in mind. Their earthly testimony was not related to Jesus, as is the case with the souls of 20.4, about whom both designations are used. (For the opinion that the phrase ἡ μαρτυρία Ἰησοῦ Χριστοῦ should be understood as an objective genitive, see Traugott Holtz, *Die Christologie der Apokalypse des*

One clue may be found at the end of the book, where Jesus tells John that he has sent his 'messenger' (ἄγγελος) in order to bear witness to the congregations (22.16). From this observation it is possible to argue that Jesus should be understood as the subject of ἐσήμανεν in 1.1.[6] In this way there is thus a correspondence between the beginning and end of the book. The former interpretation is also possible, however, especially since Jesus appears as the divine mediator to John in the introductory vision of 1.9-20 (with the ἄγγελος of 22.16 referring back to the mediator of Jesus' messages to the seven churches in chs. 2–3). In fact the succession of 1.1 is traditionally understood in this order: God—Jesus—an angel—John—John's listeners/readers.

With all due respect to the general exegetical opinion, recently argued for by Charles A. Gieschen in his revised doctoral dissertation, *Angelo-morphic Christology: Antecedents and Early Evidence*,[7] I want to question this understanding. In my view, the syntactic construction of Revelation's introductory phrase should preferably be taken to refer to Jesus as the messenger (the 'angel'), especially if the content of the rest of Revelation is taken into consideration. Actually, on the narrative macro-level the whole continuation of John's visionary story represents what the divinely elevated Jesus figure starts to disclose to him in 1.12-20 (cf. 1.19: 'Now write what you have seen, what is, and what is to take place after this'), and, in chs. 2–3, to the seven churches.[8] When the visions of heavenly worship commence in 4.1, it is the same voice which speaks to John as in the introductory vision in 1.10-16: the voice of Jesus, appearing to John as the 'Son of Man'. This identification of Jesus as the sender of the revelation recurs at the end of the book, in 22.16 (the angelomorphic Jesus has spoken already in 22.6-7, however; cf. v. 7: 'See, I am coming soon!'), which does not contradict that Jesus in his turn has been sent by God.[9]

Johannes [TU, 85; Berlin: Akademie-Verlag, 1962], p. 23. In this case, however, the particular parallelism between God and Jesus is lost.)

6.   Cf. Aune, *Revelation*, p. 15.

7.   AGJU, 42; Leiden: E.J. Brill, 1998; see esp. pp. 260-62, where he objects in particular against the interpretation of Robert H. Gundry, 'Angelomorphic Christology in the Book of Revelation', *SBLSP* 33 (1994), pp. 662-78 (674-78).

8.   Note how the identity of the sender in each of the seven letters is revealed by using characteristics borrowed from the Jesus figure of the introductory vision. In this way his superiority over the 'angels of the communities' is emphasized (which could be understood as an implicit polemic against angel devotion in the Christian communities of Asia Minor).

9.   Contra Gieschen, *Angelomorphic Christology*, p. 261. Though the identity of

When the 'angel' (= Jesus) refuses John's attempt to worship him, this may be not only an indication of a refusal of angel worship, but it could also point to a 'poor' Judaeo-Christian Christology: the elevation of the Jesus figure to divine status—above all angels—has not yet gone so far so as to make him the object of individual adoration and worship, which might have put monotheism at risk. The concept of an enthroned Jesus must not infringe on the absolute sovereignty of God. It is another matter when the elevated Jesus figure ('the Lamb') is praised together with God the Father (cf. 5.12-13).

If an important characteristic of the portrait of Jesus in the book of Revelation is thus that of his being elevated to the dignity of a divine mediator figure, depicted in angelomorphic language, would not such an idea be conceivable within the multifaceted framework of contemporary Judaism?[10] In recent years there has been a growing notion that Jesus (in some parts of the early Judaeo-Christian movement, at least) was revered through an attribution of combined messianic epithets or ideas and angelomorphic traits.[11] This christological development, with antecedents within Judaism itself, may eventually have paved the way for his 'deification'—without having recourse to the creative mind of Hellenistic Christianity. A significant contribution to this new direction in christological studies before the publication of Gieschen's revised dissertation was the monograph by Larry W. Hurtado, *One Lord, One God: Early Christian Devotion and Ancient Jewish Monotheism*, first published in 1988.[12] The scholarly discussion evoked by his theses, and to which he responds ten years later in the preface to the second edition of his study,[13] is highly interesting reading, and proof of this significant paradigmatic shift in scholarly attention to a central New Testament and theological issue still in need of further elucidation and argumentation.

the 'angel' of v. 16 is left without explanation, it is more likely to refer to John, to whom was given the command to write to the seven Christian churches, than to the individual 'angels of the churches' as the primary recipients of each of the seven messages of chs. 2–3.

10. This is the subject of another recent study, *Jesus and the Angels: Angelology and the Christology of the Apocalypse of John* (SNTSMS, 95; Cambridge: Cambridge University Press, 1997), by Peter R. Carrell.

11. For a survey of the exegetical discussion, see Gieschen, *Angelomorphic Christology*, pp. 12-25; cf. also Stuckenbruck, *Angel Veneration*, p. 208 n. 3.

12. Edinburgh: T. & T. Clark.

13. Edinburgh: T. & T. Clark, 1998; see especially pp. viii-xviii.

In Richard Bauckham's most valuable collection of essays on the book of Revelation, *The Climax of Prophecy: Studies on the Book of Revelation*, one chapter is devoted to 'The Worship of Jesus'.[14] Together with a thorough presentation of the subject and a careful evaluation of the rich material in early Christian literature, Bauckham argues that it is necessary to distinguish between angelolatry and devotion of the elevated Christ. In this connection it is also vital to be aware of the possibility of straining the limits of monotheism within the framework of liturgy:

> There may have been early Christian circles in which a general neglect of the limits of monotheism in worship accompanied the emergence of the worship of Jesus. But the importance of the material studied in this chapter lies in its sensitivity to the issue of monotheism in worship. So far from endorsing a general tendency to reverence intermediary beings, these writers emphasised a traditional motif designed to rule out angelolatry. At the same time they depicted the worship of Jesus in the throne-room of heaven. This combination of motifs had the effect, probably more clearly than any other Christological theme available in their world of ideas, of placing Jesus on the divine side of the line which monotheism must draw between God and creatures.[15]

With this in mind, the reflections of Stuckenbruck on the partly angelomorphic Jesus figure of Revelation may be combined with some significant observations by Alan F. Segal in his article 'The Risen Christ and the Angelic Mediator Figures in Light of Qumran'.[16] Against the background of various Jewish texts (from the Pseudepigrapha, from Qumran, and also from 'mainstream' Judaism) Segal argues that the belief of the first Christians in the elevation of Jesus to divine status after the resurrection should be understood as an expression of contemporary ideas about the transformation of the righteous after death to angelic beings.[17] The transformation of Jesus, by virtue of his resurrection from the dead—according to some parts of early Christianity also manifested by the empty tomb and his bodily appearances—signified this elevation to the highest possible, that is, divine, status and dignity. The specifically Christian novelty does not rest in the idea of a reward to the faithful witness (= the martyr) through elevation to heavenly dignity and immortality, but in the

---

14. Edinburgh: T. & T. Clark, 1993, pp. 118-49.

15. Bauckham, *The Climax of Prophecy*, pp. 148-49.

16. In J.H. Charlesworth (ed.), *Jesus and the Dead Sea Scrolls* (New York: Doubleday, 1992), pp. 302-328.

17. See esp. pp. 304-308.

combination of this with the idea of Jesus as a crucified Messiah. In Segal's opinion there must have been a creative dialectic between historical facts and the hermeneutic process, in which the combination of certain scriptural passages may have provided an impetus for the development of Christology.

Among the scriptural passages which seem to have played a significant role in the development of these ideas Segal refers especially to Ps. 110.1-2, the elevation of the Davidic scion ('The LORD says to my lord, "Sit at my right hand until I make your enemies your footstool").[18] The possibility of combining this text with the enthroning of the 'Son of Man' in Dan. 7.9-13 is evident, as well as with the promise of Dan. 12.3 to 'those who lead many to righteousness', who will be transformed and be 'like the stars forever and ever', that is, attain immortality.[19] Another element in this process of hermeneutical application of scriptural passages to the risen and glorified Jesus is represented by the actualization of the promise in Exod. 23.21 that an angel of the Lord, carrying the divine name, was to lead the people of Israel during their desert wanderings. In this way the earthly Jesus is retroactively ascribed divine status, since the risen Christ could be regarded—and revered—as a manifestation of the divinity.[20]

In particular, Segal draws attention to two texts from the pseudepigraphical and Qumranite literature in order to illuminate the Danielic motif of transformation to angelic or divine status: 4QM[a] and *1 En.* 70–71.[21] The latter text depicts the transformation of Enoch as he is elevated into the celestial world, where he can behold all the heavenly secrets. As he is brought forth to the throne of God his divine elevation and status—far above the angels—is confirmed (*1 En.* 71.14-17). In the former text an

18. See also Stuckenbruck, *Angel Veneration*, pp. 128-36, who strongly emphasizes the significance of this psalm for the development of early Christology (cf. esp. his survey of its use in the New Testament and in other early Christian texts, together with a brief bibliography, pp. 128-29, n. 208).

19. Note, however, that Dan. 12.3 includes all the righteous in this transformation. Cf. the promise of *2 Bar.* 51.10 that those who are saved 'will be like the angels and be equal to the stars', and 51.12 that 'the excellence of the righteous will then be greater than that of the angels'.

20. Segal, 'The Risen Christ', pp. 320-22.

21. Segal, 'The Risen Christ', pp. 305-308. Though these chapters from *1 Enoch* belong to that part of the Enoch traditions ('The Book of the Similitudes', *1 Enoch* 37–71) of which there are no fragments among the Qumran fragments, Segal points out that a similar concept of the elevation of the righteous and their transformation into angelic status is to be found in other parts of *1 Enoch* for which there is Qumranite evidence (cf. *1 En.* 104.2, 4).

unidentified subject speaks about his elevation to communion with and equal dignity as the *'elim* of the heavenly host. As Segal conjectures, inspired by Morton Smith, we may here have an important confirmation of the Qumranite idea of a mystical union, within a liturgical framework, between chosen, blessed and holy human beings and angels/celestial beings.[22]

This is not the place to go further into the subject of a communion between angels and human beings. But I would like to take the occasion to reflect more synthetically on some observations pertaining to the question of ideological and/or theological contacts between the book of Revelation and the texts from Qumran. In his study *Angels at Qumran: A Comparative Study of 1 Enoch 1–36; 72–108 and Sectarian Writings from Qumran*, Maxwell J. Davidson makes the observation that the great interest in angels in these chapters of *1 Enoch* (of which fragments have been found at Qumran) does not seem to have any correspondence in the other parts of this composite work.[23] Concluding from this observation that the Enochic traditions may not have been originally authored by the Qumranites, he offers some reflections as to possible tendencies in the ideological development within Qumranite Judaism and in its relations to its Jewish context.[24] Of particular interest is his suggestion that there may have been a declining Qumranite interest in the Enochic traditions:

> Furthermore, we might also speculate that it was because of such major differences in outlook that the Enochic books became of lessened interest to the Qumran community as time went on ... Initially they may have been of some importance to the newly formed sect, because of such things as the 364-day calendar proposed by the Enochic astronomical writings and the hope expressed for the righteous. Perhaps once the calendar had become well established within the life of the sect, the need to appeal to the *Astronomical Book* may have correspondingly diminished. Similarly, as the sect produced its own writings with their distinctive eschatology, the rather

22. See Smith's article 'Two Ascended to Heaven: Jesus and the Author of 4Q491', in J.H. Charlesworth (ed.), *Jesus and the Dead Sea Scrolls* (New York: Doubleday, 1992), pp. 290-301. Note, however, that the figure of *1 En.* 71 was identified as the archangel Michael by Maurice Baillet in his edition of this fragment in *Quaran Cave 4, III* (DJD, 7; Oxford: Clarendon, 1982), pp. 26-29.

23. JSPSup, 11; Sheffield: Sheffield Academic Press, 1992. As he is careful to point out (pp. 29-30), this observation was already made by J.T. Milik in his edition of the Aramaic Enoch fragments, *The Books of Enoch: Aramaic Fragments of Qumrân Cave 4* (Oxford: Clarendon Press, 1976).

24. Davidson, *Angels at Qumran*, pp. 320-22.

different Enochic traditions might have grown less significant for a community in which priestly traditions were of such importance.[25]

A most stimulating and provocative study on this matter has recently been published by Gabriele Boccaccini: *Beyond the Essene Hypothesis: The Parting of the Ways between Qumran and Enochic Judaism*.[26] As the title of his book indicates, in Boccaccini's opinion there was a schism in Essene Judaism between an 'Enochian' and a Qumranite party.[27] From my perspective, within the framework of this article, the question of whether early Christian theological thinking and the main New Testament characters themselves could be fitted into an ideological/theological development within ancient Judaism of the kind which Boccaccini suggests, is of special interest. Thus, for example, one of Boccaccini's fascinating suggestions is his explanation of the fact that nothing from *1 En.* 37–71 has been found among the Qumran fragments. According to him, the reason is that this particular (pre-Christian) Enochic tradition was not shaped until after the rupture between Enochic and Qumranite Judaism, which occurred roughly around the turn of the era. This would explain why the content of these chapters differs in several important aspects from Qumranite ideas, namely as regards messianic expectation and concepts concerning the 'Son of Man', but also concerning the relation between free will and determinism.[28]

Boccaccini's proposal about *1 Enoch* 37–71 (in particular if he is right about the dating and ideological setting of these chapters) has interesting consequences for the picture of ideological development within ancient Judaism and early Christianity, especially in combination with the above-mentioned observations of Davidson. As regards angelology, the implication is that the Judaism of the Qumran texts does not seem to bother too much about the direct intervention of angels in human affairs, but rather that a fundamental dualism is emphasized within its deterministic conception of the world. When, at roughly the same time, the earliest Christian

25. Davidson, *Angels at Qumran*, p. 322.
26. Grand Rapids: Eerdmans, 1998.
27. See, e.g., 'his brief summary of this hypothesis (p. 16): My claim is that Enochic Judaism is the modern name for the mainstream body of the Essene party, from which the Qumran community parted as a radical, dissident, and marginal off-spring. Subsequently, Enochic/Essene Judaism polemically rejected the ideas of the Qumran Essenes, continued to exist side by side with its radical progeny, contributed to the birth of the parties of John the Baptist and Jesus, and even survived Qumran for some time after the destruction of the temple in 70 CE'.
28. Boccaccini, *Beyond the Essene Hypothesis*, pp. 144-49; cf. pp. 130-31.

writings give multiple evidence for the belief in angels as mediators between God and human beings (together with an attestation of contemporary Jewish ideas about the Messiah and the Son of Man), is it possible to claim that the New Testament theologians as a rule stand closer to 'Enochic' than to Qumranite Judaism? But is it not also reasonable to surmise that there may have been a similar wide scope of ideas and opinions among the early Christians as that witnessed by contemporary Jewish sources? After all, the more or less conflict-laden plurality of early Christian ideas is merely a reflection of tensions and conflicts that may already be found in contemporary Judaism.

The aim of these reflections, in combination with observations collected from recent scholarly studies, has been to call attention to the renewed discussion about the development of Christology within the earliest Jesus movement. The devotion of the elevated Jesus as expressed in the book of Revelation is one important element in this process, especially when it is put into the context of contemporary Jewish angelology and apocalyptic speculation about the elevation of certain particularly blessed human beings to heavenly glory and dignity.[29] But in view of the great differences between the book of Revelation and the rest of the New Testament writings concerning both style and content—in this particular case with focus on Christology—and in consideration of the similarities that exist between Revelation and the Qumran writings, the question about the place of Revelation as regards its theological/ideological milieu within contemporary Judaism must also be deemed as relevant.[30] In response to, and as a further development of Boccaccini's theories concerning the tension between 'Enochic' and Qumranite Judaism, I would therefore suggest that

29. Cf. the chapter on 'The Christian Mutation' in Hurtado, *One Lord, One God*, pp. 99-114, in which he points out and analyses six features of this change in traditional Jewish monotheism: '(1) hymnic practices, (2) prayers and related practices, (3) use of the name of Christ, (4) the Lord's Supper, (5) confession of faith in Jesus, and (6) prophetic pronouncements of the risen Christ' (p. 100). See also Gieschen's conclusions on the implications of his study for understanding the growth of early christology, *Angelomorphic Christology*, pp. 349-51.

30. On the similarities between Revelation and the conceptual world of the *Songs of the Sabbath Sacrifice* (4QshirShabb[a-h] [4Q400-407]) from Qumran and Masada, see, e.g., my article 'L'Apocalypse entre judaïsme et christianisme: Précisions sur le monde spirituel et intellectuel de Jean de Patmos', *RHPR* 79 (1999), pp. 31-50. In the same way as the Qumran texts are full of sharp polemic against fellow Jews, an intra-Jewish conflict may be detected in Revelation's harsh denouncement of the 'synagogue of Satan' in Rev. 2.9 and 3.9.

Revelation be reckoned within the sphere of the latter form of ancient Judaism.[31] Its particular way—unique among the New Testament writings —of expressing belief in, and devotion to, the resurrected and exalted Jesus is most naturally understood as a product of this milieu. The implications thereof are of significant importance, not only for the picture of how early Christology developed within various forms of earliest Christianity. Our conception of the theological restrictions within ancient Judaism is questioned by this example of devotion to a divine agent which challenges the limits of monotheism.

---

31. As I understand him, Boccaccini (cf. *Beyond the Essene Hypothesis*, p. 194) does not seem to be sensitive enough of the plurality among the first Christian confessors in this respect.

FEMINIST RECEPTION OF THE NEW TESTAMENT: A CRITICAL RECEPTION

Jorunn Økland

Reception history closes off options of reading virtually any tradition, and…an important task of criticism is to re-open the options that have been suppressed.[1]

Women Receiving the New Testament

The term 'reception' is very apt to describe how Christian people in our Northern European culture meet the Bible: it is just there—we have never been asked to acknowledge its presence. We are born into a culture that has been severely marked by the Bible, and many of us have even been members of a Christian church from when we were born. The (biblical) fundaments of our culture and church were given long before we had any possibility to call them into question.

In one of her outstanding articles, Anne-Louise Eriksson sketches the following 'impossible choice' for Christian women of our culture: Either to embrace the sacred texts that reduce, wipe out or openly disdain women's lives, and consider these texts normative; or to say that these sacred texts threaten the process towards full humanity for women, therefore their normativity has to be rejected.[2] I recognize the 'impossible choice' Eriksson describes as part of a more hypothetical theological argument, but many have never experienced that they have such a choice. I agree more with those who consider it an illusion to believe that we make choices concerning our origins. Before we are grown-up, educated and mature enough possibly to make the impossible choice Eriksson

---

1. D. Boyarin, *Carnal Israel: Reading Sex in Talmudic culture* (The New Historicism: Studies in Cultural Poetics, 25; Berkeley: University of California Press, 1993), p. 22.

2. A.-L. Eriksson, 'Bibelns auktoritet och kvinnors erfarenhet's in P. Block *et al.* (eds.), *Om tolkning. V. Bibeln som auktoritet* (Tro & Tanke; Stockholm: Svenska kyrkans forskningsråd, 1998), pp. 134-46 (136).

describes, the Bible and its discourses of gender have shaped us—directly or indirectly—in such a profound manner that it would be an illusion to believe that we could uproot ourselves from our origins and choose not to let them nourish—or poison—us anymore.[3] When feminist theologians continue to talk about a choice, they legitimize the idea of the autonomous subject, 'man as mushroom',[4] who can exist independently of culture and other people, and therefore freely chooses to enter or exit social contracts. But no such subject has ever existed in flesh and blood. It is significant that it was not until I had studied for a long time, and become shaped in the image of the European disembodied and disembedded ideal 'man of letters', that I could even imagine such hypothetical situations of choice concerning the biblical fundaments of the culture and church that is part of me. That is why I will recast Eriksson's situation of choice as a situation of constant dilemma for the Christian woman-identified person: on the one hand the Bible *gives* her a cultural and religious identity; the Bible is an authority in the sense that she stands in a continuing discourse with it—if not, she would neither know who she is nor where she comes from. On the other hand, as a woman, the Bible *denies* her an identity as fully human. I think it is a task for feminists therefore to reflect critically on how it is possible to deal with the dilemma in question, through bringing to light what kind of baggage we carry in terms of biblically sanctioned gender structures. There is no way out of the dilemma, but the Christian woman can still insist on being a 'favorite daughter': 'Favorite sons and daughters who refuse to sanctify their father's house have their uses. Persistently to critique a structure that one cannot not (wish to) inhabit is the deconstructive stance'.[5]

I will continue by exploring the relation between the female reader and the text without asking for any essential meaning in the text itself—this time. Let us take Mt. 5.27-28 as an example: 'You have heard that it was said, "You shall not commit adultery". But I say to you that every one who

---

3. Cf. the criticisms made particularly by Jewish and Muslim feminists against the so-called 'secular' stance: This stance is so profoundly determined by Christian ways of thinking that the term 'post-Christian' is at least more honest about its origins. From a Jewish or Muslim point of view, the post-Christians are as Christian as any.

4. S. Benhabib, 'The Generalized and the Concrete Other: The Kohlberg-Gilligan Controversy and Feminist Theory', in S. Benhabib and D. Cornell (eds.), *Feminism as Critique: Essays on the Politics of Gender in Late-Capitalist Societies* (Feminist Perspectives; Cambridge, MA: Polity Press, 1987), pp. 77-95 (84).

5. G. Spivak, *Outside in the Teaching Machine* (New York: Routledge, 1993), p. 284.

looks at a woman lustfully has already committed adultery with her in his heart'.[6] What happens inside the head of a 10-year-old Norwegian girl—or a grown-up woman—who reads these verses from the Bible as part of her daily meditation?

First possibility: Hopefully she thinks 'this does not concern me. These are words from one man to other men; this is speech between men'.

Second possibility: The grown-up woman thinks, 'Oh, I must not fall in love with married women', for she is a lesbian who is reading the New Testament for the first time. This reading of the Norwegian version is fully possible, since the grammatical male gender of the Greek text is neutralized. But when she continues to read some verses further down, she still realizes that Jesus is not talking to women like her (5.31-32): 'It was also said, "Whoever divorces his wife, let him give her a certificate of divorce". But I say to you that every one who divorces his wife, except on the ground of unchastity, makes her an adulteress; and whoever marries a divorced woman commits adultery.' Thus the woman reading the Norwegian version realizes the male addressees also of 5.27-28. The passage as a whole does not address women who desire other women, and our lesbian woman has just found another passage that renders her invisible.

Third possibility: A subtle process of interpretation and reception is activated in both women. This process 'sits in the spine' of most women living in cultures where the male gaze and point of view dominates the cultural expressions, and it is a dual process: partly they identify with and adjust to the female figures in the text; partly they start to adjust the gender of the text itself to make it fit them and their experience. This possibility is the most likely, as I see it.

For in our culture the Bible is canon, a book we live with, struggle with and refer to when we want to speak about our cultural identity. We expect it to have something to say to us, a Word of God. This implies that even if we do not belong to the (gender-)group the texts are addressed to, we *make sense* of the texts so that they speak to us anyway. Since the texts of the Bible with few exceptions have an implied male author or speaker, and an implied male addressee, this women's reading strategy, or process of interpretation, has developed by necessity. If the cited words by Jesus are going to have something to say at all to women, they *have to* interpret, transform and/or step into the object role in the text, and identify with the woman who is looked upon lustfully by men. If the message of this text to grown-up men is that they should not look at women lustfully, its message

6.   Biblical citations are from the RSV.

to the little girl must be that since Jesus problematizes the lustful gaze of the man and not that of the woman, and simultaneously describes the woman as the desired, it is the role of woman to be desired, not to desire. This message is confirmed by very many other texts in our culture that speak from the standpoint of the male gaze. By continually reading biblical texts and other texts that speak from a male position and to a male audience, the little girl quickly learns to adjust to this male–male axis of communication which at the same time is a message in itself: It is men who gaze, desire and speak, and women who are gazed upon, desired and spoken about. The sad thing is that our culture lets this biblical message stand uncorrected, so finally the little girl thinks that this is how it should be. The problem is not that men are presented as subjects and women as objects *per se*: rather it is a problem that people who identify as men do not learn to see themselves as objects and people who identify as women do not learn to see themselves as subjects, *too*, when the male–male communication axis becomes the dominant one.

The second part of the process of reception mentioned above is the adjustment of the text. Since the text does not have female implied authors and addressees, the content of the commandment is read metaphorically or transcribed: 'literally this does not concern me, but on a spiritual level or in another area of life it must', since it is written in the Bible which is the word of God to all, not only to men. One way (out of a myriad) of making sense of this text so that it speaks to women is to read it as a warning against desiring one's neighbor's wonderful house.

I chose this text from Matthew 5 because its gender is very explicit. However, feminists have shown that the implied author or speaker in almost all biblical texts are male, and that as a necessary consequence, the texts negotiate sex-specific, male problems which male readers have mistaken for universal problems. It is no coincidence that the text in question speaks about somebody's wife and not somebody's husband (5.31-32).

Also, I labeled this reception process a *women's* process. But men in our culture also are driven into similar, although not equally fundamental, processes of reception. For example, it is a problem for both male and female Norwegians to read texts addressed to poor people, slaves and persecuted Christians without starting to transcribe and/or move the meaning of the text on to a different level. The difference is that women *constantly* must adjust the fundamental dynamic between the implied sender and receiver of the text, and transform the gendered issues. Very many utterings in the Bible that men still can read literally, women must adjust in order to make them relevant and sensible.

Feminists Receiving the New Testament

The feminist reception of the New Testament is a critical reception. It comes closest to the first possibility sketched above. If the two females presented above were feminists, they would say that 'this text has contributed to my formation, but strictly speaking it has nothing to do with me; this is speech between men about "women"'. In their reception of the text they do not ignore it, but historicize and contextualize it, and thus decenter it from its historically elevated position.

Hereby I have narrowed the meaning of 'feminist' so much that I have excluded most older forms of feminism from the outset. Like all descriptions and representations, my representation of 'feminism' is also simultaneously normative: I express what I think a feminist reception should be, and will continue to do so a little more, before I present readings by scholars with other views on what 'feminism' consists of. What we probably all will agree in is that power, privileges and positions are asymmetrically distributed between men as a group and women as a group in nearly all known societies, to men's advantage, and that such social traits should be changed.

Feminists also talk about gender. That men are humans and only women are gender or carriers of gender, is a naturalized, but phallogocentric[7] idea as old as Paul, as we will soon see. However, this idea is still going strong even if very few will maintain that men are less gendered than women after a moment's thought. Gender is a cognitive structure, a way of sorting the world into clear categories. Gender is systematically attached to humans: notions of feminine and masculine shape and reshape human bodies, but they also shape the development of societies and communities, which in turn not only reflect but also affect the gender discourse so that it develops in new directions adjusted to time, place and situation.

---

7. *Phallogocentrism* can be explained as an ideology adjusted to the value- and power-structures of patriarchal societies, that identifies penis, phallus and *logos*: the male is norm, which means that the world is interpreted according to a *logos* that is defined by the masculine: men decide what the human consists of, what is right and wrong, etc., and the female is subsumed under the male categorizations. Thus it is not the situatedness in a male body *per se* (which is insinuated as the problem in the more common term *androcentric*), but the phallogocentric *ideology* that make men and women define the male position with the human or universal position. See also discussion below on Irigaray.

Feminist readings of the Bible take as a point of departure that the biblical writings are influenced in a fundamental way by the phallogocentric discourse within which they emerged and developed, and that the texts therefore confirm and reproduce this perspective which implies that women disappear from focus for their own part and can be represented only in relation to men—as antitheses, as objects of the generosity of a male, as tools to think with when men want to think about body, desire and sexuality,[8] and so on. As in other critical hermeneutical scholarship, it is a central and integrated part of the research process to reflect theoretically and methodologically on the fact that our situatedness affects the way we read. Therefore it is part of the feminist reading project to visualize the mechanisms of interpretation that the little girl uses, and the way the masculine identity of the little boy is shaped when he reads the same text in Matthew 5.

Feminist reception of the New Testament is thus to *make visible* the gender structures in the text. It is not the feminist who brings gender to the text, but rather the feminist who receives the text and tries to grasp the implicit gender of it, including where words such as 'woman' or 'sex' do not occur.[9] Because humans are always categorized as gender—at least temporarily—texts that speak about humans or men are as gendered as texts that speak about women, even if we are not used to viewing, for example, theological anthropology as gendered speech. Feminist methods help bring to light how linguistic structures express gender, or how ideas that the text presents as obvious, natural, or divinely ordained are results

---

8.   K. King, 'A Response to: Galatians and Gender Trouble: Primal Androgyny and the First-Century Origins of a Feminist Dilemma', in D. Boyarin (ed.), *Galatians and Gender Trouble: Primal Androgyny and the First-Century Origins of a Feminist Dilemma* (Protocol of the Center for Hermeneutical Studies, NS 1; Berkeley: Center for Hermeneutical Studies, 1992), pp. 39-42.

9.   'The plights and plots of women were part of the past but are absent—for the most part—from history writing. Gender is different. Gender both was present in past time and is present in modern history writing. The problem is not that *gender* is absent from either the past or from our renderings of history; even a womanless history is simultaneously and necessarily gendered. The claim of such an absence is possible only when *gender* is mistakenly used as a simple synonym for *women*. The problem is not gender's absence, but the absence of a critical analysis of gender. A more powerful project investigates something that is present but hidden, largely through our familiarity with masculinist histories and culture' (M. Peskowitz, 'Engendering Jewish Religious History', in M. Peskowitz and L. Levitt [eds.], *Judaism since Gender* [New York: Routledge, 1997], pp. 17-39 [33]).

of long processes and struggles during which other possibilities of, for example, 'naturalness' were open.

However, what the feminist brings to the text is in many cases also an *evaluation* of the gender structures in the text in accordance with the overall goals of feminism.

Feminist Readings of 1 Corinthians with a Particular Focus on 11.2-16.

I will now give some examples of feminist readings of 1 Corinthians before I return to theoretical and methodological reflections towards the end of the essay. 1 Corinthians 11.2-16 in particular will be in focus. There are at least two levels of a text which are always gendered: the implied author/speaker and the implied reader. The implied author of 1 Cor. 11.2-16 as of other biblical texts is male. Many would say that the gender of the implied readers in this text is male; others would say that the implied readers are both male and female. In this text gender is also played out on the surface level.

1 Corinthians 11.2-16 was a popular topos before feminist exegesis became a strong trend in research, full as it is of exegetical issues. In a traditional reception of the passage, Paul's words are taken at face value and women are either invisible, reproductive tools for the Corinthian men and for Paul, or disorderly, disobedient and without respect and sensitivity. Women's disregard for the customary mode of appearance is seen as a problem. Their disorderliness is linked with their femininity or with their 'overrealized eschatology'.[10]

However, I will on purpose avoid the checklist questions of what ἐξουσία ἐπὶ τῆς κεφαλῆς means; what the role of the angels is; or in which way Paul is drawing on Jewish/rabbinic teachings on creation. Often these topics seem to be used as 'emergency exits', so that in discussions one does not have to deal with the implications of what is after all seen by most scholars as the main message of the text: 'The argument in 11.2-16 is so convoluted that we can no longer say with certainty what kind of custom or style Paul advocates for women prophets and liturgists. It is clear, however, that he does so because he wants them to know that the head or source of woman is man just as the head or source of Christ is

---

10. E.g. G. Fee, *The First Epistle to the Corinthians* (The New International Commentary on the New Testament; Grand Rapids: Eerdmans, 1987), pp. 497-98.

God'.[11] In addition: when no solutions to these exegetical problems have reached the level of common sense after so many years of discussion and intense philological research, it may be that it is the questions that are posed wrongly, or that we have to approach the answer from a different set of criteria. Particularly I find that to read this text without any use of the gender-analytical tools developed by feminist biblical scholarship is like doing rhetorical analysis without using any rhetorical theory, ancient or modern.[12]

I will present some selected feminist exegetes who write from different positions and who therefore approach the passage from different angles: Leopold Zscharnack, Elisabeth Schüssler Fiorenza, Lone Fatum and Antoinette Wire. I will to a certain extent presuppose that these are well known and need no broader presentation, in order to concentrate on their readings of the text in question. These exegetes are not disembedded and disembodied subjects who hold a static opinion all the time and in all situations: more than one have presented several and partly contradictory readings of the text. In order to show different ways of reading I have selected the most distinct reading from each. Therefore this chapter does not do the scholars themselves any justice. They serve only as outstanding representatives of different ways of reading.

Leopold Zscharnack

Feminism started over 200 years ago, after the French revolution. If we want to draw some historical lines and look at an example of early feminist *scholarship* on this text we have to look at a male feminist, since women in our part of the world had no access to academic positions until the last century. *The Woman's Bible* only offers an anecdote on this text— what is noteworthy for us today is that the revising committee did not consider the text controversial enough or important enough to find it worthwhile to comment on.[13] But Leopold Zscharnack was far ahead of his time

---

11. E. Schüssler Fiorenza, 'Rhetorical Situation and Historical Reconstruction in 1 Corinthians', *NTS* 33 (1987), pp. 386-403 (395).

12. In Gordon Fee's view, the discussion of the difficult questions mentioned 'has been further *complicated* by the resurgence in the 1960s of the feminist movement' (*The First Epistle*, p. 492, my italics).

13. E. Cady Stanton *et al.* (eds.), *The Woman's Bible* (New York: European Publishing Company, 1898), p. 159: Louisa Southworth there argues along the lines of divine inspiration. If it can be shown that Paul did not receive his message from God, but only from a myth, it cannot be authoritative. See also readings by other feminists

when he published *Der Dienst der Frau in den ersten Jahrhunderten der christlichen Kirche* in 1902.[14]

Zscharnack is highly critical of 'modern' authors who do not consider women in the Early Church. For him, it is bad scholarship to try to explain early Christianity without taking into account what an important force women were. ('Looking at the greetings attached to the New Testament letters, women seem to have contributed with a far greater contingent than the men of this service of the congregation').[15] He shows how women from the start had important positions, how they were gradually excluded from central tasks in the early Church, and how the Church fathers, misogynists as they were (p. 190), fought to reserve the clerical offices for men—and to put the female devotees into convents (p. 155).

Zscharnack reads 1 Corinthians 11 as containing two seeds that are mutually challenging, and both cannot grow simultaneously. The first seed 'containing' equality between women and men was not taken care of and fell on 'dry' or 'rocky ground'; it did not take root and did not bring forth fruit (p. 15) before possibly 1900 years later. This was the Christian seed proper. This seed is visible in 1 Cor. 11.11: 'in the Lord woman is not independent of man nor man of woman'. If this view had been consistently carried through it would have choked the other seed, which 'contained' the more widely accepted view in Antiquity. We find this view in 11.3 and 7: 'man is the head of woman' and 'a man ought not to cover his head, since he is the image and glory of God; but woman is the glory of man'. According to the latter view, the woman has at most a secondary and deduced form of godlikeness. The veil on her head should constantly keep in people's eyes and minds her humbleness and condemned position (p. 16). For Zscharnack these two views of women are mutually exclusive, and one of them is specifically Christian, while the other is taken over from the context and hence non-Christian in his eyes. The problem is only that Paul evidently does not perceive the views as mutually exclusive since he mentions both of them in the same passage!

Zscharnack's context for saying this is partly a Lutheran polemic against Catholicism; partly the quest in liberal theology for 'pure'

before 1920 in M. Selvidge, *Notorious Voices: Feminist Biblical Interpretation 1500–1920* (London: SCM Press, 1996).

14. Göttingen: Vandenhoeck & Ruprecht.

15. 'Wenn man die den NTlichen Briefen angefügten Grüsse betrachtet, so scheinen die Frauen zu diesem Gemeindedienst ein weit grösseres Kontingent gestellt zu haben als die Männer' (p. 46).

Christianity, where Lutheranism is seen as 'pure' while Catholicism is 'religion'; and partly the early feminist movement arguing for equality between the sexes alᵌo in the church. As a Lutheran, he depicts earliest Christianity as an ideal over against early Catholicism that closed the priesthood to women. An opening of the priesthood for women would differentiate the Lutheran Church from the Catholic Church and make it more similar to the ideal—the earliest church. Thus, in his work we see how gender as a structure, a way of sorting the world into clear categories (cf. definition above), also corresponds to Zscharnack's structuring of the relationship between confessions.

In other respects Zscharnack has a very nuanced comparative perspective. He compares early Christianity with other pre-Christian religions and shows how Christianity in some ways represented a turn to the worse for women. After a few centuries, women under Christianity were left with two alternatives: either domestic invisibility or monastic cloisture. And when discussing how Christianity *could* have been an improvement for women, he adds that the position of women in Judaism *also* improved in the Roman era: 'Especially when comparing the Jewish estimation of the woman in recent times with the estimation of the woman in first Christianity, it could be doubted, if there really here exist any progress'.[16] 'So it is more a formulation caused by dogmatical than historical interest when one claims that it is first in Christianity, and that from the begining, that the dignity of the woman has been fully acknowledged and practically validated' (p. 5).[17]

This is an insight that Zscharnack's successors seem to have forgotten. This insight was brought back into scholarly focus again first through the work of Bernadette Brooten[18] and then through Jewish feminist scholarship on Antiquity with its inherent and partly also explicit critique of Christian feminist biblical scholarship.

16. 'Gerade wenn man die jüdische Schätzung der Frau in jüngerer Zeit vergleicht mit der Schätzung der Frau im alten Christentum, so erhebt sich doch ein Zweifel daran, ob hier wirklich ein Fortschritt vorliegt' (p. 4)

17. 'So ist es eine mehr durch dogmatische als durch historische Interessen veranlasste Formulierung, wenn man behauptet, dass die Würde der Frau erst im Christentum, aber in ihm auch von Anfang an zur vollen Erkenntnis und zu praktischer Geltung gekommen ist' (p. 5).

18. Most significantly B. Brooten, *Women Leaders in the Ancient Synagogue: Inscriptional Evidence and Background Issues* (BJS, 36; Chico, CA: Scholars Press, 1982).

Elisabeth Schüssler Fiorenza

If Zscharnack's ideas sound familiar even to one that has not read his book, it is probably because similar ideas are discussed and developed in the early works[19] of Elisabeth Schüssler Fiorenza. She argued extensively and thoroughly that women were central in the earliest Christian movement. She further developed a picture of earliest Christianity as a 'discipleship of equals', which means an 'egalitarian countercultural, multifaceted movement'[20] that existed before the later church absorbed the gender hierarchy and patriarchy of the non-Christian cultural environment. Schüssler Fiorenza was an alert reader of the texts' empty spaces, fissures and discontinuities. She not only brought to attention the fragility of the texts, but also prepared the way for more recent feminist critiques maintaining that in phallogocentric texts, women can only be visible in the 'gaps, contradictions or margins'.[21]

Schüssler Fiorenza continues to shape feminist biblical discourse not only through her past work, but also through her continuous (mainly hermeneutical) contributions to the field. For one who came into theology after *In Memory of Her* was published, it is difficult to understand what was said in both feminist and mainstream scholarship before its emergence since she has launched new models for understanding early Christianity. The traditional view in scholarship—that women were marginal in the early Christian movement—she ascribes partly to the fact that the androcentric sources scarcely mention women, and partly to the fact that androcentric scholarship has regarded these filtered sources as objective descriptions. Schüssler Fiorenza holds that although the biblical writings are androcentric and have been molded in a patriarchal culture, they are nevertheless also women's

---

19. The early article 'Word, Spirit and Power: Women in Early Christian Communities', in R.R. Ruether and E. McLaughlin (eds.), *Women of Spirit: Female Leadership in the Jewish and Christian Traditions* (New York: Simon & Schuster, 1979), pp. 29-70, contains in germ Schüssler Fiorenza's historical and hermeneutical reflections which are developed with greater clarity and length in her main works: *In Memory of Her: A Feminist Theological Reconstruction of Christian Origins* (New York: Crossroad, 1983); and *Bread not Stone: The Challenge of Feminist Biblical Interpretation* (Boston: Beacon Press, 1984). I understand her later book, *But She Said: Feminist Practices of Biblical Interpretation* (Boston: Beacon Press, 1992), as an attempt to waterproof and update her earlier works.

20. 'Word, Spirit and Power', p. 31.

21. This was first pointed out by the French feminist philosophers (see T. Moi, 'Introduction', in *idem* [ed.], *French Feminist Thought* [Oxford: Basil Blackwell, 1987], pp. 1-13 [5]).

writings in the sense that women have been present in all human history, but invisibly for the men who kept the records. She tries to read the New Testament as source also to women's history, to reconstruct the historical communities and the circumstances *behind* the text, and to reconstruct the history of early Christianity as a history of both women and men. She tries to show how women were in the center of the Jesus movement and in the early Christian missionary movement in the Roman-Hellenistic world. In her 1983 book, then, the New Testament is a historical record, even if it is a fragmentary one.

Schüssler Fiorenza's readings of 1 Corinthians 11 are found both in *In Memory of Her* and in her article 'Rhetorical Situation and Historical Reconstruction in 1 Corinthians'. In the more recent article, Schüssler Fiorenza looks at the letter-text from a rhetorical-analytical perspective. However her basic views in this article are so similar to those Wire develops in her book that I will let this position be represented by Wire below, and let Schüssler Fiorenza speak through *In Memory of Her*. There Schüssler Fiorenza uses Gal. 3.27-29 as a feminist hermeneutic key to Pauline texts. She reads the creed as a communal Christian self-definition that proclaims that in Christ all distinctions of religion, race, class, nationality and gender are insignificant: 'All the baptized are equal' (p. 213). The confrontations between the Christian groups and the surrounding cultures are interpreted as results of the historical reality of this new form of egalitarian community. Since equality was not merely an ideal, women also influenced the shaping of the Christian communities. 1 Corinthians 11 and other texts show that women had leadership roles in the movement on an equal basis with men: 'Without question they [women] were equal and sometimes even superior to Paul in their work for the gospel' (p. 161).

Since women and men were equal, Corinthian men and women did not have conflicting interests or different codes of behavior, thus there was no need for Paul to discuss women's and men's issues separately throughout the letter. The passages that directly mention women do so because these women were exceptional or their actions had become a problem:

> These texts must not be taken to be all the available information on women in early Christianity. Thus we no longer can simply assume that only 1 Cor.11.2-16 speaks about women prophets, while the rest of chapters 11-14 refer to male charismatics and to male prophets. The opposite is the case. In 1 Corinthians 11-14 Paul speaks about the worship of all Christians, men and women, and he singles out women in 11.2-16 only because their behavior constituted a special problem'.[22]

22. Schüssler Fiorenza, *In Memory of Her*, p. 45.

The Corinthian Christian group Schüssler Fiorenza characterizes as a pneumatic, ecstatic community that understood the significance of the Spirit and of Jesus Christ in terms of Sophia theology, as the pre-Pauline christological hymns indicate. Since in this theology Sophia was conceived as a semihypostatic divine female figure, women probably were especially attracted to become devotees (pp. 219-20). Their cultic behavior, which constituted the special problem Paul addresses in 1 Corinthians 11, was ecstatic, similar to the worship of oriental deities, where 'disheveled hair would be quite common' (p. 226).

'The Corinthian pneumatics presumably took over such a fashion because they understood their equality in the community and their devotion to Sophia-Spirit by analogy to the worship of Isis...and her associations—like the Christian communities admitted women and slaves to equal membership and active participation' (pp. 227-28). In principle, then, Schüssler Fiorenza's Paul agrees with the Corinthians, but he is afraid that the Christian cult may be confused with this mystery cult or the other one. His main purpose in the passage is therefore to preserve the Christian pneumatic service in proper and restrained forms, so that it should not be confused with orgiastic, secret cultic celebrations that disturbed public decency and order.

If the Christians confessed upon entering the community that there was no longer any distinction between male and female, and if equality was already realized in the communities, what about those statements in this passage that speak against the equality of women and men in worship? Partly Schüssler Fiorenza does not agree that this is the case: '11.2-16 does not deny women's prophecy and prayer in the worship assembly but insists that in the Christian community women and men are equal' (p. 233). Partly she argues that such statements are grounded in Paul's missionary interests: the worship should not be too offensive to possible converts. By 'converts' she must mean male converts, since women were attracted to Christianity anyway because of the female Sophia-'goddess' and the freedom of women in this cult. 'It is not theology but concern for decency and order which determines Paul's regulation concerning the behavior of pneumatic women and men in the worship service of the community' (p. 233). Thus, Schüssler Fiorenza sees decency and order not as theological concerns, but as social or practical concerns that have nothing to do with theology. Therefore she can maintain that the passage is 'not directed against the spiritual freedom and charismatic involvement of women in the community' (p. 236).

Probably unintentionally, Schüssler Fiorenza presents Paul as one who again and again[23] sacrifices the realization of the Christian ideal, and the freedom of the female Christians in the community, on the altar of mission for the sake of new male converts in need of decency and order. For her reluctance to draw the consequences of this in her historical reconstruction of early Christianity, she has been criticized by many, including Lone Fatum.

Lone Fatum

Lone Fatum's main publication on 1 Cor. 11.3-9 is the article 'Image of God and Glory of Man: Women in the Pauline Congregations'.[24] Her discussion partners are traditional historical-critical exegetes and feminist theologians, in particular Schüssler Fiorenza, with whom she also discusses in the article 'Tango med en tidsel'.[25] In the latter article, Fatum positions herself within 'elendighedsforskning' or, literally translated, 'misery research',[26] that she views as the necessary implication of a historical and critical feminist consciousness. In all of her articles she attacks the bias in 'dignity research' and pleas for unapologetic readings.

Fatum writes from within a context in which feminist exegetes had tried to prove that biblical texts may leave room for both affirmation and liberation of women (as we have already seen an example of), basing themselves on the supposition that Christian faith and biblical religion and spirituality are in themselves neither suppressive nor misogynist. Fatum wants to come beyond this apologist interpretation, an interpretation that

23. The verses 14, 33b-36 Schüssler Fiorenza reads as Pauline, but holds that they only concern the non-Christian and maybe also Christian women married to Christian men (pp. 231-33).

24. L. Fatum, 'Image of God and Glory of Man: Women in the Pauline Congregations', in K. Børresen (ed.), *Image of God and Gender Models* (Oslo: Solum, 1991), pp. 56-137. A revised, shorter version was published as 'Women, Symbolic Universe and Structures of Silence: Challenges and Possibilities in Androcentric Texts', *ST* 43 (1988), pp. 61-80.

25. L. Fatum, 'Tango med en tidsel—om at finde værdigheden i elendighedsforskningen', in I. Brohed, U. Görman and T.N.D. Mettinger (eds.), *Feministteologi i dag. Sju föreläsningar til Kerstin Aspegrens minne* (Religio, 30; Lund: Teologiska Institutionen i Lund, 1989), pp. 85-105.

26. A feminist research trend in the 1980s, a reaction against 'værdighedsforskning' (dignity research), i.e. the quest for the 'glorious past' of women, for female agency and dignity.

makes for example Paul appear as women's friend through harmonization, excuse or even misinterpretation.

In her article of 1991, 'Image of God', Fatum gives an overview of how traditional exegesis has negotiated the meaning of 1 Corinthians 11 in relation to the baptismal formula and 1 Cor. 14.33-36. She finds both feminist and malestream exegesis guilty of an uncritical treatment of Gal. 3.28, since this verse is read as an expression of an absolutely positive affirmation of women. The cost is a satisfactorily consistent understanding of 1 Cor. 11.2-16, which is often interpreted 'negatively', although this text is also seen to represent an acceptable compromise between different views of women (p. 57). Thus Fatum criticizes the tendency we see in Schüssler Fiorenza, Wire, and others, to use Gal. 3.28 as a hermeneutic key to the understanding of New Testament texts on gender and women. Paul does not give any indications that he considers this uttering of such primary importance. Fatum holds that the fact that Paul writes 1 Cor. 11.3-9 without involving Gal. 3.28 calls for a reconsideration of what, in his own view, were the theological and practical consequences of Gal. 3.28. In clear words: The pre-pauline baptismal formula cannot be taken as the quintessence of Paul's theology.

It is noteworthy that Fatum also considers 1 Cor. 11.2-16 incoherent, awkward and theologically confusing (p. 73) *even* if it is not read with Gal. 3.28 as hermeneutic key. Since she elsewhere comments on 1 Corinthians as a very consistent letter, ch. 11 is characterized as remarkably atypical for the letter as a whole, in this and other respects.

Fatum herself understands 11.2-16 as a piece of 'women's paraenesis', a piece of social and moral guidance concerning the behavior and appearance required of Christian women. The central issue is defined as 'the social aspects of women's conduct in relation to gender and sexuality' (p. 72), something which is socially valid inside and outside of the assembly (pp. 71-72). Thus she pays little attention to the fact that the passage is placed as introduction to chs. 11–14, a section dealing with questions related to ritual gatherings and worship. She makes some important observations that this section is actually the context of the women's paraenesis, and that in this section 'Paul urges to unity and solidarity in honour and recognition of the congregation as the temple of God' (p. 68), but in her socio-sexual approach the congregation as assembly and temple disappears.

She admits that the women obviously must have behaved quite actively and independently (p. 72). The paraenesis presupposes a group of Christian women with an emancipated awareness of themselves as women (p. 81). The presence and consciousness of these women led Paul to write this piece to reinforce male sexual control in the congregation. It is exactly these two points, in slightly different words, which are developed further by Antoinette Wire, as we shall see. The female Christians are treated as females, not as Christians. Their praying and unveiled prophesying is rejected on non-eschatological, non-christological grounds by Paul.

Paul's argument implies that woman was not created in God's image, but derived from the man.[27] Therefore woman cannot pray or prophesy before God in her own right, but only as dependent on the man. For Paul, the present implication of the order given in creation is a gendered structure of super- and subordination—the veil is then a sign of woman's subordination.

In keeping with her 'misery'-approach, Fatum is critical of Paul's ideological universe. Thus Fatum is like Zscharnack in not explaining away the 'negativity' of 1 Corinthians 11. On the other hand Fatum shares with Schüssler Fiorenza the view that the passage is obscure and confusing.

Antoinette Wire

During the last decades, many fresh interpretations of 1 and 2 Corinthians have occurred using rhetorical theory to analyze Paul's argumentation. Among these contributions Antoinette Clark Wire's *The Corinthian Women Prophets: A Reconstruction through Paul's Rhetoric* is the most challenging as I see it.[28] Wire observes that many passages in 1 Corinthians strikingly concern women directly or indirectly. Instead of regarding these passages as incidental and sporadic, directed to single persons, she interprets such passages as forming a coherent whole because they are directed to one 'party' in Corinth, 'the Corinthian women prophets'. These were some, most or all of the Christian women in Corinth, 'the women at large as the spirit moves them to prophesy' (p. 156).

Methodologically, the book contains both an analysis of the arguments in 1 Corinthians and a historical reconstruction of the Corinthian women prophets: their social situation and behavior and their thinking about religious questions. In this reconstruction she uses anthropological models to sum up and arrange the results from the rhetorical analysis. To be able to go from the analysis to a reconstruction of the women prophets, she works from the assumptions that Paul writes to persuade; that although

27.   Following Schüssler Fiorenza, and in keeping with her reading of the passage as sexual-moral paraenesis, Fatum understands 1 Cor. 14.34-36 to imply that Paul supports one set of norms for married women, and one set for unmarried women.
28.   Minneapolis: Fortress Press, 1990.

Paul focuses on other issues than women's in his letter, the letter is written with the women constantly in view, and partly addressed to them; that when Paul's argument is particularly intense, 'struggling for their assent, one can assume some different and opposite point of view in Corinth from the one Paul is stating' (p. 10). This opposite point of view Wire consistently locates within the group of women prophets.

Through this holistic reading emerges a picture of a group that had a central position in the community, exercised all kinds of leading functions, and represented other experiences of the Christian faith and thus other values and theologies than those of Paul. Their theology was based on pre-Pauline baptismal formulas, and a gender-inclusive reading of Genesis was used as point of departure for thinking about creation and new creation. They also interpreted eschatologically their experiences of community and new life, their open communication with God through prayer, tongues, prophecy, and so on. They influenced the community as a whole to such an extent that Paul could not overlook them. In short Wire depicts an ideal women's club, where Paul disturbs like the big bad wolf in a hen's paradise.

A main contribution from Wire is that she has consistently carried through her perspective in an analysis of the whole letter, not only some smaller parts, not only the 'checklist'-questions elaborated by earlier scholarship. Wire has managed to step out from many deadends and has pointed at more fruitful paths. Particularly important, she more firmly than the previously mentioned scholars reads 'our' passage within its local context in the letter.

Wire puts Paul's hierarchical way of thinking in sharp relief. She reads 1 Corinthians 11 as a display of male honor problems. In Paul's presentation of a theology of cosmic competition between man and God, Wire reads a male experience of tension between self-glory associated with woman's uncovered head and God's glory associated with undistracted worship. Therefore it is not possible for a man to give God full honor at the same time as he is himself honored. 'Woman is interpreted as a factor in the problem that man has with God, or God with man' (p. 122). In his hierarchy of heads, women are denied direct participation in Christ. Paul dissociates divine from human by appeal to what is written about God's image: 'Man as God's image and glory represents the divine side of the conflict, and woman as man's glory represents the human contention against God' (p. 132). Thus, Paul locates the threat to God's glory in the woman. The *hubris* and the conflict is within the male, between God's glory and his own glory, which he sees embodied in the woman. *She* is the one who has to carry the consequences of *his hubris*, through covering her head, even if she for her own part could have glorified God without conflict or distraction since she has no glory of her own. But since man participates in worship also, only her covering can ensure his undistracted, exclusive praise of God.

In keeping with her strategy of reconstructing the recipients from Paul's arguments, Wire also presents what might have been the Corinthian women prophets' views (p. 134). They probably did not share Paul's theology of cosmic competition. Rather they understood their active, uncovered participation in the worship as glorification of God, not as production of human glory that belongs to the male separate from God.

Wire reads vv. 2-16 as placed in the context of paraenesis concerning correct worship vs. warnings of idolatry. Wire uses this cultic location, as well as the appeals to Christ as head of man and God as head of Christ, to say something about the theology of the women prophets. 'If they did not already understand Christ as a middle figure between God and the believer they would hardly understand Paul's appeal' (p. 134). She also thinks that they rejected the male as exclusive image of God (from the exclusion of the 'not male and female' in Paul's citation of the baptismal formula in 1 Cor. 12.13).[29] Further, they understood themselves to be incorporated into the body of Christ—God's image that is not male and female—*qua* females. On this basis, they understood their prophesying uncovered and praying uncovered as speaking for God and to God directly and not via the male.

What is 'Woman'?

A problem in all the discussed contributions is the confidence of scholars that they know what Paul means by γυνή in 1 Corinthians 11; that the word is an innocent signification of people with female bodies (biologically and/ or culturally marked). This confidence *may* be well founded, but it needs to be discussed.

---

29. She also bases this hypothesis on 11.7, where Paul profits from the authority of Gen. 1.27 on creation in God's image without quoting the verse. Direct quotation 'would involve using a Greek term with generic implications for the human being created in God's image rather than his term that means "the male". And a full quote would end inclusively, "male and female he created them." In fact Paul replaces the biblical narrative of God creating according to God's image with a description of the male as God's image and glory. Whatever credibility Paul receives from this interpretation of Genesis depends on its parallels to other interpretations of that time' (p. 119).

First, few feminists today would hold that there is any female or male essence[30] or transhistorical substance. The belief in static substances behind the words 'feminine'/'woman' and 'masculine'/'man'[31] is renounced. But then it is also difficult to take for granted that Paul's uses of terms denoting human gender refer to the same things as we today put into these terms. In clear words: There is no constant entity behind the word 'woman' in the text with whom modern people can identify, borrow perspective from and draw on in an evaluation of 1 Corinthians as 'positive' or 'negative' for 'women'. Rather, we must try to find out what Paul puts in the word 'woman' in this particular text.

Second, language carries notions of gender. In the 1970s and 1980s there was a tendency to locate the patriarchal elements in the social structures behind the text, on a level that we strictly speaking do not have access to through Paul's text. This tendency also presupposes that social structures could exist independently of textual production. But it is not only the social structures behind the text that are gendered. Gender is also present in the use of language in the text itself. Gender is produced through grammar, synonyms and antonyms, idioms and expressions, and reproduced in the reader. I will discuss this last point first, and then return to the first point.

Schüssler Fiorenza does not problematize the language categories themselves and the way they work. 'Women' are women, there are no problems

30. There are strikingly many parallels between today's discussions between 'essentialists' and 'constructivists' and the discussions between realists and nominalists in the Middle Ages. An important difference is that where nominalists would say that the universal concepts designate groups of similar things, the constructivists even question the internal similarity of things covered by the same name. Even if the parallels between the nominalist controversies and modern feminist discussions already were drawn upon by Simone de Beauvoir, *The Second Sex* (trans. H.M. Parshley; London: Vintage Books, 1953), pp. 13-15, these parallels have not been sufficiently explored in later feminist theory, and I hope to come back to this topic on another occasion.

31. I do not distinguish between male/masculine and female/feminine, and I use 'gender' as a translation of the Norwegian 'kjønn', which includes both sex and gender. This is also how the historian Joan Scott uses the 'gender' term. Since Scandinavian languages as well as French do not distinguish between sex and gender from the outset, it is unnecessary for feminists with such linguistic backgrounds to go via Anglo-American poststructuralism to deconstruct the distinction between sex and gender and related concepts: T. Moi, *Hva er en kvinne: Kjønn og kropp i feministisk teori* (Oslo: Gyldendal, 1998), p. 31 n. 15 (concerning Joan Scott's 'gender', see pp. 54-55).

in the relationship between the word and the character of the reality it denotes, and therefore she can read the New Testament as 'record'—in our case of Corinthian ecstatic Sophia-worship. Women are representable in patriarchal texts; the problem is only that they are often not represented.

Fatum is more cautious, since she reads Paul's text as a normative text to the Corinthians. From the text we can reconstruct not women of the past but the author's view of women, and what set of norms for women he supports. Still it is the rhetorical purpose of the text, not the language in itself, that should alert the feminist.

Wire thinks that the more intent the speaker has to persuade, the less he can afford to misjudge or misrepresent the audience (p. 4). Thus she presupposes that Paul is in full control of his use of language, that he has a fully adequate perception of the Corinthians, that he manages perfectly to put into language, and that he is so knowledgeable of the Corinthian discourse that he knows how different words and expressions are understood there—in short, that there is one, hegemonic, univocal discourse that shapes both Paul's and all the Corinthians' (as a group) understanding of the words and ideas he uses. Thus she shares the presupposition that language is 'neutral' and unambiguous, which makes it possible to believe that the women prophets could disagree with Paul over content, but still be representable in the structures of his language.

According to the French philosopher Luce Irigaray, woman is not not-yet-represented, but rather 'non-representable' within the phallogocentric paradigm since she transcends the possibilities of representation within it.[32] Irigaray discusses canonized philosophers of Western civilization—Plato, Aristotle, Plotin, Descartes, Kant, Freud—and concludes that 'woman has not yet taken place—woman is still the place', that is, that femaleness within their discourse is produced as a basis for the exposition of the male/human. 'She is not uprooted from matter...still, she is already scattered into x number of places that are never gathered together into anything she knows of herself, and these remain the basis of reproduction—particularly of discourse—in all its forms. Woman remains this nothing at all... She must continue to hold the place she constitutes for the subject, a place to which no eternal value can be assigned...'[33] In a certain sense one has to conclude, then, that women do not have a history, and that the representations of

---

32. L. Irigaray, *Speculum of the Other Woman* (trans. G.C. Gill; Ithaca, NY: Cornell University Press, 1985); cf. K. Egeland, 'Problemet som ikke (vil) finnes', *Kvinneforskning* 23.1 (1999), pp. 80-88 (86).

33. Irigaray, *Speculum*, p. 227.

'woman' in phallogocentric texts need not have anything in common with those embodied humans we define as 'women' around us today. The word 'woman' only functions within this discourse as an empty category with changing content.

In a reading of Paul, this means that his texts cannot be read as sources to women's history. Also in his letters the word γυνή is an empty space that is filled with the likeness, opposition or complementarity of the male, all according to his purpose. Therefore, contradictory utterings on γυνή are not strange but rather something we should expect. That the utterings are inconsistent is confirmed by the fact that it evidently is possible to read so many different 'views of women' out of this text! In this light, 1 Corinthians 11 comes out not as atypical, but typical in its location of 'woman' partly as subjugated, partly as complementary to the male.

Following Irigaray, we have to ask whether Paul had a view of women at all. What could he possibly see? At most, he could see 'women' as a category of otherness in relation to the male. If we situate the passage firmly within the context of chs. 11–14 that deal with the ritual gatherings, and that according to Wire and more recently Anders Eriksson, touch many gender issues[34], these gender issues do not *necessarily* have to be linked to any 'real' women in the ritual gatherings. According to the Norwegian philosopher Kjell Soleim,

> 'Descartes may be credited...[for] destroying the microcosm-macrocosm model and thus getting rid of man's double out in space... Man could no more look at himself in the mirror of the universe in order to find his own properties reflected out there; ... And although Descartes may not have been much concerned about it, by the same token he ruined the gendered system of the universe. Since the ancient Greek philosophers, all through the Middle Ages and Renaissance, the elements constituting our world were female and male, thus heat was considered male and humidity female; in Aristotle, form was male and matter female. In substituting mathematical measurement for Aristotle's final causes and substantial forms, Descartes desexualized our world'.[35]

When gender difference was expelled from 'out there' it became entrenched in the body instead. This post-Cartesian modernity model of

34. Wire, *The Corinthian Women Prophets*; Anders Eriksson, '"Women Tongue Speakers, Be Silent": A Reconstruction through Paul's Rhetoric', *BibInt* (1998), pp. 80-104.

35. K. Soleim, '"I doubt: I am a Man": The Cartesian Subject Exposed to Sexual Difference', in I.N. Preus *et al.* (eds.), *Feminism, Epistemology, and Ethics* (Oslo: Department of Philosophy, University of Oslo, 1996), pp. 137-46 (137-38).

gender, the idea that gender has above all to do with human bodies (and particularly female bodies and sexual organs) was reinforced through psychoanalytical discourse. Feminist historians have to too great an extent brought with them to the texts the modern model of gender with its fixed notions of 'woman', 'man' and 'sexuality'. If such etic paradigms, though helpful in modernity, produce more problems than sense today, we should feel free to exchange them for new paradigms that take into account what we have learnt since then.

To continue Wire's analogy of vision,[36] when Paul in his inner eye is focusing on the problems in the Corinthian ritual gatherings, I am not so sure that the women are even in his wider field of vision. His filtering gaze only sees lack of unity, chaos and disorder. However, notions of chaos and disorder were related to notions of 'femininity', as unity was to 'masculinity' in the discourse Paul formed part of. In this dichotomizing discourse male and female each belong on their side. In many cases, therefore, it was unnecessary for Paul and other speakers to categorize phenomena as masculine and feminine explicitly—in most dichotomies, it was 'given' which pole was masculine and which pole was feminine. This makes it possible for modern readers to read the problems of disorder and splitting as also related to his discussion of 'woman' in the ritual gatherings. On the other hand, this perspective implies that when Paul was talking about 'women', he need not have been inspired by concrete happenings and actions by Corinthian 'women', he just wanted peace, order and unity in what he perceived as a chaotic assembly. If 'woman' as a location of man's opposite—in this case 'cosmic' femininity—also was a location for disorder and chaos, he had to put 'her' in her cosmically correct place.

If we return to the discussion of substances or essences, I am still disturbed by the *a priori* confidence that γυνή is compatible with what we identify as women today—particularly if one first has left the essentialist position. How is it possible to say anything about historical women and their experiences and 'point of view' if it is not possible to know anything about the women because the texts are androcentric, or if there is no female essence that makes it possible to speak transhistorically about women? And if it is not, then neither is it possible to transport today's judgments about 'positive', 'confirming', and so on, to the past.

The way Schüssler Fiorenza on the one hand criticizes essentialist notions of femininity, makes her on the other hand dependent on a static concept of 'woman' in her critique of androcentrism, as has been pointed

36. Wire, *The Corinthian Women Prophets*, p. 8.

out and criticized already by Anne-Louise Eriksson.[37] But Schüssler Fiorenza is only an example of a dilemma that concerns all forms of feminist scholarship, and this dilemma has been most sharply formulated by the historian Joan Scott. In her book *Only Paradoxes to Offer: French Feminists and the Rights of Man*,[38] she describes the struggle of the post-revolutionary French feminists for a true democracy where 'les droits de l'homme', 'rights of *man*', also would be rights of women. Scott shows how Olympe de Gouge and the others made themselves dependent on the same dichotomized way of thinking of gender that they criticized:

> Feminism was a protest against women's political exclusion; its goal was to eliminate 'sexual difference' in politics, but it had to make its claims on behalf of 'women' (who were discursively produced through 'sexual difference'). To the extent that it acted for 'women', feminism produced the 'sexual difference' it sought to eliminate. This paradox—the need both to accept and to refuse 'sexual difference'—was the constitutive condition of feminism as a political movement throughout its long history.[39]

I think I find the same dilemma in all the discussed contributions and also in my own work. Constantly, we as feminist interpreters make ourselves dependent on the same foundation that we criticize. But exactly this shows that women—feminists included—do not have a different language and other thought structures to speak in and from than those given us by contemporary discourse. We cannot not inhabit our father's house. There is no inner feminine source or feminine language, independent of time, place and culture from which we can draw our critique of patriarchy. It is exactly the language and the inherent inconsistencies in the phallogocentric discourses that give us the means to criticize it.[40] Therefore feminist critique still 200 years after Olympe de Gouge has 'only paradoxes to offer'. But we play out this dilemma in different ways:

Zscharnack argues for women's right to offices and responsibility in the church—with the argument that they deserve it because of their great

37. A.-L. Eriksson, *The Meaning of Gender in Theology Problems and Possibilities* (Uppsala Womens' Studies A. Women in Religion, 6; Stockholm: Almqvist & Wiksell, 1995).

38. Cambridge, MA: Harvard University Press, 1996.

39. Scott, *Only Paradoxes to Offer*, pp. 3-4.

40. 'It is precisely because feminism embodies paradox that it has been trivialized or consigned to marginality by those seeking to protect the foundations of whatever status quo they represent. Such protection involves denying contradiction by rendering it invisible and by displacing the source of the problem onto those who would point it out' (Scott, *Only Paradoxes to Offer*, p. 17).

sacrifices and efforts for the church! But is not a right something you have, not something you make yourself deserve?

Schüssler Fiorenza criticizes the androcentric notion of eternal feminine values, while at the same time social gender and women's social roles seem to be as firm in her work as the female essence is in, for example, Zscharnack. Also, Schüssler Fiorenza uses the gaps and lacunae in the text to postulate women's activity and leadership. But women's activity does not necessarily imply autonomy or that they are in control. Schüssler Fiorenza seems to presuppose that if she can only show that women prayed, prophesied and disheveled their hair, it follows that they were autonomous, self-representing subjects. Thereby she is caught in the same dichotomized way of thinking that she criticizes, where activity is linked with individuality, full humanity, autonomy—and strictly speaking masculinity.

Fatum says in some places that the women in the Pauline communities are inaccessible to us, because the text that speaks about them is androcentric. Simultaneously, her understanding of the self-conscious Corinthian women forms the basis for her criticism of Paul. She presupposes that they had a 'self', that there existed something like a 'point of view of the women themselves' that Paul was negative toward.[41]

The 'woman problem' in Wire is of a slightly different character because her goal is not to sort out what Paul can or cannot be used for today, but to historicize him and to place him as only one among multiple voices of early Christianity.[42] But in order to make her reconstruction of the women prophets, Wire like the others is dependent on a quite static perception of what the word 'woman' signifies—if not it would be impossible to draw on women's experiences so directly in reconstructions of the past. But could the woman prophets possibly have such a consciousness that she ascribes to them? Was a worldview accessible to them in which women and men were equal in worth, when the discourse they formed part of presented other views?

41. Fatum, 'Image of God', pp. 59, 86.
42. Wire finds the women accessible through Paul's text, since they are part of the rhetorical situation of the letter. Wire shares with Fatum a view of Paul as non-affirmative of the women in the congregation, but while Fatum holds that the women are not a part in Paul's discussion with the Corinthians, Wire thinks that he feels threatened by the women. Thus Wire is reading Paul as a source for women's subversive identity, while there is no space for such a thing in Fatum's text. In Wire's picture, it was possible for the women to contest Paul's authority because his writings did not become canonized until much later. This difference also illustrates how they relate to very different theories of patriarchy.

In this perspective, accusations back and forth of scholarly inconsistency, essentialism or bias, appear irrelevant. For myself, I try to criticize and get further from the paradoxes of the last generation, but end up in new ones. For example, in spite of my skepticism to language I do not stop speaking about the past, something I should have done if my overall goal was to be consistent. However paradoxes are everywhere—which paradoxes are legitimate or illegitimate (then classified as *inconsistencies*), visible or invisible, is only a question of who has the power of definition. I will plea that the paradox/inconsistency inherent in feminism, itself a product of the inconsistencies inherent in the modern discourse of human rights, is a legitimate one: '"women" is indeed an unstable category…this instability has a historical foundation, and.. feminism is the site of the systematic fighting-out of that instability—which need not worry us'. [43]

Conclusion

I have tried to present feminist reception as a critical reception of the biblical texts through analysis of the gender structures that are built into them. I have also tried to show that feminists can read the same text in different ways. The differences can be explained by the different periods or places they read from, but also their differing views of how the overall goals of feminism can be reached.

Some feminist theologians seem to think that in order to fuel women's struggle for full humanhood today it is necessary to give them 'a glorious past'. In 1983 Schüssler Fiorenza wanted to reclaim the past, by use of adequate hermeneutics and methods, as a past also for women. However, this procedure yielded so meager results that it is incomprehensible today how one could be so enthusiastic at the 'wow women-stage' (Elizabeth Clark's expression) in the 1970s and early 1980s. Another, in my view more fruitful, way of using the past in present arguments is to demonstrate how notions of gender have changed through the ages, according to place and situation, and how therefore gender structures and the precise content of words sich as 'man' and 'woman' are neither stable nor eternally given:

> 'The cultural reward of this analysis is not, then, the discovery or recovery
> of a golden age in the past,…but the very fact that we can show that the
> different androcentric formations functioned in entirely different fashions at

---

43. D. Riley, 'Does a Sex Have a History?', in J. Scott (ed.), *Feminism and History* (New York: Oxford University Press, repr. 1996), pp. 17-33 (20-21).

different times and places provides a kind of demystifying historization, showing that each was contingent and specific and that all are equally unsettled from the positions of transhistorical natural status'.[44]

For me, the display of historical contingency is a much better basis for optimism concerning the future than a couple of female anomalies in the Christian past, or a display of the miserable status of women in Christianity. If Schüssler Fiorenza and her sympathizers had been correct that early Christianity was a discipleship of equals, feminist exegesis would be dead by now: it would have meant that all struggle to change our gender discourses is in vain, since 2000 years of equality-thinking has not changed anything! If the Bible speaks so clearly about equality between man and woman as many maintain today, why did nobody understand this before the nineteenth century?

The New Testament is written from within a gender discourse that does not automatically make sense today. We do not make sense of the world by drawing on cosmic hierarchies that also encompass people. Paul accepted slavery, we do not. In our society, rape and pedophilia is against the law, whereas Paul in his lists of sexual vices does not discuss consent as an issue.[45] But if the New Testament writings are not politically correct when measured against modern standards, should the reception of them within feminist theology and scholarship of religion therefore be brought to an end? I consider such a view dangerous; it is an idea of displacement comparable to sticking one's head into the ground, and as misuse of feminist methods. We can say that today the mutant seed of equality between the sexes that exists in some New Testament texts has at least grown into a little plant, even if it is not flourishing yet. In the early modern environment with its discourse of equal dignity of all men, the little mutant got better growing conditions than in the Roman period with its emphasis on patriarchal rule. This implies that I see modern feminist discourse as an illegitimate child, but still a child, of biblical gender discourse.

44. D. Boyarin, *Carnal Israel: Reading Sex in Talmudic Culture* (The New Historicism: Studies in Cultural Poetics, 25; Berkeley: University of California Press, 1993), p. 243.

45. B. Brooten, *Love between Women: Early Christian Responses to Female Homoeroticism* (The Chicago Series on Sexuality, History, and Society; Chicago: University of Chicago Press, 1996), pp. 246-47, 250-51, 290-92, 294.

THE ANNUNCIATION: A STUDY IN RECEPTION HISTORY

Tord Fornberg

The Annunciation in the New Testament

The subject that I have been asked to lecture on is extremely wide: 'The Reception of the New Testament as a Continuing Process'. In order not to look too widely and thus by necessity superficially I have chosen one single text as my test case: the well-known Lukan pericope on the Annunciation for the Virgin Mary (Lk. 1.26-38). As we all know, this text has played an important role for the development of Christian theology, for Christology as well as for Mariology.[1] Countless artists have depicted the scene, and its importance for popular piety, also in Lutheran Sweden, can hardly be exaggerated. It was only the Enlightenment of the eighteenth century that caused the Virgin Mary to disappear from popular piety and folklore.[2]

The reception of the pericope in the Bible itself can be dealt with in few words. The mystery of the virginity of the young Mary is only mentioned in Matthew 1–2 and Luke 1–2. The scene with Gabriel's visit to the home of the young Mary never meets the reader of the Bible outside of Luke 1, and nowhere in the New Testament does any author betray knowledge of our pericope.

Luke does not provide his reader with a clear interpretation of the story, and scholars have sometimes stated that the Annunciation and the virgin birth are theologically mute events. This is hardly the case. There was no

---

1.   C. Ebertshäuser et al., *Mary: Art, Culture, and Religion through the Ages* (New York: Crossroad, 1998), as well as many articles in *Marienlexikon* I-VI (St Ottilien, 1988–94) are of great value for the topic of this paper.

2.   On this see E. Burman, *Mariablomster* (Stockholm: Rabén & Sjögren, 1989), on how flowers with Marian names lost these names under the influence of the eighteenth-century Swedish botanist Carl von Linné. As an example we may mention 'Vårfrudagslök' (a flower which might blossom as soon as 25 March), which he renamed 'Vårlök' and to which he gave the Latin name *Gagea lutea*, after his British colleague Gage.

Jewish expectation that any savior should enter the world in this way. Maybe the text conveys the message that Jesus was born into the world through God's direct creative act *ex nihilo*, an event that has been compared to the creation in the beginning of time. Or one may say that it was not at his baptism (Acts 10.38) or at the resurrection (Rom. 1.3-4) or at any other occasion that Jesus was enthroned as the Son of God. He is the Son of God (Lk. 1.35) from all eternity. The virgin birth has been understood as a sign comparable to the empty tomb; a sign that hints at the very specific divinity of Jesus for the eye of faith.

The Early Church

The Earliest Texts

The earliest example of the virgin birth (not the narrative about the annunciation) outside of the New Testament can be found in the writings of Ignatius of Antioch. Here we find the words: 'The virginity of Mary and her giving birth eluded the ruler of this age, likewise also the death of the Lord—three mysteries of a cry which were done in the stillness of God' (*Ignatius Ephesians* 19.1). The author continues by alluding to Matthew 2 on the wise men and the star of Bethlehem. Already in the 110s CE Ignatius knew the early stages of the development of myths around the birth of Jesus, which became so clear some two generations later in *Prot. Jas.* 11.1-3. Mary was a virgin, but even the birth of Jesus was mysterious and preserved her virginity.[3] The *Protevangelium of James* includes the earliest explicit example that the Lukan variant of the Annunciation narrative was known:

> And behold, an angel of the Lord stood before her and said: 'Do not fear, Mary, for you have found grace before the Lord of all things and shall conceive of his Word'. When she heard this she doubted in herself and said: 'Shall I conceive of the Lord, the living God, as every woman bears?' And the angel of the Lord said: 'Not so, Mary; for the power of the Lord shall overshadow you. Wherefore also that holy thing which is born of you shall be called the Son of the Highest. And you shall call his name Jesus, for he shall save his people from their sins'. And Mary said: 'Behold, (I am) the handmaid of the Lord before him: be it to me according to your word'.

---

3.   The *Odes of Solomon* and the *Ascension of Isaiah* witness that Mary remained a virgin even during the birth (*virginitas in partu*). Apocryphal traditions like those about Joachim and Anne were later suppressed by the Catholic Church, e.g. during the Renaissance and its program of *ad fontes*.

Later authors of the second century, authors such as Justin[4] and Irenaeus,[5] developed the thinking about Mary. She became a counterpart to Eve in a similar way as Paul in Romans 5 described Jesus as a second Adam who recreated what the first Adam had destroyed at the fall into sin. The connection of Eve with her role in the fall and Mary with her role in the work of salvation was made through a reference to Gen. 3.14-15, and was still more important on Latin ground, where the word-play Ave (= *chaire* in Lk. 1.28) / Eva could be made. It is then used time and again, for example, in the hymn *Ave Maris stella*, known from around the ninth century.[6]

The Early Church also saw the use of the narrative of the Annunciation by Christian artists, maybe not surprisingly because of its importance for salvation history. The scene with Mary and Gabriel is thus depicted in the Priscilla catacomb in Rome as well as in the Peter and Marcellus catacomb, where it is found for the first time introducing a Christological pictorial cycle.[7]

Support for Emergent Asceticism

Mary with her embarrassed question of how it could be that she was to bear a son soon became important for the emergent Christian asceticism. Early asceticism as it developed in the Egyptian deserts in the early fourth century could refer to several biblical figures. One of them was the apostle Paul, who had argued in 1 Corinthians 7 for celibacy as the ideal way of life for all those who want to take their faith seriously in all its eschatological character.[8] But Paul's argument for celibacy was totally different from that which later on became important. The urgent *Parousia* and the consequent haste with missionary work did not take for granted the denigration of the body and its lusts, which became so characteristic of much later theology.

Quite early the Virgin Mary stood out as a still more important biblical pattern to be imitated. Her embarrassed question how she could bear a son

---

4.   See, e.g., Justin, *Apol.* 1.33; *Dial.* 100.

5.   *Adv. Haer.* 3.22.4.

6.   Strophe 2 in *Ave Maris stella* thus reads: *Sumens illud Ave Gabrielis ore, funda nos in pace, mutans nomen Evae*. See also paintings that show how Adam and Eve are driven out of Paradise while Mary sits in a paradisiacal garden, in M. Warner, *Alone of All her Sex* (London: Quartet, 1978), p. 61.

7.   E.g. Ebertshäuser *et al.*, *Mary*, p. 224.

8.   Warner, *Alone*, pp. 55-56. See also Mt. 19.10-12 with the words about eunuchs for the kingdom of heaven.

was explained by fourth-century authors such as Gregory of Nyssa and Ambrose and somewhat later by Augustine,[9] who supposed that she had already decided to live a life in virginity. For this reason she has been looked upon as an ideal, in reality not even possible to imitate perfectly, for priests, monks and nuns who have refrained from their sexuality in order to live totally for God. We may quote from a modern Indian book on the Virgin:

> ...the religious have Mary as their model, for she was totally consecrated to God, being overshadowed by the Holy Spirit (cf. Lk 1.35), having the Lord with her (cf. Lk 1.28) and being totally in the service of God (cf. Lk 1.38, 48). To God's design Mary said *fiat* (cf. Lk 1.38) by her free and definitive choice. So is religious life a definite choice...[10]

In fact, there is a close connection between love for Mary and the emergent monasticism. Especially in the monasteries Mary was venerated as the ideal, which Christians tried to imitate, but never really succeeded. It is no coincidence that the Church can point to so many virgin martyrs. Figures from the fourth century such as Agnes and Lucy may be mentioned, as well as many later saints like Mary Goretti (1890–1902).

Influence from the Church Year
The Annunciation was soon included in the Christian calendar. Thus Byzantine Christians were familiar with the feast of the Annunciation by the fifth century, and monks who fled Islam brought it to the West. It was also moved to the spring equinox on 25 March.[11] This festival celebrated the mystery of Incarnation just as the feast of the virginity of Mary did, which soon came to be celebrated in Rome on 1 January. Thus the feast of the Annunciation emphasized the Christology of the Catholic Church in opposition to those theologians who looked upon Jesus as a Gnostic revealer of saving knowledge, a peripatetic philosopher or a shepherd. These different Christologies, however, were reflected on the Roman sarcophagi of the fourth and the fifth centuries. The pictorial cycles on these sarcophagi were often influenced by the contemporaneous non-Christian culture in a way that never was the case with the feasts of the Christian year.

---

9. R. Brown, *et al.* (eds.), *Mary in the New Testament* (Philadelphia: Fortress Press; New York: Paulist Press, 1978), pp. 114-15 but without references.
10. G. Kaitholil, *Mary: The Pilgrim of Faith* (Bombay: Saint Paul, 1993), p. 114.
11. Ebertshäuser *et al.*, *Mary*, p. 169.

The Medieval Era of the Western Church

The great Church Fathers could work with the biblical texts and comment upon them in written form.[12] But most Christians have been illiterate, even in recent times.[13] People have not been able to read the Gospels themselves but have been totally dependent upon its being read aloud in the service and its being depicted on the walls and the ceilings of the churches. Thus a biblical text such as Lk. 1.26-38 became known to Christians mainly through prayers such as Hail Mary, the Rosary, through the Creed, and by means of all the pictures showing the Annunciation that were created by artists in the service of the Church.

The Creed: The History of Salvation

For most people the text about the Annunciation was less important than the pieces of art depicting this famous event, often being the first picture in a long series of pictures. These series reflect the concentration upon Jesus' birth and his death and resurrection which is also expressed in the Apostolic and the Niceno-Constantinopolitanian Creeds. The Apostolic Creed is here closer to the Lukan text when it clearly distinguishes between the Annunciation and the birth. Thus the words of the Apostolic Creed '*conceptus est de Spirito Sancto, ex Maria Virgine*'[14] seem to imply that the Spirit became pregnant like a woman and then 'borrowed' Mary's body up to Jesus' birth. A similar concept seems to lie behind the apocryphal Gospel of the Hebrews according to which Jesus calls the Spirit his mother, and about which fathers like Origen and Jerome posed no questions.

This idea was then read into the narrative about the Annunciation by authors such as John the Damascene and by artists who painted a small

---

12. I. de la Potterie, '*Kecharitōmenē* en Lc 1.28 Etude philologique', *Bib* 68 (1987), pp. 357-82 and 480-508 (487-91), shows how Ambrose understood Mary's grace to refer to her being the mother of God's Son, and how Jerome interprets her being full of grace as a reference to the Messianic child in her bosom. Only toward the end of the era of the Early Church was the concept of *gratia* given a strictly mariological meaning.

13. It may be noted that the Swedish compulsory primary school dates from as late as 1842.

14. Warner, *Alone*, p. 38 and A. Ekenberg, *Låt oss be och bekänna* (Örebro: Libris, 1996), pp. 45-46. The Niceno-Constantinopolitan Creed does not make any clear distinction between the roles of Mary and of the Spirit with its wording *sarkōthenta ek pneumatos hagiou kai Marias tēs parthenou*.

boy flying directly from God to the Virgin Mary, even entering her body physically through her ears.[15] When Mary heard the words of the angel and accepted them by saying her *fiat*, the divine Word came to dwell in her bosom.[16]

A medieval Christian normally became acquainted with the Creed through a series of paintings on the church walls. The fact that the Creed was recited in Latin and thus could not be understood by the vast majority of the people made these pictures all the more important. The different parts of the Creed were distributed among the 12 apostles who were thought to have contributed one part each. The passage about the Annunciation was often ascribed to James the elder, maybe because of the influence from the *Protevangelium of James* on popular piety. When they painted this scene, the artists quite naturally did not distinguish between the various Gospels as is done by historical-critical scholars of today. Thus the text in Lk. 1.26-38 was often combined with Mt. 1.18-25 with its quotation from Isa. 7.14: 'Behold, a young woman shall conceive and bear a son, and shall call his name Immanuel'. In the very moment when Mary received and accepted Gabriel's words the prophecy uttered by Isaiah to King Ahaz was fulfilled and even surpassed: Mary was not only a young princess in the royal family, she was even the untouched girl whom the Septuagint had brought into the prophetic statement. Time and again the artists painted how Mary received the words from the archangel with an open book in her hand, and invariably the pages visible have the words from Isa. 7.14 written on them.

In the medieval era Mary became all the more important in the prayer life of the believers. One example is the Hail Mary, a short prayer built around a combination of Gabriel's words of greeting to Mary in Lk. 1.28 and Elizabeth's words to Mary in Lk. 1.42: 'Hail Mary...' The two texts were combined in the eighth century and have been widely used as a prayer since the eleventh century. After some additions were made, Pope Paul V received Hail Mary into the breviary as late as 1568. The breviary was enormously widespread, and it is no coincidence that many of the paintings depicting the Annunciation show a young woman who just looks up from an open book, that is, from the breviary.

In fact these pictures have a double function. On the one hand, they

15. A hymn ascribed to Venantius Fortunatus may also be mentioned (*quod aure virgo concepit*); Warner, *Alone*, p. 37.

16. K. Barth, *Die Kirchliche Dogmatik* I/2 (Zürich: Zollikon, 1938), p. 220. See also de la Potterie, '*Kecharitōmenē*', pp. 376-78, about a Byzantine hymn on an ostracon: *hē ton theou logon ... gennēsasa.*

explain how Mary could be prepared to listen to the message conveyed by the angel and say her *fiat*. On the other hand, pictures of the young Mary reading her breviary make her into a pattern to be followed by all those who look at them. This model function is strengthened by all the paintings in which Mary is shown with concrete details from the time of the artist himself, for instance when she is depicted as a wealthy Dutch housewife from the sixteenth or the seventeenth centuries. Mary then became a natural model of identification for those who ordered the paintings: wealthy businessmen in the service of the Dutch East India Company and their wives, hopefully pious and humble.[17]

The Rosary

The Rosary has often been considered as a Western parallel to the Jesus-prayer of the Eastern Church or to the mantras of Hinduism and Buddhism with their few points of prayer, repeated over and over again. Here salvation history is summarized in 15 scenes. The first two are those which are combined for the first time already in Luke 1 and then in Hail Mary, that is, the Annunciation (Lk. 1.28 and 38) and Mary's visit to Elizabeth (Lk. 1.42). The 15 scenes, which lead all the way to Mary's coronation as the Queen of heaven, combine Mariology and Christology. Mary is consistently considered together with her Son. A correct understanding of what really happened the day Gabriel visited the young Mary in her home in Nazareth is necessary for a correct Christology and vice versa. The Rosary played a role which can hardly be overemphasized for Catholic piety, and we may point to the role it played to keep the faith of the secret Japanese Catholicism alive for almost 300 years from the turn of the century in 1600.[18]

Thus a whole series of Marian events from the Bible and from the tradition of the Church were taken up, leading from the Annunciation in a humble home in a small Galilean village all the way to Mary's coronation as Queen over the whole of cosmos. This created a mighty frame of interpretation both for the Christ message of the Church and for the self-understanding of the pious Christian. Mary had been poor like so many

---

17. See, e.g., a painting by the fifteenth century artist Robert Campin, in C. Stuhl-mueller, 'Annunciation', in *New Catholic Encyclopedia*, I, pp. 562-65.

18. T. Fornberg, 'Kirishitan—ett ofrivilligt experiment i religiös inkulturering', *SEÅ* 63 (1998), pp. 273-80, and *idem*, 'Why the Queen of Heaven Married the King of the Philippines', *Swedish Missiological Themes* 87 (1999), pp. 21-28.

others, but by God's grace she was chosen for an incomparable task[19] and finally became glorified in a way that can never be grasped. But since the Rosary was not only made up of joyous and glorious mysteries (passages 1-5 and 11-15) but also of painful mysteries (passages 6-10), it was easy for all those who made the words of the Rosary their own to identify with Mary and hope for a joyful eternity. The history of art gives us many examples of this combination of joy and sorrow. To take one example: on the painting *The Annunciation* by Jan van Eyck (the 1430s) the angel radiates pure delight, while Mary lifts her hands as a symbolic gesture of suffering. This is also reflected by the motive on the floor on which they stand, showing the battle of David against the Devil in the figure of Goliath.[20] This is only one of many examples of how the Annunciation has been combined with the prophecy uttered by the old Symeon: 'Behold this child is set for the fall and the rising of many in Israel, and for a sign that is spoken against (and a sword will pierce through your own soul also), that thoughts out of many hearts may be revealed' (Lk. 2.34-35).

Biblia Pauperum

The Annunciation narrative is often taken up in the so-called *biblia pauperum*,[21] a series of biblical events, presented in chronological order, as is the case with the Creed and the Rosary.

Normally the chain of events starts with the creation of the world, then Lucifer's fall and as its consequence the fall into sin through the snake and Adam or, maybe more often, Eve.[22] The events following the fall are most often bypassed, and it is only with the events in the humble home in Nazareth that the *biblia pauperum* returns to the biblical story. After the scene with Gabriel and Mary and her *fiat* the most important events in the New Testament follow: Jesus' birth, death, resurrection and ascension, followed by the Assumption of the Virgin Mary to heaven and her coronation, almost making her into the fourth person in the Trinity.

19. Cf. Albino Luciani (Pope John Paul I), *Illustrissimi* (Boston: Little, Brown and Co., 1978), pp. 121-22 regarding a fictive epistle to King Lemuel of Massa.

20. W. Beckett, *Bonniers stora bok om måleriets historia* (Stockholm: Bonnier Alba, 1995), pp. 63-64.

21. R.P.L. Milburn, 'The "People's Bible": Artists and Commentators', in G. W.H. Lampe (ed.), *The Cambridge History of the Bible*, II (Cambridge: Cambridge University Press, 1969), pp. 280-308.

22. The tradition which put the blame for the fall into sin on Eve rather than on Adam (thus Sir. 25.24 and 1 Tim. 2.14) gained in importance in the High Medieval period.

The second characteristic of the *biblia pauperum* is the great number of references it makes to the history of Israel. The events mentioned in the Old Testament are looked upon as prophetic events prefiguring what later on took place in the Jesus story, the Annunciation being the first of these. As an example of such a *biblia pauperum* the lavishly illuminated *Codex Palatinus Latinus 871* from the fiftteenth century may be mentioned.[23] The various scenes from the salvation history beginning with the Annunciation and ending with the Coronation of the Virgin Mary are each interpreted through two Old Testament scenes which prefigure them and in addition through four prophetic figures, each one with a scriptural quotation which is given the same interpretation. The Old Testament is consistently understood with the help of typology, showing its true meaning when it is fulfilled in the Jesus story.[24] In the *Codex Palatinus Latinus 871* the following six Old Testament passages are given as prophecies pointing forward to the Annunciation in Nazareth. The two main passages are Gen. 3.14-15 about the woman and the snake and Judg. 6.36-40 on Gideon's wool. To these are added four extra passages: Isa. 7.14 on the virgin who shall conceive; Ezek. 44.2 on the gate which will remain closed; Ps. 71(72).6 on the rain which falls on the meadow; and finally Jer. 31.22 on the woman who shelters the man when God will create something new.

This very carefully thought through system aimed at an understanding of the links between the Old Testament and the New Testament. This understanding was made known to ordinary Christians through the paintings that illuminated many medieval churches, among them several churches around Lake Mälaren west of Stockholm, Härkeberga being the most well known of them. The artist Albertus Pictor of the late fifteenth century is the most famous of the artists behind these paintings.

The interpretive program in the *biblia pauperum* has a long prehistory, as is evident from other medieval books such as *Speculum Humanae Salvationis*[25] and various marginal notes, the so-called *Glossa Ordinaria*. These marginal notes were probably relatively incidental originally, and it was only later on that they began to reflect the official teaching of the church. The so-called *Speculum* refers not only to events in the Old Testa-

---

23. K.-A. Wirth (ed.), *Die Biblia Pauperum im Codex Palatinus Latinus 871 der Biblioteca Apostolica Vaticana* (Zürich: Belser, 1982).

24. Cf. how the emergent rabbinic theology emphasized the Torah and its various commandments, an interpretation which reached its definite written form in the Mishnah and the two Talmuds.

25. Milburn, 'The "People's Bible"', pp. 294-301 (297), 302-303.

ment but also sometimes to events outside of the biblical tradition. The
conclusion was evidently drawn that God's salvation plan also had been
prepared outside of the covenant with Israel. The same universalism had
been taken for granted by the Scholastic philosophers, when they referred
to Aristotle and other classical philosophers, and by an author such as
Thomas of Celano in his reference to the pagan Sibyl as an authority
together with David in his hymn *Dies irae*.[26] The plan of salvation includes the whole humankind, and at least occasionally the whole of
humankind has received a preliminary divine revelation. The preliminary
divine revelations, however, do not seem to have included any exact
knowledge of how this salvation was to start, that is the Annunciation for
the Virgin Mary. We find the following three scenes mentioned in the
Speculum: Moses and the burning bush (Exod. 3); Gideon with his wool
(Judg. 6); and Abraham's servant and Rebecca at the well (Gen. 24).

The Imitatio Mariae Ideal
Mary's answer in obedience to the words of the angel, *ecce ancilla domini*
(Lk. 1.38), shows her to be a humble servant of the Lord. She is then made
into a pattern to be imitated by the pious Christian, especially within
Franciscan piety, where humbleness was a central virtue.[27] It is no coincidence that paintings illustrating the Annunciation often show the words
ecce ancilla domini coming from Mary's mouth. Another example is provided by the famous work *De imitatione Christi* (4.17) by Thomas à
Kempis (c. 1380–1471). He emphasizes Mary's answer to the angel who
brought her the message of the mystery of Incarnation. In line with the
theme of the whole book—the Christian's humbleness and Christ-likeness
—Mary is here described as the one who already in the moment of the
Annunciation understood the real meaning of Christian humbleness. She is
made into a pattern to be followed by innumerable Christians, men as well
as women.

The Salvation Historical Pattern
The medieval typological interpretation of the Old Testament as we
encounter it in, for example, the *biblia pauperum* was very selective in its
use of Biblical passages. What had happened between the fall into sin and
the Annunciation hardly had any independent significance but pointed

---

26. Thomas of Celano was one of St Francis's earliest co-workers and thus lived in
the first half of the thirteenth century. It is supposed that he authored the *Dies irae*.
27. Warner, *Alone*, pp. 179-85.

forward to the culmination of the history of salvation. It was Mary's answer, *fiat mihi secundum verbum tuum*, which made this culmination into a reality. Her free acceptance of the words of the angel showing her preparedness for obedience made it possible for God to be born into the world and thus to save it. This perspective became evident, for example, with Bernhard of Clairvaux (1090–1153), when he consistently emphasized the biblical material and played down various apocryphal traditions of popular piety such as the *Protevangelium of James*.[28]

Medieval church art, for instance in many Swedish churches, shows unambiguously the great importance that was given to Mary's participation in the plan of salvation. Many baptismal fonts from the early medieval period as well as late medieval altar retables show various scenes from the biblical history. Frequently the first of these many scenes is the Annunciation scene, evidently understood to be the presupposition for what followed. The events surrounding the birth of Jesus are normally followed directly by his death and resurrection. As in the Creed the emphasis thus is laid on the Incarnation, made possible by Mary's free acceptance of her task, and on Jesus' death and final glorification. A variant of this progression, which is also very common, shows the Annunciation immediately followed by the meeting of Mary and her elderly relative Elizabeth. This association was made already by Luke in ch. 1 and was then taken up in the Hail Mary and thus entered the piety of the Christians.

Sometimes medieval iconography interprets the Annunciation and the mystery of Incarnation related to it with the help of an old mythical motif, the unicorn. According to the old myth, a unicorn, itself a symbol of chastity and goodness, can only be caught by an untouched girl. Thus the moment of the Annunciation and the conception in Mary's bosom has been depicted by artists who show a unicorn resting its head in Mary's lap. Such depictions from the fifteenth century can be found in some churches in the county of Uppland, among them Odensala.[29]

The Development of a High Mariology

Genesis 3.15, on how Eve's descendents shall crush the snake's head, is one of the Old Testament texts that have played the greatest role as an

28. B. Orchard, *Born to be King: The Epic of the Incarnation* (London: Ealing Abbey, 1993).

29. J. von Konow, B. Tunander and J. Bergström, 'Enhörning', in *Nationalencyklopedin*, V (Höganäs: Bra böcker, 1991), p. 522; and Burman, *Mariablomster*, p. 31.

interpretive pattern for the Annunciation scene.[30] The Hebrew wording evidently has a collective reference, later on developed in the Targums. Thus *Targo. Neaf.* reads:

> I put enmity between you and the woman, between her children and your children. And it shall happen that when her children observe the Law and the commandments, they shall aim at you, break your head and kill you. But when they fail to keep the commandments of the Law...[31]

In the Septuagint version we read the masculine pronoun *autos*, which opens up the way for an individualistic understanding of the word; a concrete male person among Eve's descendents will one day crush the head of the snake and thus nullify the consequences of the fall into sin. As was the case with Isa. 7.14, the Septuagint here prepares the way for a Christian reading of Gen. 3.15.

In the Latin tradition this development went further. The normative edition of the Vulgate reads the feminine pronoun *ipsa*, 'she',[32] which, however, is not used by Jerome. He did not yet understand the text mariologically. It is only in later manuscripts that it was understood as referring to the Church and still later to the Virgin Mary. But with the development of the high Mariology of the Middle Ages the feminine variant *ipsa* became popular as the scriptural proof needed to show that it was Mary's *fiat* that crushed the head of Satan. In spite of the fact that the Church had rejected the Pelagian heresy, Gen. 3.15 with the reading *ipsa* and Lk. 1.38 were combined to support the idea that the salvation of humanity still had been made possible by a human being, though supported by God's immeasurable grace. When the Vulgate (with *ipsa*) was declared the normative Bible of the Church, this reading became the real foundation for the continued development of Mariology.

The words *gratia plena* in Lk. 1.26 have been understood to convey the message that Mary has been given grace through which she has earned merits, which she later could forward to others. This idea is expressed in

30. E.F. Sutcliffe, 'Jerome', in G.W.H. Lampe (ed.), *The Cambridge History of the Bible*, II (Cambridge: University Press, 1969), pp. 80-101 (97-99).

31. Je mettrai une inimitié entre toi et la femme, entre tes fils et ses fils. Et il se fera que lorsque ses fils garderont la Loi et accompliont les commandements, ils te viseront, te briseront la tête et te tueront. Mais quand ils délaisseront les commandements de la Loi... Translation according to R. Le Deaut, *Targum du Pentateuques* I (SC, 265; Paris: Cerf, 1978), pp. 92-95.

32. J. Pelikan, *Mary through the Centuries* (New Haven: Yale University Press, 1996), p. 91.

hymns such as *Salve Regina* and *Ave Regina coelorum* from around 1100 CE.[33] Mary's being addressed as Queen in prayers and hymns is reflected by innumerable pictures which show how she is crowned as Queen of heaven. The concept of Mary as a queen, however, is much older than these pictures from the thirteenth century and onwards. Sometimes her queenship is combined with the Annunciation scene. This is the case with a well-known mosaic from the 430s in S. Maria Maggiore in Rome, the earliest Marian church in the Western part of the world. Mary is here depicted dressed as a Byzantine empress and sitting on a throne when Gabriel approaches her. This mosaic must be understood against the background of the council of Ephesus in 431 CE, when Mary was awarded the title *theotokos*. Thus this title became one of the instruments used for understanding the Annunciation scene. However, it is important to note that this mosaic is only one of several pictures with motifs from the childhood of Jesus. Thus its message is christological rather than mariological.[34]

In late medieval art we often find a detail which alludes to the conviction that the archangel Gabriel approached the Queen of heaven rather than a young Jewish girl. Thus it is depicted how Gabriel kneels or at least humbly bows down in front of Mary. As the Queen of heaven she is superior to Gabriel.[35]

The Division of the Western Church

The splitting-up of the Western Church in the early sixteenth century has a multi-faceted background. One may point to ecclesiastical demise with worldly popes and church dignitaries, a late medieval philosophy that tended to break up the unified scholasticism, and the Florentine Renaissance with its inheritance from antiquity and catchwords such as *ad fontes*.[36]

The study of the normative books of the church thus came to focus upon the canonical scriptures, including the pericope on the Annunciation in Luke 1, while an apocryphal story like the one in the *Protevangelium of*

33. H. Räisänen *et al.*, 'Maria/Marienfrömmigkeit', in *Theologische Realenzyklopädie*, XXII (Berlin: W. de Gruyter, 1992), pp. 115-61 (128; H. Grote). One may also note titles such as *mater misericordiae, spes nostra* and *advocata nostra*.

34. Räisänen *et al.* 'Maria', p. 158 (C. Nauerth).

35. One may compare the majestically tall angel on Duccio's painting of the Annunciation from 1278 CE with the humbly kneeling angel on Filippo Lippi's painting from the fifteenth century or on a painting by Rubens from 1609 CE.

36. Warner, *Alone*, pp. 244-45 and Pelikan, *Mary*, pp. 153-63.

James decreased in importance. This led to a very high Mariology, since the attempts at a strict exegesis of Gen. 3.15 and Lk. 1.28 proved to support an even stronger conviction of the Immaculate Conception.

Protestant theology supplemented the catchword *ad fontes* of the Renaissance with its own catchwords such as *sola scriptura* and *solus Christus*. Protestantism distanced itself from the classical Greco-Roman culture with its schools of philosophy as well as from the ecclesiastical tradition, in which Mariology often had lived its own life independent of Christology and ecclesiology. This independent life of Mariology perhaps found its clearest expression in the conviction that after her assumption into heaven Mary was crowned Queen of heaven, an idea that is difficult to find in the Bible if it is read in a historical way.[37]

Another important theme that summarized much of Protestant theology was *sola fide*, salvation through faith without any possibility of being helped by one's own qualifying acts. This conviction became of prime importance for the Protestant understanding of the figure of Mary. By necessity it ruled out her active participation in the salvation plan. Instead she was described as a pattern of faith to be followed by all Christians.[38]

In his Bible translation of 1522 Martin Luther, under the influence of the famous humanist Erasmus of Rotterdam, introduced his new understanding of Gabriel's words to the young Mary as 'Greetings to you, most beautiful', which broke with the Catholic understanding of the passage.[39] Erasmus and after him Martin Luther thus rejected the traditional interpretation according to the principle *sensus plenior* which had dominated the scene for several centuries.[40] This becomes still more evident when Luther on another occasion calls Mary *magna peccatrix*.[41]

In an Annunciation sermon Luther emphasized that God did not act in accordance with the normal order in nature in the virgin birth. Instead God gave a sign, which indicates that a totally new situation is at hand.[42] Luther's intention to be as close as possible to the thinking of the Early

37. See, e.g., de la Potterie, '*Kecharitōmenē*', p. 368. One may compare with early Protestant authors such as Flacius Illyricus, who understood the word *kecharitōmenē* with the help of the words *gratis diligo* with Mary as the object for God's action.

38. Pelikan, *Mary*, pp. 159-60.

39. Räisänen *et al.*, 'Maria' p. 135 (H. Grote) and de la Potterie, '*Kecharitōmenē*', pp. 359-60.

40. See, e.g., J. Fitzmyer, *The Gospel According to Luke (I-IX)* (AB, 28; New York: Doubleday, 1981).

41. De la Potterie, '*Kecharitōmenē*', p. 359.

42. Barth, *Dogmatik* I/2, p. 195.

Church, before the so-called *Frühkatholizismus*, became normative in Lutheranism. Thus an author such as Johann Gerhard (1582–1637) pointed to the virgin birth as a sign of God's unlimited power over nature.[43] It may be significant that this interpretation of the virgin birth, evidently independent of the emergent Catholic Church, is also expressed in the Quran with its background in Oriental, at least partly Jewish-Christian, theology.

Albrecht Bengel's well-known work *Gnomon* from 1742 may be mentioned as an example of Protestant interpretation of the Bible. He comments upon the words in Lk. 1.28 with the statement *Non ut mater gratiae, sed ut filia gratiae appellatur*,[44] of course intended to be read in an anti-Catholic way. This short note may exemplify the way in which German Protestantism actively argued against the Catholic interpretive tradition.

Another example of Protestant exegesis of the eighteenth century is given by the very extensive collection of biblical scholarship authored by Christoph Starke.[45] Starke argued openly against the Catholic understanding of the Annunciation on those points in which Protestantism had parted ways with Catholicism. However, he accepts the connection between how Eve became the instrument for sin to enter into the world while she was still a virgin, and how Mary, also a virgin, should bear the savior of this same world. But Starke went on to emphasize that Gabriel's greeting was given to Mary and that it belonged only to the historical situation described by Luke. Thus others must not use it:

> The words of the angel are a greeting at a special occasion. They cannot be used as a prayer by anyone at any occasion… The Papists have taken their *Ave Maria* from here and introduced it as a prayer only in 1090…

After having mentioned the use of the rosary the passage ends with the comment: 'Thus it is not only falsely changed into a prayer formula. In addition, it does not suit Mary any longer.' In what follows it is stated that Mary's embarrassed question in Lk. 1.34 does not at all mean that she had promised to live in chastity. Already the fact that she was engaged proves the opposite.

However, the authors and thinkers of Romanticism in the years around 1800 understood the figure of Mary against the background of the

---

43. Barth, *Dogmatik* I/2, p. 220.

44. A. Bengelius, *Gnomon Novi Testamenti [...]* (Tübingen: Schrammius, 1742), pp. 206-208.

45. C. Starke, *Synopsis Bibliothecae Exegeticae in Novum Testamentum: Kurzgefaster Auszug [...]*, IV (Leipzig: Breitkopf, 3rd edn, 1745), pp. 993-1002.

contemporary idea of woman as an exponent for 'the eternal feminine', the ideal human being who cannot become better, thus, for example, Johann Wolfgang von Goethe. Karl Barth countered much later that the virgin birth is totally at odds with nature and that it expresses God's grace toward his creation. He also distanced himself from Friedrich Schleiermacher's idea that the text about Jesus' birth shows that woman, contrary to man, does not really need any conversion.[46]

The Catholic Church

When Protestant theologians emphasized a literal interpretation of the Bible, Catholic theologians as well started to penetrate the concrete historical meaning of the biblical text, sometimes playing down the traditional understanding, based as it was on allegory and typology. We may mention Maldonatus[47] (died 1583) as an example of such a theologian. He referred to Gen. 43.23 in which Joseph comforted his brothers and Judg. 6.23 and 19.20 in which Gideon and a Levite were greeted with peace. Maldonatus sought to understand Gabriel's message to Mary with the help of Semitic idiom (Hebrew *shalom*) to mean that Mary was encouraged to feel joy over the message of peace that the angel conveyed.[48]

But the emphasis on the historical and literal meaning of the biblical text did not become normative. The influence from Catholic popular piety was too heavy. The prayers of the church and the eucharistic liturgy with their slow but steady development were mighty instruments for the preservation of centuries-old patterns of interpretation like typology and *sensus plenior*. Consequently the Annunciation became of prime importance because of its place as the introductory mystery of the Rosary. Maybe the best example of this is provided by the above-mentioned so-called *Kirishitan*, Japan's secret and, until the end of the nineteenth century, relentlessly persecuted Catholics.

During the first half of the twentieth century some cautious steps were taken toward a more historical way to interpret the Bible. It was no longer taken for granted that *kecharitōmenē* in Lk. 1.26 necessarily carried all the theology that ecclesiastical tradition had ascribed to it. No doubt, M.J. Lagrange was quite farsighted in his well-known biography of Jesus.[49]

46. Barth, *Dogmatik* I/2, pp. 197, 213. See Pelikan, *Mary*, pp. 165-75 on 'the eternal feminine'.

47. De la Potterie, '*Kecharitōmenē*', p. 362.

48. S. Lyonnet, '*Chaire kecharitōmenē*', *Bib* 20 (1939), pp. 131-41 (140).

49. M.J. Lagrange, *The Gospel of Jesus Christ* (Bangalore: Theological Publications in India, 1992 [French original 1928]), esp. pp. 15-21.

There he cautiously took up the critical questions, which were being asked in a new era, but he did this with a deep respect for the age-old tradition of the Church. He proposed that Mary had given a promise to remain a virgin, and he took for granted that Joseph had accepted this decision.[50] He considered the biblical text as basically historical, and he attempted to understand it in a way that made it relevant for a new age with its critical questions.

Protestant Preaching

Protestant preaching on the Annunciation will be exemplified by a couple of sermons by Lutheran pastors of the eighteenth and the nineteenth centuries. The 19th century saw a number of revivalist movements and the wide spread of literacy. As a consequence a great number of collections of sermons were printed and gained a wide circulation.

The famous work *Den fallna människans salighetsordning*[51] (1771) by Anders Nohrborg (1725–67) is one of the most important works from Swedish Pietism, with its emphasis on the individual's way to salvation, the so-called 'Nådens ordning'. Its first part has the subtitle 'The Reception of Grace and Blessedness through Christ' and starts with a detailed commentary on the Annunciation for the Virgin Mary. The text is interpreted in the light of Peter's confession according to Mt. 16.16, 'You are the Christ, the Son of the living God'. The message found in the text is totally christological, which, however, does not mean that the importance of the Virgin is denied. The fact that Mary bore the Son of God into the world guarantees the he is both God and man and that consequently he can atone for the sins of humanity.

Henric Schartau (1757–1825)[52] was another important revivalist preacher. Being a pastor in the university town of Lund he had a lasting influence on several generations of pastors in southwestern Sweden. Several summaries of his sermons on the Annunciation have been written down by his listeners and (posthumously) published. It is not always easy to find the connection between the underlying text and Schartau's sermons. Instead they seem to follow the principle that every sermon (as well as every single biblical text)

---

50. Thus already Thomas Aquinas; see E. Gratsch, *Aquinas' Summa* (Bangalore: Theological Publications in India, 1990), pp. 229-31.

51. A. Nohrborg, *Den Fallna Menniskans Salighets-Ordning...* (Lund: C.W.K. Gleerup, 10th edn, 1844), pp. 1-14.

52. H. Schartau (several collections of sermons and summaries of sermons).

shall express 'the whole gospel' about the salvation of humankind, of every single individual who repents. All texts, even those of such a specific character as the one about the Annunciation, express principally the same message about the individual Christian's choice of salvation or damnation.

This conclusion is quite evident when the themes of his published sermons on this text are taken into consideration:

1793 (1796, 1808)	'The great blessedness of those who have got the witness that they please God'.
1811	'The blessed condition of God's children'.
1815	'Jesus' great glory'.

An undated sermon has the theme: 'The comfort of repentant sinners, which they get from the fact that their Savior is both God and man'. To these sermons can be added a sermon on the epistle of the Annunciation day (in 1817) with the theme: 'How dangerous it is not to fear sin'.

Archbishop Johan Olof Wallin (1779–1839) once preached on Annunciation day on the theme 'The annunciation days of blessedness', focusing on how the young Mary proved to be 'worthy to listen to the heavenly greeting of peace'.[53] He continued: 'These were the words of the gospel of peace to a pure heart on this day of the annunciation of blessedness. This same gospel sounds even today for hearts which receive it in faith.' Here the Virgin Mary is made into a pattern to be followed by the individual Christian. The mysterious word about the Christian's partly unconscious existential questions reaches the Christian especially on certain days of grace, at birth, at baptism, at confirmation and one's first Eucharist (when she stands 'at the end of the calm valley of her childhood, looking forward to an unknown future'). The whole of nature then speaks with the same angelic voice as Gabriel once did. Wallin continues with a serious warning not to reject this voice. Toward the end of the sermon Wallin points to Mary's function as a pattern to be followed by everyone:

> The angels of Annunciation descend from heaven, announcing to everyone among the children of this world: Hail, you who are full of grace!…you, young and innocent…you, happy youth…you, repented slave of sin…you, tired wanderer on this earth…

In this sermon Wallin in his moralistic individualism is close to the pietistic tradition. In another sermon of 1827 on the Annunciation, Romanticism and

---

53. J.O. Wallin, *Predikningar över de årliga Sön- och Högtidsdagarnas Evangelier*, VI (Malmö: Världslitteraturens Förlag, 1930), pp. 128-45.

its ideas on what is specifically feminine have influenced him, and he finds a personification of all feminine virtues and values in Mary.[54]

Another important revivalist movement of the nineteenth century has made a deep imprint upon northern Scandinavia. It started with the Lutheran pastor Lars Levi Laestadius. One of this movement's most influential pastors was Aatu Laitinen (1853–1923) in Rovaniemi in northern Finland. He emphasized in an Annunciation sermon from 1885[55] how Mary preached about God's grace and love and how she answered in faith but still had to suffer the pains of the childbirth. When she answered, 'Behold, I am the handmaid of the Lord; let it be to me according to your word', she came 'to understand why God had let her bear his Son under her heart and be born as a human being through her'. Laitinen goes on to state that Mary could not yet really 'feel joy in the Lord' until she had been reborn much later after Jesus' death and resurrection. By combining these two Marian scenes—the one in her home in Nazareth and the one under the cross on Golgotha—she becomes a model for the Laestadian Christian and his or her way of life through his or her own conversion, necessary for every single individual.

Recent Developments

The School of Comparative Religion

The school of comparative religion with its background in critical historical exegesis quite naturally asked other questions than those posed by the above-mentioned preachers. Instead of reading the biblical text as God's message to humankind of all times, the text was understood as a document reflecting its own historical background. It was explained through what scholars knew about the historical situation and with the help of the arguments of causality characteristic of the age of Enlightenment. Thus the question about the possible background which the Annunciation may have in other religions was posed as well as its possible historicity, often answered negatively with arguments from a wide variety of old mythological parallel material.

Scholars have often hypothesized that the Annunciation scene as a whole or at least vv. 34-35 was created out of Isa. 7.14, since there might have been a need to find a possible fulfillment of this text in the New Testament. One well-known representative of this hypothesis was the

54. S.-E. Brodd, 'Exemplet af en ren och hjertlig fromhet', in H. Möller (ed.), *Johan Olof Wallin: En minnesskrift 1989* (Uppsala: Erene, 1989), pp. 162-202.

55. A. Laitinen, *Evangeliepredikningar* (Luleå: Laestadiana, 1976), pp. 193-96.

great liberal theologian Adolf von Harnack (1851–1930).[56] Other scholars[57] have answered that the Annunciation narrative cannot possibly have been created out of Isa. 7.14 and any need to find Isaiah's prophecy fulfilled in the Jesus story. The main argument for this denial is that the Isaiah text was not read as a messianic prophecy in contemporaneous Judaism.

Martin Dibelius (1883–1947) accepted a mythological understanding of the virgin birth but did not want to interpret it as a *hieros gamos*-motif. According to Dibelius, the Early Church did not take up Hellenistic concepts of divine sons. This was done only later when the Church expressed its message in the vocabulary and concepts of Greek culture.[58]

Fundamentalism

Fundamentalism[59] in the strict sense of the word emerged in the 1890s among conservative Protestants in the United States. It must be understood as a reaction against the emergence of modern science and critical biblical scholarship. This scholarship was not rejected because of its deficiencies but because it was considered as part of the threat against the faith of past generations that the modern time with its secularist patterns of thought meant. The biblical word was put forward as the single authority against everything that was new. Five points were singled out as the main points in this defense of the Christian faith, among them the virgin birth. This can hardly be distinguished from the Annunciation narrative. The virgin birth stands out as a naked fact without any real theological meaning in itself, but it must be 'believed', purely because it is to be read in the biblical text. Being a nature miracle the virgin birth was looked upon as historically impossible by many 'modern' scholars, for which reason it had to be defended as a test case of the absolute trustworthiness of the Bible.

Historical-Critical Commentaries on Luke from the End of the 1950s

There is no need here to describe the work that has been done by historical-critical scholars with the Annunciation pericope.[60] Every biblical text is studied in its own right. Thus, ideas from Matthew 1 with the quotation of Isa. 7.14 are not allowed to influence the understanding of Luke 1, and

---

56. A. von Harnack, 'Zu Lk 1,34-35', *ZNW* 2 (1901), pp. 53-57.
57. E.g. O. Piper, 'The Virgin Birth', *Interpretation* 18 (1964), pp. 131-48 (138-39).
58. Thus already Justin, *Dial.* 69-70.
59. J. Barr, *Fundamentalism* (London: SCM Press, 2nd edn, 1981), pp. 238-39.
60. See, e.g., Brown *et al.* (eds.), *Mary*, pp. 127-28, for a summary.

historical questions are dealt with seriously. Apologetic arguments are no longer allowed to influence the scholar in his or her work. It is of course another matter to what degree scholars really succeed in living up to their ideals. In reality there is often a clear connection between the religious or ideological background of a scholar and the results that he or she reaches.

Two examples will be given of Protestant commentaries, where it is clearly visible that the respective authors consciously argue against Jewish or Catholic patterns of interpretation. Thus Walter Grundmann, who became deeply involved in Nazism, quite naturally silently distanced himself from this in his commentary on Luke, written in the post-war Communist East Germany.[61] His idea that Mary was Aryan and not Jewish has now been left out as untenable. However, he still emphasizes that what took place in Nazareth was at odds with all possibilities within Judaism, especially the fact that Gabriel addressed a woman. He refers to a late Talmudic passage as support: 'It is not at all proper to greet a woman', evidently taken from Billerbeck's not always impartial collection of texts.[62] Grundmann also argues against Catholic authors who state that Mary was astounded by the message from the angel because she had already promised to live in chastity, a proposal that may also be ideologically biased. He describes this idea as 'a dogmatically governed makeshift solution'. In his argument that the virgin birth tradition is late he is opposed by commentator the Howard Marshall,[63] who considers it as early. This is not surprising since contrary to Grundmann, Marshall normally ascribes a high degree of historical trustworthiness to the gospel tradition, even if he expresses himself cautiously in this case. Marshall continues by emphasizing how traditional Catholic scholars have not been able to liberate themselves from theological presuppositions when they interpret this text.

While Protestant biblical exegesis quickly adjusted to the ideology of the Enlightenment with its critical questions to the biblical text, the real change in Catholic exegesis did not take place until the 1950s. The battle of Modernism at the turn of the century led to a situation of suspicion toward all attempts to work without presuppositions with biblical texts. As late as about 1960 conservative theologians in the Vatican forbade the

---

61. W. Grundmann, *Das Evangelium nach Lukas* (THKNT, 3; Berlin: Evangelische Verlagsanstalt, 4th edn, 1966), pp. 53-61.

62. *B. Qid.* 70a.

63. H. Marshall, *The Gospel of Luke* (NIGTC; Exeter: Paternoster Press, 1978), pp. 62-77.

progressive scholar Stanislas Lyonnet to teach, ironically enough under the pontificate of the progressive Pope John XXIII. Lyonnet had earlier published an article in *Biblica* in which he had argued that the introductory greeting *chaire* is to be translated 'rejoice' (in the salvation that has been made a reality through the birth of this child).[64] There is no doubt that he moved strictly within the boundaries of church tradition as regards the understanding of the Annunciation. But still his cautious historical and theological questions were sensitive for those who wanted to keep everything as it had been for centuries during the years that led up to the Second Vatican Council.

During the Council (1962–65) it became clear that the Fathers rejected the documents that had been written by the various preparatory committees, and the Catholic Church accepted the methods and results which had been accepted by Protestant theologians and scholars for several decades. In fact, it was Pope Pius XII who had made possible this new development in Catholicism through his encyclical *Divino afflante Spiritu* of 1943. This encyclical stressed the importance of the literary genres of the biblical texts and tended to play down the importance of interpretive models such as typology and *sensus plenior*. The mariological interpretation of the phrase *gratia plena*, when used about Mary as *mater gratiae*, can be considered as such a *sensus plenior*, in which the medieval authors went ahead of the probable historical meaning of the Lukan text.[65]

Josef Schmid was one of those German Catholic scholars who soon took up the 'Protestant' historical-critical interpretation of the word *kecharitōmenē*, thus in his commentary on Luke from 1960. Anton Vögtle went still further when he characterized the Annunciation as a theological motif without any historical basis.[66] Among American authors we may mention Joseph Fitzmyer and Raymond Brown,[67] who in spite of their faithfulness to the church have expressed the new perspectives with great force.

---

64. Lyonnet, '*Chaire*', pp. 131-41. See also references in, e.g., Marshall, *Luke*, p. 65, H. Schürmann, *Das Lukasevangeliums* I (Leipzig: St Benno, 1970), p. 39 and Fitzmyer, *Luke*, pp. 344-45.

65. Cf., e.g., Schürmann, *Das Lukasevangelium*, p. 45, where he states that we cannot find the Immaculate Conception in the biblical text through a philological-historical study but only thanks to the faith of the Church.

66. A. Vögtle, 'Offene Fragen zur lukanischen Geburts- und Kindheitsgeschichte', *Bibel und Leben* 11 (1970), pp. 51-67 (52-64).

67. See, e.g., R. Brown, *The Birth of Messiah* (New York: Doubleday, 1977), pp. 334-55.

Official Catholic Documents

The official documents of the Catholic Church from the last decades express both the traditional Catholic view and the historical-critical view. Thus the Council Decree on Revelation, *Verbum Dei* 7-10,[68] distinguishes between the original historical meaning, as it can be deduced with the help of modern Western exegesis, and the *sensus plenior* of a more or less technical sense, which the church later found in the text. Many normative theologians thus take the traditional faith of the church for granted and explain it with the help of modern scholarly theology. A good example is the textbook on the Creed that was written by (now) Cardinal Joseph Ratzinger in the years following the Council.[69]

In his apostolic encyclical *Marialis Cultus* (1974) Pope Paul VI expressed the traditional Catholic conviction that Mary said her *fiat* of her own free will at the Annunciation and thus actively contributed to the salvation of humanity. This is also valid for the encyclicals that have been authored by Pope John Paul II, for example, *Redemptoris mater* (1987) and *Mulieris dignitatem* (1988), as well as for the new Catechism.[70]

Modern Interpretations of Ancilla Domini

It is quite evident that Mary's answer *ecce ancilla domini* has normally been understood as an expression of her humble obedience to God's will. But in our own time many Christians have posed the question if this really conveys the true message that poor and harassed people can find in Mary's words to Gabriel. Liberation theologians from the so-called Third World countries and after them feminist theologians from North America and Western Europe[71] have pointed to a new combination of texts: Mary's words to Gabriel are now read in the light of her words in the Magnificat (Lk. 1.51-53):

---

68. W. Abbott and J. Gallagher, *The Documents of Vatican II* (London: Geoffrey Chapman, 1966).

69. J. Ratzinger, *Introduction to Christianity* (San Francisco: Ignatius, 1990 [German original 1968]), especially pp. 205-213.

70. *Catechism of the Catholic Church* (London: Geoffrey Chapman, 1994), pp. 108-114.

71. Many authors may be mentioned, e.g. Samuel Rayan from India, Tissa Balassuriya from Sri Lanka, Elisabeth Schüssler Fiorenza from the USA and Kari Börresen from Norway.

He has shown strength with his arm, he has scattered the proud in the imagination of their hearts, he has put down the mighty from their thrones, and exalted those of low degree; he has filled the hungry with good things, and the rich he has sent away empty.

Through this combination of texts we get a new picture of Mary, who is no longer an ideal of humility but rather of strength and willpower in this world. In this way Mary becomes a pattern of life for all those who want to make justice a present reality in this world. She stands out as a model for everyone, men as well as women, but especially for women who can identify with her in the unjust conditions of their lives but still have the power to rise up and fight for what is just and fair.

Thus a new combination of Marian texts will lead to a new image of Mary, an image that has hardly been seen before. We are reminded that biblical interpretation has never reached its end. A new age poses new questions and finds new answers. The encounter between the young Mary and the archangel Gabriel is reread from a new perspective and is found to convey a new message. The study of the Bible is always carried on in the crosscurrent between what is old and well known and what points to the future with all its challenges.

TRANSLATION AS INTERPRETATION[*]

Thor Strandenæs

Translation as Interpretation: The Problem

In Front of the Text

It is a fact that readers of the Bible have always needed interpretation. The original readers needed interpretation in order to bring the subject matter in contact with their religious and cultural universe. The same goes for modern Bible readers. The extent to which such interpretation is necessary may vary. But pure knowledge of a language or the ability to read it has never been sufficient for understanding biblical texts, even in New Testament times. Thus, in Acts 8.30-31 Philip asks the Ethiopian official, 'Do you understand what you are reading?' and receives the answer, 'How can I, unless someone guides me?'[1] Here, the verb ὁδηγέω obviously refers to systematic biblical teaching or an exposition of the Old Testament texts with regard to their messianic message and their bearing on the person and work of Jesus. In this essay, however, I will not pursue the issue of interpretation or exposition of the biblical texts as such, but deal specifically with the relation of interpretation to translation in the preparation of Bible versions for modern readers.

There are many translators and theologians who have shown the extent to which translation both involves interpretation and is itself, to a certain degree, also to be regarded as interpretation. While dealing with the question of how to translate the divine names David Cunningham has pointed out that: 'to translate is to interpret, and one never translates without remainder. There must be multiple names for God, for there are many

*   This is a revised and enlarged edition of my contribution in seminar group 4 on hermeneutical problems. I am thankful for the constructive critique and suggestions received there.

1.   Likewise Jesus expounds the Old Testament scriptures to the Emmaus walkers, Lk. 24.27; cf. also Jn 16.13.

languages—among which there can never be exact replication, but always interpretation.'[2]

Thus interpretation is involved in translation. And rather than challenging the title of this chapter, I shall presuppose its truth and proceed to ask: what does it *imply* that translation is regarded as interpretation?

What Kind of Translation?
Before proceeding further it is necessary to determine on which kind of translation we should focus. As Sjölander has observed, the time has probably passed for ever when one version alone will entirely dominate the scene, and the existent multiplicity of versions has its advantages as it enables readers to choose versions which suit their ability and stylistic tastes.[3]

Some purposes may be combined in one version, others not.[4] If one settles for a linguistic translation, this excludes a cultural-historical one. The former aims at bringing the reader of today back to the ancient texts, making him or her understand what they meant to their contemporary readers. The latter aims at answering the question: what meaning do these texts have in the different cultural contexts in which people live today? Although both purposes meet valid needs it is advisable to take as our point of departure that the mainstream version(s) must be linguistic translation(s), rather than cultural-historical. There are at least three important reasons for this. First, if ordinary Bible readers who are not trained in Greek or Hebrew are to discuss issues in the Bible with people belonging to other linguistic groups or faiths, they must as far as possible be able to turn to versions representing similar or identical attitudes to translation. Otherwise a dialogue might soon be impossible. This has some analogy with Origen's compilation of *Hexapla* for the purpose of fruitful discussion of matters of faith in the Old Testament with Jewish rabbis.[5] Second,

2.   D.S. Cunningham, 'On Translating the Divine Name', *TS* 56 (1995), pp. 415-40 (426).

3.   P. Sjölander, 'Some Aspects of Style in Twentieth-century English Bible Translation: One-man versions of Mark and the Psalms' (Doctoral dissertation; University of Umeå, 1979), p. 180.

4.   W.L. Wonderly, *Bible Translations for Popular Use* (Helps for Translators, 7; London: United Bible Societies, 1968), pp. 28-31, has listed factors that affect different types of translations and shown the relation between linguistic situations and types of translation.

5.   This 85-volume work was made to meet the need of Christians who, unable to

the translation must present a text which is not a historical falsification, making Bible readers believe matters to be different, better or worse than that expressed in the originals. Third, the translation must contribute to preserving continuity in the reception history of texts, between modern readers and readers in the past. After all, Scripture is a religious, historical and culturally relevant document for both past and modern times.[6]

With a linguistic translation in mind, what will be the sense of 'interpretation'? It is true that 'exegesis' and 'hermeneutics' are used almost indistinguishably by some writers and may both be included in the term 'interpretation'. In a linguistic translation, however, interpretation is used in its sense of historical-linguistic exegesis. This distinguishes it from hermeneutics, which must be reserved for the cultural-historical interpretation, a task which belongs to the teacher, preacher, philosopher or sociologist in their attempt to bridge the historical and cultural gap between modern and ancient readers, when asking what is the meaning or relevance of these documents to the lives of modern people. I am not in any way suggesting that interpretation in the first sense is a neutral process, free from ideological or theological bias, and will deal with this aspect shortly.

In the Text and behind the Text[7]
First of all, the process of translating obviously involves coming to grips with the meaning of the originals. Before one translates a historical document one must establish—as far as possible—the meaning it carried for the original readers. Translators must therefore possess sufficient knowledge of the language of the original text as well as the culture in which it was communicated, including such socio-political, religious and cultural factors as are relevant to deciphering its meaning. When establishing the

read and understand Hebrew, needed proof to meet accusations that their Scripture quotations were not contained in the original Hebrew text.

6.   Its religious, historical and cultural relevance is demonstrated in the presentation by Tord Fornberg in the previous article in this volume.

7.   In his instructive book *Contextual Bible Study* (Pietermaritzburg: Cluster Publications, 1993), p. 24, Gerald West distinguishes between three modes of reading the Bible critically: 1) reading behind the text—focusing on the historical and sociological context; 2) reading the text itself—focusing on the literary and narrative context; and 3) reading in front of the text—focusing on the major metaphors, themes and symbols that are projected by the text. The first two modes are oriented toward the past, the times contemporary to the composition of the biblical texts, and represent the historical-exegetical approach. The third mode focuses on present times and readers and represents cultural-historical translation.

historical meaning of texts interpretation therefore plays a necessary part of the process. Quite often interpretation involves choosing between two or more possible referential meanings in the original text. A classic example is the possible ways of rendering ἐντὸς ὑμῶν in Lk. 17.21: 'within you' or 'in the midst of you'.[8] In some languages a choice is necessary which is not called for in others. Such choices in translation may often express different schools of New Testament interpretation.

In the Authorized Version of 1611 (AV), the English Revised Version of 1881 (RV) (as well as The American Standard [edition of the English revised] Version of 1901 [ASV], the rendering 'the kingdom of God is within you' reflects a non-eschatological sense. The kingdom of God, understood individualistically as growing and developing from within each person, fits the tenets of modern liberal theology as well as a more mystic understanding which was preferred in medieval times until well beyond the Reformation.

In the Revised Standard Version (1946 and 2nd edn. 1971, RSV), the New English Bible (1961 and 2nd edn. 1970, NEB) *et alii*, 'the kingdom of God is among you' has been used, a translation that is open to both a present and future meaning. Here an eschatological dimension has been introduced.

The different choices show that theological orientations or beliefs bear on the choices which translators make. Robert P. Carroll reflects this point well when he states that Bible translation…is an attempt to provide as accurate a translation as possible, *within the constraints set by the prevailing ideology of the group translating and publishing the Bible'*.[9] Carroll goes on to say that the cultural and ideological biases of the old Bible translations are more easily detectable, since they appear as notes and annotations to the text. But a translation without accompanying notes can be a very misleading document, since it appears to be neutral. Modern translations also carry the biases of the translators. It is therefore necessary that readers—and translators—should be aware that any act of translation represents but *one* interpretation of Scripture. In some modern versions

8.   The former can be found in the Authorized Version, the Revised Version, the New International Version and the Good News Bible; the latter in the Revised Standard Version, the Jerusalem Bible, likewise in the Norwegian Bible Society Bibelen (1978 edition: 'iblant dere').

9.   R.P. Carroll, 'Cultural Encroachment and Bible Translations: Observations on Elements of Violence, Race and Class in the Production of Bibles in Translation', *Semeia* 76 (1996), pp. 39-53 (47).

this awareness has led the translators/publishers to include a preface wherein the guiding principles are made known. Two examples of this in English are the prefaces to the New International Version (NIV) and Today's English Version (TEV). But the discussions which these versions have caused show that the prefaces to each of them could have contained even more relevant information. Each group of translators therefore followed up with such information later.[10] This shows how important it is that principles which guide a translation are spelled out and known to its readers.

Second, interpretation also involves choosing between several possible ways of rendering into the receptor language(s), as Cunningham stated at the beginning of this article. Even when taking for granted the basic principle of deWaard and Nida, *that translating means translating meaning*,[11] translation is a process which involves deciding between multiple possible choices in the receptor language(s). Since each language has its own genius,[12] the kind and number of choices which must be made varies from one receptor language to another. In languages such as Shona, East Nyanja, Yao, Lomwe and Marathi, a term that covers both 'within' and 'among' is recorded for Greek ἐντός.[13] In English as well as other languages, however, this is not the case, and a choice between the two must be made when translating, as with the ἐντὸς ὑμῶν in Lk 17.21. Thus, the translators must be as familiar with the cultures and languages of the original texts as with those of the receptor groups.

In the very act of translating, translators are aware that the number of choices may not, after all, be that many, since words and clusters of words are translated in a specific literary context. As stated by Ernst R. Wendland,

> One finds that words used in their primary sense in the Scriptures, i.e., that meaning which is the most relevant culturally and which collocates with the largest and most diverse group of items, usually present little problem in the process of message transfer, except in cases where that particular meaning

10. *Questions and Answers about the New Translation.* (New York: International Bible Society, [no date]), and E.A. Nida, *Good News for Modern Man* (Waco, TX: Word Books 1977).

11. J. deWaard and E.A. Nida, *From One Language to Another: Functional Equivalence in Bible Translating* (London: Thomas Nelson, 1986), pp. 60-77.

12. E.A. Nida and C.R. Taber, *The Theory and Practice of Translation* (UBS Helps for Translators; Leiden: E.J. Brill, 1974), pp. 3-5.

13. J. Reiling and J.L. Swellengrebel, *A Translator's Handbook on the Gospel of Luke* (London: United Bible Societies, 1971), p. 588.

or sense is unknown in the R[eceptor]L[anguage] environment. It is the
secondary senses and extended (including nonliteral) usages which cause
special difficulty due to the inevitable incompleteness of lexical equivalence between languages.[14]

I shall return later to some of the challenges which such secondary
senses and extended usages represent for translators.

Interpreting before Translating

When discussing translation theoretically it is tempting to presume that
translation precedes interpretation. After all, translators should struggle
with the texts themselves, not study them through filters provided by
exegetes and commentators. When engaging in actual translation work,
however, one soon discovers that translating is an involved process in
which interpretation plays an important role. After all, the translators must
be as certain as possible that they have grasped the intended meaning of
the author of a text or of the participating subjects of a discourse. This can
only be done adequately by means of commentaries which shed light on
linguistic, historical, religious and other sociocultural aspects of the texts.[15]

E.R. Hope has demonstrated how textual analysis is an integral part of
the translation process. In his analysis of the book of Jonah he points out
how the study of pragmatics has made it possible to be much more objective when establishing the intended meaning of the biblical author than
often assumed.[16] For the translator, as well as the exegete, it is important
to be able to describe adequately the presuppositions derived from the total
culture and belief system of the author, or those of the participating
subjects of the discourse. More important still is the ability to recognise
their influence in the interpretation of texts. Another kind of presuppositions is also mentioned by E.R. Hope, namely, those which arise from the
discourse itself: 'Each individual speech act becomes part of the context of
the subsequent set of sentences, and influences the interpretation of those
sentences by creating additional presuppositions'.[17]

14. E.R. Wendland, *The Cultural Factor in Bible Translation* (UBS Monograph
Series, 2; London: United Bible Societies, 1987), p. 57.
15. Some valuable assistance for Bible translators have been provided by the
United Bible Societies in the *Helps for Translators Series* which includes *Technical
Helps*, *Handbooks* and *Guides* to each of the scriptural books.
16. E.R. Hope, 'Pragmatics, Exegesis and Translation', in P.E. Stine (ed.), *Issues in
Bible Translation* (UBS Monograph Series, 3; London: United Bible Societies, 1988),
pp. 113-28 (113, 117-18).
17. Hope, 'Pragmatics', p. 118.

This not only demonstrates how closely connected interpretation is with translation. It shows the importance as well of understanding a Scripture portion as a whole before proceeding to the act of translating it. For this purpose interpretation is necessary. As deWaard & Nida said:

> ...a translation should faithfully reflect who said what to whom under what circumstances and for what purpose and should be in a form of the receptor language which does not distort the content or misrepresent the rhetorical impact or appeal...[18]

Another effect which a thorough interpretation has on translation is the awareness it creates in the translators for searching carefully such semantic structures in the receptor language as may adequately render the meaning of the originals. Thus interpretation both facilitates a better understanding of the originals and paves the way for better communication in the receptor language.

In the following I shall give three examples from the New Testament of how translators may be tempted to tamper with the texts. All are concerned with the problem of so-called *corrective translation* and demonstrate how important it is to maintain the distinction between interpretation in its sense of exegesis or analysis and interpretation in the sense of hermeneutics.

Three Examples of Corrective Translation

Male Dominant View of History and Events in the New Testament
The first example concerns the problem of a male dominant view of history and events or, to put it in other words, whether ridding the New Testament text of a male dominant view of history and events is justified in translation. It is a fact that in many texts a male point of view is taken. In the New Testament letters the addressees are the *hoi adelphoi*, 'the brothers', and God is addressed as 'father'. Some have insisted on introducing so-called inclusive language solutions, replacing the former with 'brothers and sisters' and the latter with 'father and mother'.[19] But this means introducing cultural anachronisms and contextual distortions, both of which are to be avoided if one is to be faithful to the sense of the

---

18. DeWaard and Nida, *From One Language to Another*, p. 40.

19. DeWaard and Nida have rightly pointed out that to translate the latter 'as both "father and mother" is to create a bisexual God, not a sexually neutral God' (*From One Language to Another*, p. 24).

originals. Although one may take for granted that the early church of Philippi and Thessaloniki included women and not only men, 1 Thessalonians constantly addresses the 'brothers' (e.g. 2.1, 17; 4.1, 13).[20] In Philippi Paul and his fellow travellers, having been released from prison, went to Lydia's house, where they met 'the brothers' (Acts 16.40).[21] This obviously reflects the contemporary social customs: the male members of society were the public figures and official receivers of correspondence.

Moreover, by anachronistically replacing 'father' with 'father and mother' one forgets that religious language is highly figurative and rich in metaphors and that the word 'father' itself carries metaphoric meaning, a meaning it must maintain in the context in order not to create distortion of meaning in the translated text. Whether or not 'father' carries the right associative meaning to a reader who has herself/himself been mentally or physically abused by her/his father, or is thoroughly disappointed by him, must be clarified in a consequent hermeneutical process. As deWaard and Nida sum up: 'In addition to letting the Scriptures speak for themselves, it is essential to accurately reflect the cultural contexts of biblical times, whether ideological, sociological, or ecological'.[22]

Oppressive Political Tendencies in the New Testament
The second example concerns oppressive political tendencies, or rather whether one is justified in making use of the New Testament translation for the purpose of political oppression.

An example of this is the translation of portions of Scripture prepared by missionaries for the Panare Indians of the Venezuelan interior, where *hoi Ioudaioi* was translated by 'the Panare', a totally anachronistic choice.[23] The Panare Indians were thereby made personally responsible for the killing of Jesus, giving them 'the guilt for an act utterly unconnected with

---

20. The reference to 'all the believers' in 1 Thess. 5.26 demonstrates that the letter itself makes conscious distinctions. In other of his letters, the apostle Paul sends specific greetings to female members of the congregation, e.g., in Col. 4.15 and Rom. 16.3-15.

21. For a study of *adelphoi* and its context in 1 Thessalonians, see B. Johansen, *To All the Brethren: A Text-Linguistic and Rhetorical Approach to 1. Thessalonians* (ConBNT, 16; Stockholm: Almqvist & Wiksell, 1987).

22. DeWaard and E.A. Nida, *From One Language to Another*, p. 24.

23. N. Lewis, *The Missionaries: God against the Indians* (New York: Penguin, 1990), pp. 209-210; cf. N. Lewis, *Unreasonable Behaviour: An Autobiography* (London: Vintage, 1992), pp. 192-201.

them'.[24] This kind of diachronic translation, albeit practised by some in biblical exposition and preaching, is a falsification when it comes to rendering historical documents.[25] At the same time this is an example of how people in power, in this case some missionaries, are able to use their influence to manipulate and change the message of a version so that it stigmatizes an identified group. In recent times the history of apartheid in Africa has demonstrated how detrimental such an attitude is in general as well as with regard to instances of translation. Thus, translation must show accountability with regard to historical and sociocultural matters in the texts.

Arousing, Maintaining, Furthering or Preventing Anti-Semitism in Translation?

The third example concerns the problem of inherent anti-Semitism in New Testament texts, or rather whether ridding the New Testament text of supposed anti-Semitic tendencies is permissible in a translation.

One of the issues that has been encountered in dialogues between Jews and Christians is how the New Testament contributes to anti-Semitic feelings and movements in churches and society. If a translator wishes to lessen the degree to which the texts arouse anti-Semitic feelings, the danger of corrective translation occurs. In a provocative study Tina Pippin has pointed out some of the problems encountered in rendering the 71 references to *Ioudaioi* in the Gospel of John.[26]

1   By keeping the literal meaning 'the Jews', one perpetuates the hateful polemic.
2   By referring 'to Judeans or Jewish religious authorities, one dilutes the force of the ethnic verbal warfare'—a warfare resulting in 'so much more than a first-century dispute'.
3   By translating *hoi Ioudaioi* as 'Judahites' or 'the religious authorities'—depending on the context—one covers for the text.
4   By keeping [the Jews] surrounded by brackets as translation, the difficulties, context and history of text must be explained by glosses in accompanying notes (in the margins or between the lines).

24. Carroll, 'Cultural Encroachment', p. 45.

25. As remarked by Carroll ('Cultural Encroachment', p. 46), they were only following the customary missionary practice of making their audience personally responsible for the death of Christ.

26. T. Pippin, '"For Fear of the Jews": Lying and Truth Telling in Translating the Gospel of John', *Semeia* 76 (1996), pp. 81-97 (93).

Among the four options, Pippin prefers the fourth, but does not leave the issue with this, stating that:

> Any of these choices is vague and problematic, the cultural context of John's gospel is indeterminate, and 'equivalent' meanings in English are bound up in a dangerous and violent memory. I want to expose that memory and raise awareness about the ethical issues and stakes.[27]

She therefore approves of the basic principle adopted at the Stony Point consultation, 'that to best combat anti-semitism, one must interpret, not just translate or substitute'.[28] Basically, however, Pippin thinks that the very act of translating John 8 itself is a betrayal of the Jews and that the translator commits a crime in the very act of translating it, saying: 'The root of the problem of anti-jewishness is in the text, in the mouth of Jesus, and in Christianity itself... It is the responsibility of translators and readers to transform this history, this gospel message.'[29] Thus, she opts for a principle of corrective translation.

It should be stated here that Pippin in her argumentation is uncritically dependent on the controversial thesis of Rosemary Radford Ruether, namely that the New Testament is anti-Judaic and therefore anti-Semitic.[30] Truly, throughout history individual texts or the entire New Testament have been defined by some readers as anti-Judaic or even anti-Semitic.[31] However, in his comprehensive analysis, António Barbosa da Silva has demonstrated that Ruether's thesis is only partly true. His conclusion is that the New Testament is anti-Judaic *only* in the senses described as follows:[32]

27. Pippin 'For Fear of the Jews', p. 93.
28. *Bible Translation Utilization Committee, 1993.3*, quoted by Pippin, '"For Fear of the Jews"', p. 93.
29. Pippin, '"For Fear of the Jews"', p. 94.
30. R. Radford Ruether, *Faith and Fratricide: The Theological Roots of Anti-Semitism* (A Crossroad Book; New York: The Seabury Press, 1974) pp. 88-89.
31. Logically, however, the word 'Semitic' covers a much wider range of peoples than the Jews. It cannot therefore be used in any way to describe the realities to which 'Jew/the Jews' refer in the New Testament.
32. A. daSilva, *Is there a New Imbalance in Jewish-Christian Relations? An Analysis of the Theoretical Presuppositions and Theological Implications of the Jewish-Christian Dialogue in the Light of the World Council of Churches' and the Roman Catholic Church's Conceptions of Inter-Religious Dialogue* (Studia Missionalia Uppsaliensia, 56; Uppsala, 1992), p. 132. In the opinion of daSilva, Radford Ruether's thesis is not true with respect to the assertion that 'the New Testament is anti-Judaic, i.e., against Judaism in all its forms or expressions throughout the entire history of Judaism'.

(ii)   the New Testament is anti-Judaic, i.e., against *only* the form in which Judaism expressed itself in New Testament times, especially with regard to some Pharisees and Sadducees.

(iii)   The New Testament has (a) *always* been read as anti-Judaic, or the New Testament (b) has *sometimes* been read as anti-Judaic.

Da Silva's analysis shows that although the New Testament may be characterized as anti-Judaic in these senses, it is not thereby itself anti-Jewish.[33]

The question, however, is: does the extensive process of *righting the wrongs* in the Bible really belong to the translators, rather than to the commentators, interpreters and expositors of historical texts? As already hinted at in the two previous examples, I think not. That writers of exegetical works, when interpreting these historical documents, should be free to comment on the possible wrongs inherent in the texts themselves and/or in their *Nachgeschichte*, I think is justified. But, engaging in political, racial, gender- and class oriented purifying or re-interpretation of the texts in translation itself is a degree of hermeneutic work which results in emending the documents rather than translating them. Righting the wrongs, therefore, should belong to the dialogue in the wake of the translated texts, to humane behavior and to illuminating comments accompanying the texts in modern versions. This in turn may prepare the grounds for a changed attitude.

Greenstein, in a response to Pippin which challenges the principle of corrective translation, has given two reasons for keeping the effort of translation distinct from that of hermeneutics: 'privileging the source, and affording the reader more options in making sense of the translated text'.[34] This means that the translator is obliged to translate every occurence of the Greek Ἰουδαῖος / Ἰουδαῖοι *in context*, paying attention to its possible semantic domains as well as to the bearings the given context has on determining which of these meanings it carries there. In other words the translator ought to minimize the use of filters which prevent modern readers from coming as close as possible to the historical document and judging for themselves its quality and contents. And, since often the translated text is the basis on which the common Bible reader founds his or her opinions, its text should be accessible with all its greatness and limitations.

From what we have seen so far translation as interpretation is a matter of degree rather than of principle, since all translation work employs

33. daSilva, *Is there a New Imbalance*, pp. 132-46.
34. E.L. Greenstein, 'On the Ethics of Translation', *Semeia* 76 (1996), pp. 127-34 (129).

interpretation to some extent. Translators of historical texts, and particularly of scriptural texts, should however—and here I follow Greenstein—[35] avoid incorporating a high degree of hermeneutics into a rendering. The degree to which the Bible is used in interfaith dialogues and is challenged there by critics of historical principles of translation calls for editions where annotations at the bottom of pages or on separate pages—as in study editions—become the rule rather than the exception.

Rewriting the history of Christianity by cleansing its texts from mistakes and all traces of oppressive activities is not possible, unless the purpose is deception. Likewise, the texts of Christianity—including the Bible—cannot be amended or stripped of their human weaknesses, sociocultural embedding, and limitations without transforming them into entirely new and different documents, thereby deceiving the readers. If Christianity cannot accept the humiliating fact that such limitations which characterize humankind also apply to the Scriptures, it denies the historical nature of its own documents.

Interpreting the Readers and the Readers' Culture

Bridging Two or More Cultures

The sociocultural background and worldview of the intended readers condition their perception and understanding of Scripture.[36] In fact, the diversities in the practices and beliefs of different cultures represent the main difficulties in translation. Thus in addition to interpreting the originals and their cultural contexts, translators are faced with the need for interpreting the culture of the readers as well. This is necessary if translators are to fulfill their obligation: 'Translating consists in reproducing in the receptor language *the closest natural equivalent* of the source language message, first in terms of meaning, and secondly in terms of style'.[37]

Ernst R. Wendland has aptly shown that the problem affecting many translators is not that they are overly contextualized in the direction of the receptor culture; more frequently it is a matter of being undercontextualized.[38] He points out two major reasons for this deficiency:

---

35. Greenstein, 'On the Ethics of Translation', p. 129.
36. Wendland (*The Cultural Factor in Bible Translation*) has devoted particular attention to this challenge to translation.
37. Nida and C.R. Taber, *The Theory and Practice of Translation*, p. 12.
38. See Wendland, *The Cultural Factor in Bible Translation*, p. 192, for this and the following.

—a literal method of translation, which places more emphasis upon the S[ource] L[anguage] form of the message than upon its contemporary meaning in the R[eceptor] L[anguage]; and

—a lack of cultural awareness generally, with regard to the biblical context as well as that of the translators themselves and their constituency.

The result is a text which does not communicate to receptors as it should, either formally (i.e., the language is unnatural) or functionally (i.e., the communicative intentions of the original source are not realized).

Interpreting the readers and their culture is therefore an obligation for any translator. This is not less true in the case of translating metaphors and other figurative extensions of meaning.

Basically, figurative language is employed whenever non-figurative use of language would not be able to express the same as adequately. One should therefore take care not to lose this dimension of the originals when translating.[39] But the fact that figurative meanings tend to be 'culture specific' makes it all the more challenging for translators to deal with them.[40] This does not mean that one is left with only the choice of a literal translation in case of figurative language. Wonderly has listed five techniques for handling metaphors in translation.

—use literal translation, if the reader is likely to understand it
—convert the metaphor to simile, that is: make explicit the figurative nature of the expression
—convert a metaphor to a nonmetaphor
—combined treatment, which means: retaining the metaphor or converting it into a simile and supplementing it with a non-figurative statement of the meaning implicit in the figure

39. In the case of, e.g., Revelation it would conflict with the character and nature of the original text to reduce significant metaphors or all metaphors to non-metaphors. The object of the translator must be to make the words and expressions in the receptor language function as metaphors in the same way as they do in the original. Rather than avoiding totally the use of the Chinese word *lung* (= 'dragon') for the Greek δράκων in Rev. 12.3 (and subsequent instances in Rev. 12–13)—due to its overall positive connotations in the Han-Chinese language and wider cultural context— a qualifier should be sought which maintains the use of figurative language. Lü Chen-chung overcame this problem in his translation (1968) by employing a qualifying word, *lü* (= 'perverse'). He thereby managed to preserve the notion of evil as well as the metaphor.

40. deWaard and Nida, *From One Language to Another*, p. 153; for dealing with literal and figurative meanings see the entire section, pp. 152-58.

> —convert a metaphor to a different metaphor, that is: making use of a
> well-known metaphor instead of an unfamiliar one which people are not
> likely to understand[41]

And of these five techniques, only the third implies avoiding figurative language. The entire problem posed by figurative language shows how necessary it is for a translator to be able to interpret both the meaning of figurative extension of language in the originals as well as the effect which any solution is likely to have on potential readers and hearers.[42]

Are the Words and Concepts Really that Culturally Unfamiliar?
A special challenge to the Bible translator is the translation of the name of God in the Bible.[43] The UBS Statement 'How to translate the Name' includes five options for translating biblical divine names, namely transliteration, translating as 'Lord', translating the meaning of *YHWH*, using a name from the culture, and translating *YHWH* and *Elohim* in the same way.[44] A sixth option is also possible: the use of a combination from the other five options.

To indigenous inhabitants of a culture transliteration suggests that there is no existing name of God in the culture which adequately renders the biblical name. But it also implies that the god to whom the Bible refers was not known by another name and therefore did not exist in this culture prior to the arrival of the religions of the Book: Judaism, Christianity, Islam. The theological implications of this from the perspective of a traditional trinitarian Christian faith are obvious: the Creator is introduced together with the Book only!

Mojola has told us, that in the Iraqw-language of Tanzania, the Swahili word *Mungu* had been employed in the New Testament translation of 1977 for ὁ θεός. In the trial edition of Genesis and the book of Ruth the Iraqw

41. Wonderly, *Bible Translations for Popular Use*, pp. 121-28.

42. deWaard and Nida (*From One Language to Another*, p. 152) have shown the importance of being concerned with the corresponding literal significance of figurative meaning, since there is always a factor of psychological awareness involved.

43. For a long time H. Rosin, *The Lord is God: The Translation of the Divine Names and the Missionary Calling of the Church* (Amsterdam: Nederlandsch Bijbelgenootschap, 1956) was the standard work dealing with this problem. In recent years the discussion has been raised anew in R.P. Sharleman (ed.), *Naming God* (New York: Paragon House, 1985) and in *The Bible Translator* (e.g. *BT* 43 (1992), pp. 403-406).

44. 'How to Translate the Name: Statement by the "Names of God" Study Group, U.B.S. Triennial Translation Workshop, Victoria Falls, Zimbabwe, 8–21 May 1991', *BT* 43 (1992), pp. 403-406.

name *Looa* was employed for God. A favorable reception on behalf of the iraqw Christians was expected, but many found it unacceptable as a rendering for the name of God. Their protest went along two lines. First, *Looa* is associated with the sun; some people may even identify her with the sun.[45] To this Mojola comments: 'There is no doubt that the Iraqw see Looa as the supreme God. The sun is understood to be only a symbol of the supreme God. It is not itself God, but God's eye. This is similar to the Akan of Ghana who speak of God, *Nyame*, as "the Giver of light or sun"'.[46]

Secondly *Looa* in Iraqw-religion is described as feminine, while in the Greek and Hebrew testaments God is generally described as masculine. However, with regard to the overall qualities appropriated to *Looa*, they correspond well with God as described in the Bible: *Looa* is kind, merciful, the creator and protector, the giver of life, children, and blessing. She cares for her children, nourishes and protects them. She represents light, grace and motherhood.[47] As we know, both Old Testament and New Testament use the metaphor of God as mother, for example in Isa. 49.13-15 and Mt. 23.37 / Lk. 13.34. The good qualities of God are referred to as *Looa*. In *Iraqw*, however, the supreme evil is conceived of as fatherhood. Darkness, vengeance, death, destruction and evil are all connected with fatherhood, *Neetlangw*.[48] It seems therefore that *Neetlangw* cannot be used and that there is a lot more to lose by adopting the foreign name for god—the Swahili *Mungu*—than using *Looa*. The Great Mother was also a well-known deity in Asia Minor and Greece in New Testament times, but could not challenge the notion of God as father, and in particular as father of the Son, Jesus Christ. This—and the ecumenical problem of referring to God as 'she', when most cultures, including the New Testament original text, refer to him as 'he'—still remains unsolved. While awaiting a solution, Mojola reminds the translators:

> The point is that both fatherhood and motherhood are metaphors, linguistic pictures, necessarily grounded and bound in time and space, and in particular historical cultures, subject to the circumstances of human cultural and linguistic change. It may be pointed out that the truths these metaphors convey are still valid and relevant. But how these truths are to be represented,

45. A.O. Mojola, 'A "Female God" in East Africa: The Problem of Translating God's Name among the Iraqw of Mbulu, Tanzania', *BT* 46 (1995), pp. 229-36 (232).
46. Mojola, 'A "female" God in East Africa', p. 233.
47. Mojola, 'A "female" God in East Africa', p. 235.
48. Mojola, 'A "female" God in East Africa', pp. 234-35.

pictured, and communicated is a function of particular cultures and languages.[49]

Theologically speaking, the issue is whether or not God—as known in the Bible—is only introduced to a culture and a language upon the arrival of Christianity. Is it really necessary to borrow the name of God from Swahili, Greek, Hebrew or any other language if one is to identify the God of the Bible? Since religious language is generally agreed to be essentially metaphorical and used often in a non-literal sense, the gender question seems to be a much lesser problem than having to introduce a god into a culture who is a total stranger, even as creator. The fear of using the indigenous name may become an unnecessary obstacle for introducing Christian faith. As Mojola puts it:

> It should be noted that in general the use of God's name in the indigenous language and culture has helped to develop strong point of contact between the new faith and the indigenous traditional faith. It provides continuity and a basis for conversation between the new and the old. It provides a strong basis for giving a Christian meaning to existing forms and beliefs—adding, subtracting, or changing them as necessary. It makes possible a less hurtful transformation of the old and an easier translation to the new.[50]

Thus, translation as an act of inculturation of religious texts also reflects theological choices. In the case of translating the name of God the issue at stake is not purely linguistic.

The choice may in fact decide whether or not the biblical God is to be considered interesting or even relevant at all for people in the receptor culture. Although a historical document, the Bible is also a collection of religious texts, and as such is in dialogue with peoples of different cultures and times. In spite of all the socio cultural differences, humankind shares some basic needs and abilities which either facilitate communication or prevent it. Common human experience from life is used to interpret new or familiar information. In making the Bible understood to readers in a different culture, translators must aim at communicating at the same 'wavelength' as the intended readers. The effect of interpretation depends on the ability to distinguish clearly and communicate effectively the intended meaning of the original texts. In doing so, one always depends on common human experience in one culture to communicate to the other. In the cases of figurative language and the name and concept of 'God' one constantly

---

49. Mojola, 'A "female" God in East Africa', p. 236.
50. Mojola, 'A "female" God in East Africa', p. 231.

depends on recognizing the familiar as well as the unfamiliar, and must use the familiar to express the unfamiliar.[51] As an interpretive process, translation cannot do without this.

Translation as Contextualizing

In dealing with our topic it seems wise, finally, also to address another area of theological contextualization,[52] more specifically, the field of liturgical contextualization. Here the results of the *Worship and Culture* program of the Lutheran World Federation may be of help. In dealing with the question of inculturating the Christian liturgy in specific cultures, the studies have revealed that—among several possible methods—there are basically two main approaches to inculturation, namely the method of creative assimilation and the method of dynamic equivalence:[53]

> Creative assimilation tends to introduce new elements, while dynamic equivalence, which is a type of translation, confines itself to transmitting the content of a liturgical rite in a new cultural pattern. One thing to remember is that these two methods can overlap and need each other for a fuller effect.[54]

Transferred to the field of translation, one may say that whereas dynamic equivalence is an adequate way to go about translating, creative assimilation belongs to the process of exposition and of making the significance of the texts understood in the modern cultural context where they are read. This is further illustrated in Chupungco's definition of liturgical inculturation.[55]

---

51. Isomorphs are commonly used features of similarity and contrast in communication. Basically they are of two types, those which preserve information and those which alter information. (deWaard and Nida, *From One Language to Another*, pp. 63-71).

52. S.B. Bevans, *Models of Contextual Theology* (Maryknoll, NY: Orbis Books, 1992), presents five models for contextual theology.

53. These roughly correspond to the anthropological model and the translation model of Bevans (Bevans, *Models of Contextual Theology*), respectively, representing opposite ends of a spectrum.

54. A.J. Chupungco, 'Two Methods of Liturgical Inculturation's in S.A. Stauffer (ed.), *Christian Worship: Unity in Cultural Diversity* (Geneva: The Lutheran World Federation, 1996), pp. 77-94 (94).

55. For a fuller treatment of the term 'inculturation', see A.J. Chupungco, *Liturgical Inculturation: Sacramentals, Religiosity, and Catechesis* (Collegeville, MN: Liturgical Press, 1992), pp. 13-36.

It is a process whereby pertinent elements of a local culture are integrated into the worship of a local church. Integration means that culture influences the way prayer texts are composed and proclaimed, ritual actions are performed, and the message expressed in art forms. Integration can also mean that local rites, symbols and festivals, after due critique and Christian reinterpretation, become part of the liturgical worship of a local church.

One result of inculturation is that the liturgical texts, symbols, gestures and feasts evoke something from the people's history, traditions, cultural patterns and artistic genius. We might say that the power of the liturgy to evoke local culture is a sign that inculturation has taken place.[56]

Something is always lost when translating, but then something new is also gained. If what is gained makes the translation stand out as being in no rapport whatsoever with the original, the translation itself is bad or the interpretive activity has gone too far. In a consistent cultural-historical translation this could be the case: one might not be able to recognize the stories of the Bible from one culture to another.

Nida and Taber define cultural translation as opposed to linguistic translation as 'a translation in which the content of the message is changed to conform to the receptor culture in some way, and/or in which information is introduced which is not linguistically implicit in the original'.[57] Linguistic translation, however, is

a translation in which only information which is linguistically implicit in the original is made explicit and in which all changes of form follow the rules of back transformation and transformation and of componential analysis;...Only a linguistic translation can be considered *faithful*.[58]

To use the parallel of liturgical inculturization: In a cultural translation the drive is toward creative assimilation; in a linguistic translation toward functional (or dynamic) equivalence. But whereas most linguistic translations will always move somewhere between creative assimilation and functional equivalence, good translations will abide by functional equivalence and leave the creative assimilation to the field of biblical interpretation or textual exposition. In this sense translation presupposes interpretation without being reduced to mere interpretation.

---

56. Chupungco, 'Two Methods of Liturgical Inculturation', p. 77.
57. Nida and Taber, *The Theory and Practice of Translation*, p. 199.
58. Nida and Taber, *The Theory and Practice of Translation*, p. 203.

Conclusion: Thesis Confirmed and Modified

In the presentation above I have drawn attention to several aspects of interpretation in Bible translating. They are not intended to be exclusive in any way, but are nevertheless representative. Although 'exegesis' and 'hermeneutics' are used almost indistinguishably by some writers, I have used interpretation to refer to the role of the linguistic translator, as distinct from that of the cultural-historical one, as played by the teacher/preacher, the philosopher or the sociologist.

In this essay 'interpretation' is used in the sense of understanding and choosing between possible ways of understanding the originals. It is also used when looking for adequate renderings in the receptor language. When dealing with religious concepts and figurative language in religious documents such as the Bible the ability to interpret both original and receptor cultures is important for an adequate result.

I have also maintained that translation of historical and religious documents must not include so-called corrective interpretation, intended to rectify or polish away any unsympathetic impression left by the originals on modern readers. This must be so, since the role of the translator is to preserve the original authenticity of the documents throughout the translation process. Translators must therefore leave to biblical hermeneutics the discussion of how to interpret texts from Antiquity to modern times. This is also a kind of translation process, but of a cultural-historical and not linguistic kind. This does not mean that readers of a translation should be left without such information which may enable them—on the one hand— to understand better the socio political, historical and religious environment of the texts, and—on the other—to become more aware of problems which these texts have caused in the course of history, and still cause. This information must be provided but should be found in exegetical notes in the margins. And such notes, I think, must be provided plentifully. In this way informed readers will be able to enter discussions on questions related to, for example, elements of violence, race, gender and class in the Bible, even when their discussion partners have no proficiency in the original languages of the Bible.

Thus the thesis of this chapter is both confirmed and modified: translation is interpretation, but not mere interpretation. In mainstream versions the role of the translator is to provide a linguistic translation based on an exegetical interpretation of the originals, faithfully preserving and not altering their message. It is the role of hermeneutics to provide a cultural-historical interpretation which bridges the historical, cultural and religious gap between the original readers and the present. Such kind of interpretation is to be done *in front of the text*, which is the next step and which must not be confused with translation itself.

BIBLIOGRAPHY

Abegg, M.G., '*Paul,* "Works of the Law" and MMT', *BARev* 20 (1994), pp. 52-55.

–'4QMMT C27, 31 and Works Righteousness', DSD 6 (1999), pp. 139-47.

Abbott, W., and J. Gallagher, *The Documents of Vatican II* (London: Geoffrey Chapman, 1966).

Aejmelaeus, L., *Die Rezeption der Paulusbriefe in der Miletrede (Apg 20.18-35)* (Annales Academiæ Scientiarum Fennicæ, B/232; Helsinki: Suomalainen Tiedeakatemia, 1987).

Alexander, L., *The Preface to Luke's Gospel: Literary Convention and Social Context in Luke 1.1-4 and Acts 1.1* (SNTSMS, 78; Cambridge: Cambridge University Press, 1993).

Allison, D.C., *The New Moses: A Matthean Typology* (Philadelphia: Fortress Press, 1993).

Arnim, H.v. (ed.), *Stoicorum Veterum Fragmenta*, III (Lipsiae, 1903).

Aune, D.E., Revelation *1–5* (WBC, 52; Dallas: Word Books, 1997).

—*The New Testament in its Literary Environment* (LEC, 8; Philadelphia: Westminster Press, 1987).

Bachmann, M., '*4QMMT* und Galaterbrief, *ma'ase ha-torah* und *erga nomou*', *ZNW* 89 (1998), pp. 91-113.

Baillet, M. (ed.), *Qumran Cave 4, III* (DJD, 7; Oxford: Clarendon Press, 1982).

Baltensweiler, H., 'Das Gleichnis von der selbstwachsenden Saat (Mk 4.26-29) und die theologische Konzeption des Markusevangelisten', in F. Christ (ed.) *Oikonomia: Heilsgeschichte als Thema der Theologie* (Festschrift Oscar Cullmann; Hamburg: Herbert Reich Evang. Verlag, 1967), pp. 69-75.

Barr, J., *Fundamentalism* (London: SCM Press, 2nd edn, 1981).

Barth, K., *Die Kirchliche* Dogmatik I/2 (Zürich: Zollikon, 1938).

Bauckham, R., *The Climax of Prophecy: Studies on the Book of Revelation* (Edinburgh: T. & T. Clark, 1993).

Bauer, W., and K. Aland, *Wörterbuch zum griechischen Neuen Testament* (Berlin: W. de Gruyter, 6th edn, 1988).

Bäumer, R., and L. Scheffczyk (eds.), *Marienlexikon* (6 vols.; St Ottilien: EOS Verlag, 1988–1994).

Baumgarten, A.I., 'Crisis in the Scrollery: A Dying Consensus', *Judaism* 44 (1995), pp. 399-413.

Baumgarten, J.M., 'Sadducean Elements in Qumran Law', in E. Ulrich and J.C. VanderKam (eds.), *The Community of the Renewed Covenant* (Notre Dame, IN: University of Notre Dame Press, 1994), pp. 27-36.

—'The "Halakha" in MMT', *JAOS* 116 (1996), pp. 512-16.

Baur, F.C., *Paulus, der Apostel Jesu Christi* (Stuttgart: Becher & Müller, 1845) [= 2nd ed., vol. I, Leipzig: Fues's Verlag, 1866]).

Beale, C.K., 'Revelation', in Carson and Williamson (eds.), *It is Written: Scripture Citing Scripture*, pp. 318-36.

Beaton, R., 'Messiah and Justice: A Key to Matthew's Use of Isaiah 42.1-4?', *JSNT* 75 (1999), pp. 5-23.

Becker, J., *Jesus von Nazareth* (Berlin: W. de Gruyter, 1996).

Beckett, W., *Bonniers stora bok om måleriets historia* (Stockholm: Bonnier Alba, 1995).

Beld, A., 'Romans 7.14-25 and the Problem of *akrasia*', *Religious Studies* 21 (1985), pp. 495-515.

Bengelius, A., *Gnomon Novi Testamenti [...]* (Tübingen: Schrammius, 1742).

Benhabib, S., 'The Generalized and the Concrete Other: The Kohlberg-Gilligan Controversy and Feminist Theory', in S. Benhabib and D. Cornell (eds.), *Feminism as Critique: Essays on the Politics of Gender in Late-Capitalist Societies* (Feminist Perspectives; Cambridge, MA: Polity Press, 1987), pp. 77-95.

Berger, K., *Qumran und Jesus: Wahrheit unter Verschluss?* (Stuttgart: Quell, 1993).

–*Theologiegeschichte des Urchristentums: Theologie des Neuen Testaments* (UTB für Wissenschaft: Grosse Reihe; Tübingen: Francke, 1994).

Betz, H.D., *Galatians* (Hermeneia; Philadelphia: Fortress Press, 1979).

Betz, O., 'The Qumran Halakhah Text Miqsat Ma'ase Ha-Torah (4QMMT) and Sadducean, Essene, and Early Pharisaic Tradition', in D.R.G. Beattie and M.J. McNamara (eds.), *The Aramaic Bible: Targums in their Historical Context* (JSOTSup, 166; Sheffield: JSOT Press, 1994), pp. 176-202.

Bevans, S.B., *Models of Contextual Theology* (Maryknoll NY: Orbis Books, 1992).

Black, M. (ed.), *Apocalypsis Henochi Graeci* (PVTG, 3; Leiden: E.J. Brill, 1970).

Blomberg, C.L., *Interpreting the Parables* (Leicester: Apollos, 1990).

Boccaccini, G., *Beyond the Essene Hypothesis: The Parting of the Ways between Qumran and Enochic Judaism* (Grand Rapids: Eerdmans, 1998).

Boucher, M., *The Mysterious Parable: A Literary Study* (CBQMS, 6; Washington: Catholic Biblical Association, 1977).

Boyarin, D., *Carnal Israel: Reading Sex in Talmudic culture* (The New Historicism: Studies in Cultural Poetics, 25; Berkeley: University of California Press, 1993).

Braun, H., *Spätjüdisch-häretischer und frühchristlicher Radikalismus: Jesus von Nazareth und die essenische Qumransekte* (BHT, 24; 2 vols.; Tübingen: J.C.B. Mohr [P. Siebeck], 1957; 2nd edn, 1969).

Broadhead, E.K., *Naming Jesus: Titular Christology in the Gospel of Mark* (JSNTSup, 175; Sheffield: Sheffield Academic Press, 1999).

Brodd, S.-E., 'Exemplet af en ren och hjertlig fromhet', in H. Möller (ed.), *Johan Olof Wallin: En minnesskrift 1989* (Uppsala: Erene, 1989), pp. 162-202.

Brooten, B., *Love between Women: Early Christian Responses to Female Homoeroticism* (The Chicago Series on Sexuality, History, and Society; Chicago: University of Chicago Press, 1996).

—*Women Leaders in the Ancient Synagogue: Inscriptional Evidence and Background Issues* (BJS, 36; Chico, CA: Scholars Press, 1982).

Brown, R., *The Birth of Messiah* (New York: Doubleday, 1977).

Brown, R., *et al.* (eds.), *Mary in the New Testament* (Philadelphia: Fortress Press; New York: Paulist Press, 1978).

Bruce, F.F., *The Epistle to the Galatians: A Commentary on the Greek Text* (NIGTC; Exeter: Paternoster Press, 1982).

Bultmann, R., *Die Geschichte der synoptischen Tradition* (FRLANT, 29; Göttingen: Vandenhoeck & Ruprecht, 9th edn, 1997).

—'Römer 7 und die Anthropologie des Paulus' (1932), in *idem*, *Exegetica: Aufsätze zur Erfor-*

schung des Neuen Testaments (ed. E. Dinkler; Tübingen: J.C.B. Mohr [Paul Siebeck], 1967), pp. 198-209.

Burman, E., *Mariablomster* (Stockholm: Rabén & Sjögren, 1989).

Byrskog, S., *Jesus the Only Teacher: Didactic Authority and Transmission in Ancient Israel, Ancient Judaism and the Matthean Community* (ConBNT, 24; Stockholm: Almqvist & Wiksell, 1994).

—'Matthew 5.17-18 in the Argumentation of the Context', *RB* 104 (1997), pp. 557-71.

—'Slutet gott, allting gott: Matteus 28.16–20 i narrativt perspektiv', in B. Olsson, S. Byrskog and W. Übelacker (eds.), *Matteus och hans läsare—förr och nu: Matteussymposiet i Lund den 27–28 april 1996* (Religio, 48; Lund: Teologiska institutionen, 1997), pp. 85-98.

—*Story as History—History as Story: The Gospel Tradition in the Context of Ancient Oral History* (WUNT, 123; Tübingen: Mohr Siebeck, 2000).

Byrne, B., *Romans* (Sacra Pagina, 6; Collegeville, MN: Liturgical Press, 1996).

Callaway, P.R., '4QMMT and Recent Hypotheses about the Origin of the Qumran Community', in *Mogilany 1993: Papers on the Dead Sea Scrolls* (Krakow: Enigma Press, 1996) pp. 15-29.

Cansdale, L., *Qumran and the Essenes: A Re-Evaluation of the Evidence* (Texte und Studien zum Antiken Judentum, 60; Tübingen: J.C.B. Mohr, 1997).

Caquot, A., 'Un exposé polémique de pratique sectaires (4QMMT)', *RHPR* 76 (1996), pp. 257-76.

Carrell, P.R., *Jesus and the Angels: Angelology and the Christology of the Apocalypse of John* (SNTSMS, 95; Cambridge: Cambridge University Press, 1997).

Carroll, R.P., '*Cultural Encroachment* and Bible Translations: Observations on Elements of Violence, Race and Class in the Production of Bibles in Translation', *Semeia* 76 (1996), pp. 39-53.

Carson, D.A. and H.G.M. Williamson (eds.), *It is Written: Scripture Citing Scripture* (Festschrift Barnabas Lindars; Cambridge: Cambridge University Press, 1988).

Chatman, S., *Story and Discourse: Narrative Structure in Fiction and Film* (Ithaca, NY: Cornell University Press, 1978).

Chilton, B.D., *The Isaiah Targum: Introduction, Translation, Apparatus and Notes* (The Aramaic Bible, 11; Edinburgh: T. & T. Clark, 1987).

Chupungco, A.J., *Liturgical Inculturation: Sacramentals, Religiosity, and Catechesis* (Collegeville, MN: Liturgical Press, 1992).

—'Two Methods of Liturgical Inculturation', in S.A. Stauffer (ed.), *Christian Worship: Unity in Cultural Diversity* (Geneva: The Lutheran World Federation, 1996), pp. 77-94.

Collins, J.J., *The Scepter and the Star: The Messiahs of the Dead Sea Scrolls and Other Ancient Literature* (New York: Doubleday, 1995).

Conzelmann, H., *Die Apostelgeschichte* (HNT, 7; Tübingen: J.C.B. Mohr, 1963).

—*Die Mitte der Zeit: Studien zur Theologie des Lukas* (BHT, 17; Tübingen: J.C.B. Mohr 5th edn, 70, 1964).

Crossan, J.D., *In Parables: The Challenge of the Historical Jesus* (Sonoma, CA: Polebridge Press, 1994)

Cullmann, O., *Die Christologie des Neuen Testaments* (Tübingen: Mohr Siebeck, 5th edn, 1975).

Cunningham, D.S., 'On Translating the Divine Name', *TS* 56 (1995), pp. 415-40.

Dalman, G., *Arbeit und Sitte in Palästina* (7 vols.; BFCT; Gütersloh: C. Bertelsmann, 1928–42).

Barbara da Silva, A., *Is there a New Imbalance in Jewish-Christian Relations? An Analysis of* the Theoretical Presuppositions and Theological Implications of the Jewish-Christian Dialogue in the Light of the World Council of Churches' and the Roman Catholic Church's Conceptions of Inter-Religious Dialogue* (Studia Missionalia Uppsaliensia, 56; Uppsala, 1992).

Davidson, M.J., *Angels at Qumran: A Comparative Study of 1 Enoch 1-36, 72-108 and Sectarian Writings from Qumran* (JSPSup, 11; Sheffield: Sheffield Academic Press, 1992).

Davies, P.R., 'Halakah at Qumran', in *Sects and Scrolls: Essays on Qumran and Related Topics* (Atlanta: Scholars Press, 1996), pp. 113-26.

Davies, W.D., *The Setting of the Sermon on the Mount* (Cambridge: Cambridge University Press, 1964).

—'Was There Really a Qumran Community?', *Currents in Research: Biblical Studies* 3 (1995), pp. 9-35.

de la Potterie, I., '*Kecharitōmenē* en Lc 1.28: Etude philologique', *Bib* 68 (1987), pp. 357-82, 480-508.

de Beauvoir, S., *The Second Sex* (trans. H.M. Parshley; London: Vintage Books, 1953).

deWaard, J., and E.A. Nida, *From One Language to Another: Functional Equivalence in Bible Translating* (London: Thomas Nelson, 1986).

Dodd, C.H., *The Parables of the Kingdom* (London: Nisbet & Co., 3rd edn, 1936).

Dombrowski, B.W.W., '4QMMT after DJD X: Qumran Cave 4. Part V', *The Qumran Chronicle* 5 (1995), pp. 151-71.

Donahue, J.R., *The Gospel in Parable* (Philadelphia: Fortress Press, 1990).

Dormeyer, D., 'Mt 1.1 als Überschrift zur Gattung und Christologie des Matthäus-Evangeliums', in C.M. Tuckett, G. Van Belle and J. Verheyden (eds.), *The Four Gospels 1992* (Festschrift F. Neirynck; 3 vols.; BETL, 100A-C; Leuven: Leuven University Press, 1992), II, pp. 1361-83.

Dunn, J.D.G., *A Commentary on the Epistle to the Galatians* (London: A. & C. Black, 1993).

—*Romans 1-8*, I (WBC, 38A, Dallas: Word Books, 1988).

—'4QMMT and Galatians', *NTS* 43 (1997), pp. 147–53.

Ebertshäuser, C. *et al.*, *Mary: Art, Culture, and Religion through the Ages* (New York: Crossroad, 1998).

Egeland, K., 'Problemet som ikke (vil) finnes', *Kvinneforskning* 23.1 (1999), pp. 80-88.

Eisenman, R.H., *James the Just and the Habbakuk Pesher* (Leiden: E.J. Brill, 1986).

Eisenman, R.H., and M.O. Wise, *The Dead Sea Scrolls Uncovered* (Shaftesbury: Element Books, 1992).

Ejrnæs, B., 'Pesher-litteraturen fra Qumran', in N. Hyldahl and T.L. Thompson (eds.), *Dødehavsteksterne og Bibelen* (FBE, 8; Copenhagen: Museum Tusculanum, 1996), pp. 27-39.

Ekenberg, A., *Låt oss be och bekänna* (Örebro: Libris, 1996).

Engberg-Pedersen, T., 'Galatians in Romans 5-8 and Paul's Construction of the Identity of Christ Believers', in T. Fornberg and D. Hellholm (eds.), *Texts and Contexts: Biblical Texts in their Textual and Situational Contexts* (Festschrift Lars Hartman; Oslo: Scandinavian University Press, 1995), pp. 477-505.

—*Paul and the Stoics* (Edinburgh: T. & T. Clark; Louisville, KY: Westminster/John Knox Press, 2000).

Eriksson, A., '"Women Tongue Speakers, Be Silent": A Reconstruction through Paul's Rhetoric', *BibInt* 6 (1998), pp. 80-104.

—'Bibelns auktoritet och kvinnors erfarenhet', in P. Block *et al.* (eds.), *Om tolkning. V. Bibeln som auktoritet* (Tro & Tanke; Stockholm: Svenska kyrkans forskningsråd, 1998), pp. 134-46.

—*The Meaning of Gender in Theology. Problems and Possibilities* (Uppsala Womens' Studies A. Women in Religion, 6; Stockholm: Almqvist & Wiksell, 1995).

Erlemann, K., 'Adolf Jülicher in der Gleichnisforschung des 20. Jahrhunderts', in Ulrich Mell (ed.), *Die Gleichnisreden Jesu 1899–1999: Beiträge zum Dialog mit Adolf Jülicher* (BZNW, 103; Berlin: W. de Gruyter, 1999), pp. 5-37.

Eshel, H., '4QMMT and the History of the Hasmonean Period', in Kampen and Bernstein (eds.), *Reading 4QMMT*, pp. 53-65.

Evans, C.F., *Saint Luke* (TPI New Testament Commentaries; London: SCM Press; Philadelphia: Trinity Press International, 1990).

Fatum, L., '*Image of God* and Glory of Man: Women in the Pauline Congregations', in K. Børresen (ed.), *Image of God and Gender Models* (Oslo: Solum, 1991), pp. 56-137.

—'Tango med en tidsel—om at finde værdigheden i elendighedsforskningen', in I. Brohed, U. Görman and T.N.D. Mettinger (eds.), *Feministteologi i dag: Sju föreläsningar til Kerstin Aspegrens minne* (Religio, 30; Lund: Teologiska Institutionen i Lund, 1989), pp. 85-105.

—'Women, Symbolic Universe and Structures of Silence: Challenges and Possibilities in Androcentric Texts', *ST* 43 (1988), pp. 61-80.

Fee, G., *The First Epistle to the Corinthians* (NICNT; Grand Rapids: Eerdmans, 1987).

Fiebig, P., *Die Gleichnisreden Jesu im Lichte der rabbinischen Gleichnisse des neutestamentlichen Zeitalters: Ein Beitrag zum Streit um die 'Christusmythe' und eine Widerlegung der Gleichnistheorie Jülichers* (Tübingen: J.C.B. Mohr [Paul Siebeck], 1912).

Fitzmyer, J., *The Gospel According to Luke (I-IX)* (AB, 28; New York: Doubleday, 1981).

Flusser, D., 'Die Gesetzwerke in Qumran und bei Paulus', in P. Schäfer (ed.), *Geschichte—Tradition—Reflexion*. I. *Iudentum* (Festschrift M. Hengel zum 70. Geburtstag; Tübingen: J.C.B. Mohr, 1996), pp. 395-403.

Fornberg, T., 'Kirishitan—ett ofrivilligt experiment i religiös inkulturering', *SEÅ* 63 (1998), pp. 273-80.

—'Why the Queen of Heaven Married the King of the Philippines', *Swedish Missiological Themes* 87 (1999), pp. 21-28.

Fuchs, E., *Hermeneutik* (Tübingen: J.C.B. Mohr [Paul Siebeck], 4th rev. edn, 1970).

Gatzweiler, K., 'Les récits de miracles dans l'Évangile selon saint Matthieu', in M. Didier (ed.), *L'Évangile selon Matthieu: Rédaction et théologie* (BETL, 29; Gembloux: Duculot, 1972), pp. 209-220.

Geist, H., *Menschensohn und Gemeinde: Eine redaktionskritische Untersuchung zur Menschensohnprädikation im Matthäusevangelium* (FzB, 57; Würzburg: Echter Verlag, 1986).

Gerhardsson, B., 'Gottes Sohn als Diener Gottes: Messias, Agape und Himmelsherrschaft nach dem Matthäusevangelium', *ST* 27 (1973), pp. 73-106.

—'Sacrificial Service and Atonement in the Gospel of Matthew', in R.J. Banks (ed.), *Reconciliation and Hope: New Testament Essays on Atonement and Eschatology* (Festschrift L.L. Morris; Exeter: Paternoster Press, 1974), pp. 25-35.

—*The Mighty Acts of Jesus According to Matthew* (trans. R. Dewsnap; Scripta Minora, 1978-79.5; Lund: C.W.K. Gleerup, 1979).

Gese, H., 'Erwägungen zur Einheit der Biblischen Theologie', *ZTK* 67 (1970), pp. 417-36; repr. in H. Gese, *Vom Sinai zum Zion: Alttestamentliche Beiträge zur biblischen Theologie* (BevT, 64; Munich: Chr. Kaiser Verlag, 1974), pp. 11-30.

Gieschen, C.A., *Angelomorphic Christology: Antecedents and Early Evidence* (AGJU, 42; Leiden: E.J. Brill, 1998).

Golb, N., *Who Wrote the Dead Sea Scrolls? The Search for the Secret of Qumran* (New York: Charles Scribner's Sons, 1995).

Goranson, S., 'Essene Polemic in the Apocalypse of John', in J. Kampen (ed.), *Legal Texts and Legal Issues: Proceedings of the Second Meeting of the International Organization for Qumran Studies Cambridge 1995* (Festschrift Joseph M. Baumgarten; Leiden: E.J. Brill, 1997), pp. 453-60.

Gratsch, E., *Aquinas' Summa* (Bangalore: Theological Publications in India, 1990).

Greenstein, E.L., 'On the Ethics of Translation', *Semeia* 76 (1996), pp. 127-34.

Grelot, P., 'Les oevres de la Loi', *RevQ* 16 (1994), pp. 441-48.

Gruenwald, I., '*4QMMT*: Its Significance for the Study and Understanding of Ancient Judaism and Early Christianity' (seminar paper presented at the SNTS meeting in Copenhagen, 1998).

Grundmann, W., *Das Evangelium nach Lukas* (THKNT, 3; Berlin: Evangelische Verlagsanstalt, 4th edn, 1966).

Græsholt, G., 'Er Filon bare et sidespor?', *DTT* 56 (1993), pp. 19-34.

Gundry, R.H., 'Angelomorphic Christology in the Book of Revelation', *SBLSP* 33 (1994), pp. 662-78.

Haenchen, E., *Die Apostelgeschichte* (Kritisch-exegetischer Kommentar über das Neue Testament, 3; Göttingen: Vandenhoeck & Ruprecht, 13th edn, 1961) (= idem, *The Acts of the Apostles* [Philadelphia: Westminster Press, 1971]).

Hahn, F., *Christologische Hoheitstitel: Ihre Geschichte im frühen Christentum* (FRLANT, 83; Göttingen: Vandenhoeck & Ruprecht, 4th edn, 1974).

Hallbäck, G., *Apostlenes Gerninger* (Det Danske Bibelselskabs Kommentarserie; Copenhagen: Det Danske Bibelselskab, 1993).

Harding, M., 'On the Historicity of Acts: Comparing Acts 9.23-5 with 2 Corinthians 11.32-3', *NTS* 39 (1993), pp. 518-38.

Harnack, A. von, 'Zu Lk 1,34-35', *ZNW* 2 (1901), pp. 53-57.

Harnisch, W., *Die Gleichniserzählungen Jesu: Eine hermeneutische Einführung* (UTB für Wissenschaft: Uni-Taschenbücher, 1343; Göttingen: Vandenhoeck & Ruprecht, 1985).

Harrington, D.J., *Wisdom Texts from Qumran* (London: Routledge, 1996).

Hedrick, C.W., *Parables as Poetic Fictions: The Creative Voice of Jesus* (Peabody, MA: Hendrickson, 1994).

Held, H.J., 'Matthew as Interpreter of the Miracle Stories', in G. Bornkamm, G. Barth and H.J. Held (eds.), *Tradition and Interpretation in Matthew* (trans. P. Scott; London: SCM Press, 2nd edn, 1982), pp. 165-299.

Hengel, M., 'Jesus als messianischer Lehrer der Weisheit und die Anfänge der Christologie', in *Sagesse et religion: Colloque de Strasbourg* (Bibliothèque des centres d'études supérieures spécialisés; Paris: Presses universitaires de France, 1979), pp. 147-88.

Hill, D., 'Son and Servant: An Essay on Matthean Christology', *JSNT* 6 (1980), pp. 2-16.

Holtz, T., *Die Christologie der Apokalypse des Johannes* (TU, 85; Berlin: Akademie-Verlag, 1962).

Hope, E.R., '*Pragmatics*, Exegesis and Translation', in P.E. Stine (ed.), *Issues in Bible Translation* (UBS Monograph Series, 3; London: United Bible Societies, 1988), pp. 113-28.

Hruby, K., 'La notion d'ordination dans la tradition juive', *Maison Dieu* 102 (1970), pp. 30-56.

Hübner, H., *Biblische Theologie des Neuen Testaments* (3 vols.; Göttingen: Vandenhoeck & Ruprecht, 1990, 1993, 1995).

—'New Testament Interpretation of the Old Testament', in Sæbø (ed.), *Hebrew Bible/Old Testament*, pp. 332-72.

—'Vetus Testamentum und Vetus Testamentum in Novo receptum: Die Frage nach dem Kanon des Alten Testaments aus neutestamentlicher Sicht', *JBT* 3 (1988), pp. 147-62; repr. in *idem, Biblische Theologie als Hermeneutik* (ed. A. & M. Labahn; Göttingen: Vandenhoeck & Ruprecht 1995), pp. 175-90.

Hurd, J.C., *The Origin of I Corinthians* (London: SPCK, 1965 [repr Macon, GA: Mercer University Press, 1983]).

Hurtado, L.W., *One Lord, One God: Early Christian Devotion and Ancient Jewish Monotheism* (Edinburgh: T. & T. Clark, 2nd edn, 1998 [1988]).

Hyldahl, N., *Die paulinische Chronologie* (AthD, 19; Leiden: E.J. Brill, 1986).

—*The History of Early Christianity* (Studies in the Religion and History of Early Christianity, 3; Frankfurt: Peter Lang, 1997).

—*Udenfor og indenfor: Sociale og økonomiske aspekter i den ældste kristendom* (Tekst & Tolkning, 5; Monografier udgivet af Institut for Bibelsk Eksegese; Copenhagen: G.E.C. Gad, 1974).

Irigaray, L., *Speculum of the Other Woman* (trans. G.C. Gill; Ithaca, NY: Cornell University Press, 1985).

Jeremias, J., *Jesu Verheissung für die Völker* (Stuttgart: W. Kohlhammer, 1956).

—*The Parables of Jesus* (trans. S.H. Hooke; London: SCM Press, 3rd rev. edn, 1972).

Jervell, J., 'Das gespaltene Israel und die Heidenvölker: Zur Motivierung der Heidenmission in der Apostelgeschichte', *ST* 19 (1965), pp. 68-96 (= 'The Divided People of God: The Restoration of Israel and Salvation for the Gentiles', in *idem, Luke and the People of God: A New Look at Luke–Acts* [Minneapolis: Augsburg, 1972], pp. 41-74).

Johansen, B., *To All the Brethren: A Text-Linguistic and Rhetorical Approach to 1. Thessalonians* (ConBNT, 16; Stockholm: Almqvist & Wiksell, 1987).

Jülicher, A., *Die Gleichnisreden Jesu* (Tübingen: J.B.C. Mohr [Paul Siebeck], 1899; repr. 1910).

Jüngel, E., *Paulus und Jesus: Eine Untersuchung zur Präzisierung der Frage nach dem Ursprung der Christologie* (Hermeneutische Untersuchungen zur Theologie, 2; Tübingen: J.C.B. Mohr [Paul Siebeck], 4th edn, 1972).

Kaitholil, G., *Mary: The Pilgrim of Faith* (Bombay: Saint Paul, 1993).

Kampen, J., '*4QMMT* and New Testament Studies', in Kampen and Bernstein (eds.), *Reading 4QMMT*, pp. 129-44.

Kampen, J., and M.J. Bernstein (eds.), *Reading 4QMMT: New Perspectives on Qumran Law and History* (SBL Symposium Series, 2; Atlanta: Scholars Press, 1996).

Käsemann, E., *An die Römer* (HNT, 8a; Tübingen: J.C.B. Mohr [Paul Siebeck], 1973).

Keck, L.E., 'Toward a Renewal of New Testament Christology', *NTS* 32 (1986), pp. 362-77.

King, K., 'A Response to: Galatians and Gender Trouble: Primal Androgyny and the First-Century Origins of a Feminist Dilemma', in D. Boyarin (ed.), *Galatians and Gender Trouble: Primal Androgyny and the First-Century Origins of a Feminist Dilemma* (Protocol of the Center for Hermeneutical Studies, NS 1; Berkeley: Center for Hermeneutical Studies, 1992), pp. 39-42.

Kingsbury, J.D., *Matthew as Story* (Philadelphia: Fortress Press, 2nd edn, 1988).

—*Matthew: Structure, Christology, Kingdom* (Minneapolis: Fortress Press, 2nd edn, 1989).

Klauck, H.J., *Allegorie und Allegorese in synoptischen Gleichnistexten* (NTAbh, NS 13; Münster: Aschendorff, 1978).

Knohl, I., 'Reconsidering the Dating and Recipient of MMT', *Hebrew Studies* 37 (1996), pp. 119-25.

Konow, J.von, B. Tunander and J. Bergström, 'Enhörning', in *Nationalencyklopedin*, V (Höganäs: Bra böcker, 1991).

Kümmel, W.G., *Das Bild des Menschen im Neuen Testament* (Zürich: Zwingli-Verlag, 1948).

—*Römer 7 und das Bild des Menschen im Neuen Testament* (Munich: Chr. Kaiser Verlag, 1974).

—*Römer 7 und die Bekehrung des Paulus* (Leipzig: J.G. Hinrichs'sche Buchhandlung, 1929).

Lagrange, M.J., *The Gospel of Jesus Christ* (Bangalore: Theological Publications in India, 1992 [French original 1928]).

Laitinen, A., *Evangeliepredikningar* (Luleå: Laestadiana, 1976).

Le Deaut, R., *Targum du Pentateuque*, I (SC, 265; Paris: Cerf, 1978).

Lentz, J.C., Jr, *Luke's Portrait of Paul* (SNTSMS, 77; Cambridge: Cambridge University Press, 1993).

Lewis, N., *The Missionaries: God against the Indians* (New York: Penguin, 1990).

—*Unreasonable Behaviour: An Autobiography* (London: Vintage, 1992).

Lincoln, A.T., 'Matthew—A Story for Teachers?', in D.J.A. Clines, S.E. Fowl and S.E. Porter (eds.), *The Bible in Three Dimensions: Essays in Celebration of Forty Years of Biblical Studies in the University of Sheffield* (JSNTSup, 87; Sheffield: JSOT Press, 1990), pp. 103-125.

Lindemann, A., *Paulus im ältesten Christentum: Das Bild des Apostels und die Rezeption der paulinischen Theologie in der frühchristlichen Literatur bis Marcion* (BHT, 58; Tübingen: J.C.B. Mohr, 1979).

Linton, O., '*The Third Aspect*: A Neglected Point of View. A Study in Gal. i-ii and Acts ix and xv', *ST* 3 (1949), pp. 79-95.

Lohse, E., *Die Ordination im Spätjudentum und im Neuen Testament* (Göttingen: Vandenhoeck & Ruprecht, 1951).

Luciani, A., *Illustrissimi* (Boston: Little, Brown and Co., 1978).

Lüdemann, G., *Das frühe Christentum nach den Traditionen der Apostelgeschichte. Ein Kommentar* (Göttingen: Vandenhoeck & Ruprecht, 1988).

Luz, U., *Das Evangelium nach Matthäus*, III (EKKNT, 1; Zürich: Benziger Verlag, 1997).

—'Eine thetische Skizze der matthäischen Christologie', in C. Breytenbach and H. Paulsen (eds.), *Anfänge der Christologie* (Festschrift F. Hahn; Göttingen: Vandenhoeck & Ruprecht, 1991), pp. 221-35.

—'The Son of Man in Matthew: Heavenly Judge or Human Christ', *JSNT* 48 (1992), pp. 3-21.

Lyonnet, S., '*Chaire kecharitōmenē*', *Bib* 20 (1939), pp. 131-41.

Marshall, H., *The Gospel of Luke* (NIGTC; Exeter: Paternoster Press, 1978).

Martínez, F.García, *The Dead Sea Scrolls Translated* (Leiden: E.J. Brill, 1994).

—*The People of the Dead Sea Scrolls* (Leiden: E.J. Brill, 1995).

—'4QMMT in a Qumran Context', in J. Kampen and M.J. Bernstein (eds.), *Reading 4QMMT: New Perspectives on Qumran Law and History* (Atlanta: Scholars Press, 1996), pp. 15-27.

Medala, S., 'Some Remarks on the Official Publication of MMT', *Qumran Chronicle* 4 (1994), pp. 193-202.

—'The Character and Historical Setting of 4QMMT', *The Qumran Chronicle* 4 (1994), pp. 1-27.

Meyer, P.W., '*The Worm* at the Core of the Apple: Exegetical Reflections on Romans 7', in R.T. Fortna and B.R. Gaventa (eds.), *The Conversation Continues: Studies in Paul and John* (Festschrift J. Louis Martyn; Nashville: Abingdon Press, 1990), pp. 62-84.

Milburn, R.P.L., *'The "People's Bible"'*: Artists and Commentators', in G.W.H. Lampe (ed.), *The Cambridge History of the Bible*, II (Cambridge: Cambridge University Press, 1969), pp. 280-308.

Milik, J.T., and M. Black, *The Books of Enoch: Aramaic Fragments of Qumrân Cave 4* (Oxford: Clarendon Press, 1976).

Minnen, P.van, 'Paul the Roman Citizen', *JSNT* 56 (1994), pp. 43-52.

Moi, T., *Hva er en kvinne: Kjønn og kropp i feministisk teori* (Oslo: Gyldendal, 1998).

—'Introduction', in *idem* (ed.), *French Feminist Thought* (Oxford: Basil Blackwell, 1987), pp. 1-13.

Mojola, A.O., 'A "female" God in East Africa: The Problem of Translating God's Name among the Iraqw of Mbulu, Tanzania', *BT* 46 (1995), pp. 229-36.

Mosbech, H., *Sproglig Fortolkning til Apostlenes Gerninger* (Copenhagen: Gyldendal, 2nd edn., 1945).

Moyise, S., *The Old Testament in the Book of Revelation* (JSNTSup, 115; Sheffield: Sheffield Academic Press, 1995).

Mulder, M.J. (ed.), *Mikra: Text, Translation, Reading and Interpretation of the Hebrew Bible in Ancient Judaism and Early Christianity* (CRINT, 2.1; Assen: Van Gorcum, 1988).

Müller, M., 'Die Septuaginta als die Bibel der neutestamentliche Kirche', *KD* 42 (1996), pp. 65-78.

—'Jøder og jødedom som teologisk problem i oldkirken', N.P. Lemche and M. Müller (eds.), *Fra Dybet* (Festschrift John Strange; FBE, 5; Copenhagen: Museum Tusculanum, 1994), pp. 180-92.

—*The First Bible of the Church: A Plea for the Septuagint* (JSOTSup, 206; CIS, 1; Sheffield: Sheffield Academic Press, 1996).

—'The Hidden Context: Some Observations to the Concept of the New Covenant in the New Testament', in T. Fornberg and D. Hellholm (eds.), *Texts and Contexts* (Festschrift Lars Hartman; Oslo: Oslo University Press, 1995), pp. 649-58.

—'The Theological Interpretation of the Figure of Jesus in the Gospel of Matthew: Some Principal Features in Matthean Christology', *NTS* 45 (1999), pp. 157-73.

Munck, J., *Paulus und die Heilsgeschichte* (Acta Jutlandica, 26.1; Copenhagen: Munksgaard, 1954).

Names of God Study Group, 'How to Translate the Name: Statement by the "Names of God" Study Group, UBS Triennial Translation Workshop, Victoria Falls, Zimbabwe, 8–21 May 1991', *BT* 43 (1992), pp. 403-406.

Newman, J., *Semikhah (Ordination): A Study of its Origin, History and Function in Rabbinic Literature* (Manchester: Manchester University Press, 1950).

Nickelsburg, G.W.E., *Jewish Literature between the Bible and the Mishnah: A Historical and Literary Introduction* (Philadelphia: Fortress Press, 1981).

Nida, E.A., *Good News for Modern Man* (Waco, TX: World Books, 1977).

Nida, E.A., and C.R. Taber, *The Theory and Practice of Translation* (UBS Helps for Translators; Leiden: E.J. Brill, 1974).

Nohrborg, A., *Den Fallna Menniskans Salighets-Ordning ...* (Lund: C.W.K. Gleerup, 10th edn, 1844).

Novakovic, L., 'Jesus as the Davidic Messiah in Matthew', *HBT* 19 (1997), pp. 148-91.

—'Jesus as the Son of David within Matthew's Narrative' (ThM dissertation, Rüschlikon, CH: The International Baptist Theological Seminary, 1995).

Orchard, B., *Born to be King: The Epic of the Incarnation* (London: Ealing Abbey, 1993).

Osten-Sacken, P.van der, *Römer 8 als Beispiel paulinischer Soteriologie* (FRLANT, 112; Göttingen: Vandenhoeck & Ruprecht, 1975).

Otzen, B., 'Das Problem der Apokryphen', *SJOT* 10 (1996), pp. 258-70.

—*Judaism in Antiquity: Political Developments and Religious Currents from Alexander to Hadrian* (The Biblical Seminar, 7; Sheffield: Sheffield Academic Press, 1990).

Paffenroth, K., 'Jesus as Anointed and Healing Son of David in the Gospel of Matthew', *Bib* 80 (1999), pp. 547-54.

Parsons, M.C., 'Reading a Beginning/Beginning a Reading: Tracing Literary Theory in Narrative Openings', *Semeia* 52 (1990), pp. 11-31.

Pedersen, S., 'Scandinavian New Testament Conferences, 1978–1994', in Gunnlaugur A. Jónsson *et al.* (eds.), *The New Testament in its Hellenistic Context* (Studia theologica islandica, 10; Reykjavik, Hásleóli Íslands: 1996), pp. 15-36.

Pelikan, J., *Mary through the Centuries* (New Haven: Yale University Press, 1996).

Peskowitz, M., 'Engendering Jewish Religious History', in M. Peskowitz and L. Levitt (eds.), *Judaism since Gender* (New York: Routledge, 1997), pp. 17-39.

Piper, O., 'The Virgin Birth', *Interpretation* 18 (1964), pp. 131-48.

Pippin, T., '"For Fear of the Jews": Lying and Truth Telling in Translating the Gospel of John', *Semeia* 76 (1996), pp. 81-97.

Powell, M., *What is Narrative Criticism? A New Approach to the Bible* (London: SPCK, 1993).

Qimron, E., and J. Strugnell, *Miqsat Ma'ase Ha-Torah* (DJD, 10; Oxford: Clarendon Press, 1994)

Rad, G.von, *Theologie des Alten Testaments* (2 vols.; Munich: Chr. Kaiser Verlag, 1957, 1960).

Rau, E., 'Jesu Auseinandersetzung mit Pharisäern über seine Zuwendung zu Sünderinnen und Sündern: Lk 15.11-32 und Lk 18.10-14a als Worte des historischen Jesus', *ZNW* 89 (1998), pp. 5-29.

—*Reden in Vollmacht: Hintergrund, Form und Anliegen der Gleichnisse Jesu* (FRLANT, 149; Göttingen: Vandenhoeck & Ruprecht, 1990).

Räisänen, H., *Paul and the Law* (WUNT, 29; Tübingen: J.C.B. Mohr, 2nd edn, 1987).

Räisänen, H. *et al.*, 'Maria/Marienfrömmigkeit', in *Theologische Realenzyklopädie*, XXII (Berlin: W. de Gruyter, 1992), pp. 115-61.

Rasmussen, G., '*Den rigtige rækkefølge*: Et indblik i Lukas-skrifternes redaktionelle tilblivelse', in Lone Fatum and Mogens Müller (eds.), *Tro og historie* (FBE, 7; Copenhagen: Museum Tusculanums Forlag, 1996), pp. 206-214.

Ratzinger, J., *Introduction to Christianity* (San Francisco: Ignatius, 1990 [German original 1968]).

Reiling, J., and J.L. Swellengrebel, *A Translator's Handbook on the Gospel of Luke* (London: United Bible Societies, 1971).

Reiser, M., 'Die Stellung der Evangelien in der antiken Literaturgeschichte', *ZNW* 90 (1999), pp. 1-27.

Ricoeur, P., 'Stellung und Funktion der Metapher in der biblischen Sprache', in Paul Ricoeur and Eberhard Jüngel (eds.), *Metapher: Zur Hermeneutik religiöser Sprache. Mit einer Einführung von Pierre Gisel* (Evangelische Theologie, Sonderheft; Munich: Chr. Kaiser Verlag, 1974), pp. 45-70.

Riesner, R., *Die Frühzeit des Apostels Paulus: Studien zur Chronologie, Missionsstrategie und Theologie* (WUNT, 71; Tübingen: J.C.B. Mohr, 1994).

—*Jesus als Lehrer: Eine Untersuchung zum Ursprung der Evangelien-Überlieferung* (WUNT 2.7; Tübingen: Mohr Siebeck, 3rd edn, 1988).

Riley, D., 'Does a Sex Have a History?', in J. Scott (ed.), *Feminism and History* (New York: Oxford University Press, repr. 1996), pp. 17-33.

Rösel, M., *Übersetzung als Vollendung der Auslegung: Studien zur Genesis-Septuaginta* (BZAW, 223; Berlin: W. de Gruyter, 1994).

Rosin, H., *The Lord is God: The Translation of the Divine Names and the Missionary Calling of the Church* (Amsterdam: Nederlandsch Bijbelgenootschap, 1956).

Ruether, R.R., *Faith and Fratricide: The Theological Roots of Anti-Semitism* (A Crossroad Book; New York: The Seabury Press, 1974).

Sanders, E.P., *Judaism: Practice and Belief 63 BCE—66 CE* (London: SCM Press; Philadelphia: Trinity Press International, 1992).

Sanders, J.A., *The Psalms Scroll of Qumrân Cave 11* (DJD, 4; Oxford: Clarendon Press, 1965).

Schawe, E., 'Gott als Lehrer im Alten Testament: Eine semantisch-theologische Studie' (PhD dissertation, University of Fribourg Press, 1979).

Schäfer, P., 'Die Torah der messianischen Zeit', *ZNW* 65 (1974), pp. 27-42.

Schiffman, L.H., 'Origin and Early History of the Qumran Sect', *BA* 58 (1995), pp. 37-48.

—*Reclaiming the Dead Sea Scrolls* (Philadelphia: Doubleday Anchor Bible, 1994).

Schnackenburg, R., '"Siehe da mein Knecht, den ich erwählt habe..." (Mt 12.18): Zur Heiltätigkeit Jesu im Matthäusevangelium', in L. Oberlinner and P. Fiedler (eds.), *Salz der Erde—Licht der Welt. Exegetische Studien zum Matthäusevangelium* (Festschrift W. Vögtle; Stuttgart: Katholisches Bibelwerk, 1991), pp. 203-222.

Schröter, J., 'Markus, Q und der historische Jesus. Methodische und exegetische Erwägungen zu den Anfängen der Rezeption der Verkündigung Jesu', *ZNW* 89 (1998), pp. 173-200.

Schürmann, H., *Das Lukasevangelium*, I (Leipzig: St Benno, 1970).

Schüssler Fiorenza, E., *Bread not Stone: The Challenge of Feminist Biblical Interpretation* (Boston: Beacon Press, 1984).

—*But She Said: Feminist Practices of Biblical Interpretation* (Boston: Beacon Press, 1992).

—*In Memory of Her: A Feminist Theological Reconstruction of Christian Origins* (New York: Crossroad, 1983).

—'Rhetorical Situation and Historical Reconstruction in 1 Corinthians', *NTS* 33 (1987), pp. 386-403.

—'Word, Spirit and Power: Women in Early Christian Communities', in R.R. Ruether and E. McLaughlin (eds.), *Women of Spirit: Female Leadership in the Jewish and Christian Traditions* (New York: Simon & Schuster, 1979), pp. 29-70.

Schwartz, D.R., 'MMT, Josephus and the Pharisees', in Kampen and Bernstein (eds.), *Reading 4QMMT*, pp. 67-80.

Scott, B.B., *Hear Then the Parable: A Commentary on the Parables of Jesus* (Minneapolis: Augsburg–Fortress, 1990).

Scott, J. *Only Paradoxes to Offer: French Feminists and the Rights of Man* (Cambridge, MA: Harvard University Press, 1996).

Segal, A.F., 'The Risen Christ and the Angelic Mediator Figures in Light of Qumran' in J.H. Charlesworth (ed.), *Jesus and the Dead Sea Scrolls* (New York: Doubleday, 1992), pp. 302-328.

Seidelin, P., 'Der Ebed Jahwe und die Messiasgestalt im Jesajatargum', *ZAW* 35 (1936), pp. 194-231.

Selvidge, M., *Notorious Voices: Feminist Biblical Interpretation 1500–1920* (London: SCM Press, 1996).

Shanks, H., 'Is the Title "Rabbi" Anachronistic in the Gospels?', *JQR* 53 (1962/63), pp. 337-45.

Sharleman, R.P. (ed.), *Naming God* (New York: Paragon House Press, 1985).

Sider, J.W., *Interpreting the Parables: A Hermeneutical Guide to Their Meaning* (Studies in Contemporary Interpretation; Grand Rapids: Zondervan, 1995).

Silberman, N.A., *The Hidden Scrolls* (New York: Grosset/Putnam, 1994).

Sjölander, P., 'Some Aspects of Style in Twentieth-Century English Bible Translation: One-man versions of Mark and the Psalms' (Doctoral dissertation; University of Umeå, 1979).

Smiga, G.M., 'Preaching at Risk: Interpreting Paul's Statements on the Law', *New Theology Review* 9 (1996), pp. 74-95.

Smith, D. Moody, 'The Use of the Old Testament in the New', in J.M. Efird (ed.), *The Old Testament in the New and Other Essays* (Festschrift William Franklin Stinespring; Durham, NC: Duke University Press, 1972), pp. 3-65.

Smith, M., 'Two Ascended to Heaven: Jesus and the Author of 4Q491', in J.H. Charlesworth (ed.), *Jesus and the Dead Sea Scrolls* (New York: Doubleday, 1992), pp. 290-301.

Snodgrass, K., 'Spheres of Influence as a Possible Solution to the Problem of Paul and the Law', in S.E. Porter and C.A. Evans (eds.), *The Pauline Writings: A Sheffield Reader* (The Biblical Seminar, 34; Sheffield Readers, 2; Sheffield: Sheffield Academic Press, 1995), p. 154-74.

Soleim, K., '"I doubt: I am a Man": The Cartesian Subject Exposed to Sexual Difference', in I.N. Preus *et al.* (eds.), *Feminism, Epistemology, and Ethics* (Oslo: Department of Philosophy, University of Oslo, 1996), pp. 137-46.

Spivak, G., *Outside in the Teaching Machine* (New York: Routledge, 1993).

Stambaugh, J.E., and D.L. Balch, *The New Testament in its Social Environment* (LEC, 2; Philadelphia: Westminster Press, 1986).

Stanton, E.C. *et al.* (eds.), *The Woman's Bible* (New York: European Publishing Company, 1898).

Starke, C., *Synopsis Bibliothecae Exegeticae in Novum Testamentum: Kurzgefaster Auszug [...]*, IV (Leipzig: Breitkopf, 3rd edn, 1745).

Stegemann, H., *Die Essener, Qumran, Johannes der Täufer und Jesus: Ein Sachbuch* (Freiburg: Herder, 4th edn, 1994).

Stegemann, W., 'War der Apostel Paulus ein römischer Bürger?', *ZNW* 78 (1987), pp. 200-29.

Stendahl, K., *Paul among Jews and Gentiles and Other Essays* (Philapelphia: Fortress Press, 1976).

Stone, M.E. (ed.), *Jewish Writings of the Second Temple Period: Apocrypha, Pseudepigrapha, Qumran Sectarian Writings, Philo, Josephus* (CRINT, 2.2; Assen: Van Gorcum; Philadelphia: Fortress Press, 1984).

Stowers, S.K., *A Rereading of Romans: Justice, Jews, and Gentiles* (New Haven: Yale University Press, 1994).

Strack, H.L., and G. Stemberger, *Introduction to the Talmud and Midrash* (Edinburgh: T. & T. Clark, 1991).

Strauss. D.F., *Das Leben Jesu: kritisch bearbeitet*, I (Tübingen, 1835; repr. Darmstadt: Wissenschaftliche Buchgesellschaft, 1969).

Stuckenbruck, L.T., *Angel Veneration and Christology: A Study in Early Judaism and in the Christology of the Apocalypse of John* (WUNT, 70; Tübingen: J.C.B. Mohr [Paul Siebeck], 1995).

Stuhlmacher, P., *Schriftauslegung auf dem Wege zur biblischen Theologie* (Göttingen: Vandenhoeck & Ruprecht, 1975).

—*Versöhnung, Gesetz und Gerechtigkeit: Aufsätze zur biblischen Theologie* (Göttingen: Vandenhoeck & Ruprecht, 1981).

—*Biblicasche Theologie des Neuen Testaments* (2 vols.; Göttingen: Vandenhoeck & Ruprecht, 1992, 1999).

—*Wie treibt man Biblische Theologie* (Biblisch-Theologische Studien, 24; Neukirchen–Vluyn: Neukirchener Verlag, 1995).

Stuhlmueller, C., 'Annunciation', *New Catholic Encyclopedia*, I, pp. 562-65.

Sutcliffe, E.F., 'Jerome', in G.W.H. Lampe (ed.), *The Cambridge History of the Bible*, II (Cambridge: Cambridge University Press, 1969), pp. 80-101.

Sæbø, M. (ed.), *Hebrew Bible/Old Testament: The History of its Interpretation*, I.1 (Göttingen: Vandenhoeck & Ruprecht, 1996).

Talmon, S., 'The Community of the Renewed Covenant: Between Judaism and Christianity', in E. Ulrich and J.C. VanderKam (eds.), *The Community of the Renewed Covenant* (Notre Dame, IN: University of Notre Dame Press, 1994), pp. 3-24.

Theissen, G., 'Der Bauer und die von selbst Frucht bringende Erde: Naiver Synergismus in Mk 4.26-29?', *ZNW* 85 (1994), pp. 167-82.

—*Psychologische Aspekte paulinischer Theologie* (FRLANT, 131; Göttingen: Vandenhoeck & Ruprecht, 1983).

Tomson, P.J., *Paul and the Jewish Law* (CRINT; Assen: Van Gorcum; Philadelphia: Fortress Press, 1990).

Tronier, H., 'Allegorese og universalisme—erkendelse som gruppemarkør hos Filon og Paulus', in N.P. Lemche and H. Tronier (eds.), *Etnicitet i Bibelen* (FBE, 9; Copenhagen: Museum Tusculanum, 1998), pp. 67-107.

—'Loven og dæmonmagterne ifølge Galaterbrevet—en hermeneutisk forklaring', in L. Fatum and M. Müller (eds.), *Tro og historie* (Festschrift Niels Hyldahl; FBE, 7; Copenhagen: Museum Tusculanum, 1996), pp. 264-84.

—*Transcendens og transformation i Første Korintherbrev* (Tekst & Tolkning, 10; Copenhagen: Akademisk Forlag, 1994).

—'Virkeligheden som fortolkningsresultat—om hermeneutikken hos Filon og Paulus', in M. Müller and J. Strange (eds.), *Det gamle Testamente i jødedom og kristendom* (FBE, 4; Copenhagen: Museum Tusculanum, 1993), pp. 151-82.

Ulfgard, H., 'L'Apocalypse entre judaïsme et christianisme: Précisions sur le monde spirituel et intellectuel de Jean de Patmos', *RHPR* 79 (1999), pp. 31-50.

—*The Story of Sukkot: The Setting, Shaping, and Sequel of the Biblical Feast of Tabernacles* (BGBE, 34; Tübingen: J.C.B. Mohr [P. Siebeck], 1998).

VanderKam, J.C., *The Dead Sea Scrolls Today* (Grand Rapids: Eerdmans, 1994).

VanderKam, J., and E. Ulrich (eds.), *The Community of the Renewed Covenant : The Notre Dame Symposium on the Dead Sea Scrolls* (Christianity and Judaism in Antiquity series, 10; Notre Dame, IN: University of Notre Dame Press, 1994).

Vermes, G., *The Complete Dead Sea Scrolls in English* (Harmondsworth: Penguin Books, 1997).

Via, D.O., Jr, *The Parables: Their Literary and Existential Dimension* (Philadelphia: Fortress Press, 1974).

Viviano, B.T., 'Rabbouni and Mark 9.5', *RB* 97 (1990), pp. 207-218.

Vögtle, A., 'Offene Fragen zur lukanischen Geburts- und Kindheitsgeschichte', *Bibel und Leben* 11 (1970), pp. 51-67.

Vollenweider, S., *Freiheit als neue Schöpfung: Eine Untersuchung zur Eleutheria bei Paulus und in seiner Umwelt* (FRLANT, 147; Göttingen: Vandenhoeck & Ruprecht, 1989).

Wallin, J.O., *Predikningar över de årliga Sön-och Högtidsdagarnas Evangelier*, VI (Malmö: Världslitteraturens Förlag, 1930).

Warner, M., *Alone of All her Sex* (London: Quartet, 1978).

Weder, H., *Die Gleichnisse Jesu als Metaphern: Traditions- und redaktionsgeschichtliche Analysen und Interpretationen* (FRLANT, 120; Göttingen: Vanderhoek & Ruprecht, 3rd edn, 1984).

Weiss, H.-F., *Der Brief an die Hebräer* (KEK, 13; Göttingen: Vandenhoeck & Ruprecht, 1991).

Wendland, E.R., *The Cultural Factor in Bible Translation* (UBS Monograph Series, 2; London: United Bible Societies, 1987).

West, G., *Contextual Bible Study* (Pietermaritzburg: Cluster Publications, 1993).

Wilckens, U., *Der Brief an die Römer*, II (EKKNT, 6; Neukirchen–Vluyn: Venus, Neukirchener 1980).

Winninge, M., *Sinners and the Righteous: A Comparative Study of the Psalms of Solomon and Paul's Letters* (ConBNT, 26; Stockholm: Almqvist & Wiksell, 1995).

Wire, A.C., *The Corinthian Women Prophets: A Reconstruction through Paul's Rhetoric* (Minneapolis: Fortress Press, 1990).

Wirth, K.-A. (ed.), *Die Biblia Pauperum im Codex Palatinus Latinus 871 der Biblioteca Apostolica Vaticana* (Zürich: Belser, 1982).

Wonderly, W.L., *Bible Translations for Popular Use* (Helps for Translators, 7; London: United Bible Societies, 1968).

Wright, N.T., '*4QMMT* and Paul: The Contexts of Justification' (seminar paper from the SNTS meeting in Copenhagen, 1998).

Zimmermann, A.F., *Die urchristlichen Lehrer: Studien zum Tradentenkreis der διδάσκαλοι im frühen Urchristentum* (WUNT, 2.12; Tübingen: Mohr Siebeck, 2nd edn, 1988).

Zimmermann, J., *Messianische Texte aus Qumran: Königliche, priesterliche und prophetische Messiasvorstellungen in den Schriftfunden von Qumran* (WUNT, 2.104; Tübingen: Mohr Siebeck, 1998).

Zscharnack, L., *Der Dienst der Frau in den ersten Jahrhunderten der christlichen Kirche* (Göttingen: Vandenhoeck & Ruprecht, 1902).

INDEX

NEW TESTAMENT

OTHER ANCIENT REFERENCES

INDEX OF AUTHORS

JOURNAL FOR THE STUDY OF THE NEW TESTAMENT
SUPPLEMENT SERIES